ATLANTA

TRAY BUTLER

Contents

▶ **Discover Atlanta** **19**
Planning Your Trip 20
Explore Atlanta 22
• The Two-Day Best of Atlanta . . . 22
• Top 10 for Kids 23
• Food to Please the Soul 24

▶ **Sights** **25**
Downtown 27
Midtown 36
Buckhead 41
Little Five Points and
  East Atlanta 42

▶ **Restaurants** **43**
Downtown 45
Midtown 48
Buckhead 55
Virginia-Highland 61
Little Five Points and
  East Atlanta 63
Decatur 68
Greater Atlanta 70

▶ **Nightlife** **73**
Live Music 75
Dance Clubs 78
Bars 79
Brewpubs 83
Jazz Clubs 84
Lounges 85
Gay and Lesbian 86

▶ **Arts and Leisure** **88**
The Arts 90
Festivals and Events 101
Sports and Recreation 106

▶ **Shops** **113**
Books and Music 116

Clothing, Accessories, and
  Shoes 118
Gifts and Specialty 122
Home Furnishings and Accents . . 125
Markets 127
Shopping Malls 128
Spas and Salons 129

▶ **Hotels** **131**
Downtown 133
Midtown 136
Buckhead 139
Virginia-Highland 141
Little Five Points and
  East Atlanta 142
Decatur 144

▶ **Excursions from Atlanta** **145**
Marietta and Vicinity 148
Stone Mountain 154
Lake Lanier and Vicinity 157
Athens 159

▶ **Background** **163**
The Setting 163
History 165
Government and Economy 171
People and Culture 173

▶ **Essentials** **178**
Getting There 178
Getting Around 180
Tips for Travelers 182
Health and Safety 184
Information and Services 185

▶ **Resources** **188**
Suggested Reading 188
Internet Resources 190

▶ **Index** **193**

Maps

▸ Map 1: Downtown...........4-5

▸ Map 2: Midtown 6-7

▸ Map 3: Buckhead...........8-9

▸ Map 4:
Virginia-Highland..........10-11

▸ Map 5: Little Five Points
and East Atlanta...........12-13

▸ Map 6: Decatur...........14-15

▸ Map 7: Greater Atlanta ...16-17

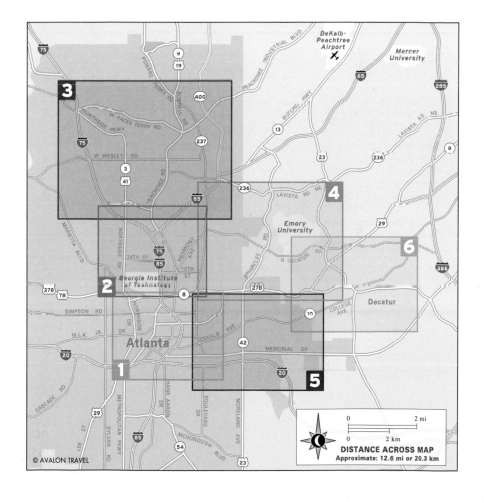

MAP 1 DOWNTOWN

SEE MAP 5

⭐ SIGHTS

5	GEORGIA AQUARIUM	36	GEORGIA CAPITOL MUSEUM
6	WORLD OF COCA-COLA		
8	CENTENNIAL OLYMPIC PARK	39	HISTORIC OAKLAND CEMETERY
16	INSIDE CNN TOUR	46	ATLANTA CYCLORAMA AND CIVIL WAR MUSEUM
26	UNDERGROUND ATLANTA		
32	MARTIN LUTHER KING JR. NATIONAL HISTORIC SITE	47	ZOO ATLANTA

🍴 RESTAURANTS

2	FRENCH AMERICAN BRASSERIE	31	ROLLING BONES BARBECUE
12	PASCHAL'S	34	SLICE
18	TED'S MONTANA GRILL	35	NO MAS! CANTINA
20	SUN DIAL RESTAURANT, BAR & VIEW	38	DADDY D'Z
22	THRIVE	40	RIA'S BLUEBIRD
28	CITY GRILL	41	SIX FEET UNDER
		43	GRANT CENTRAL PIZZA

🌙 NIGHTLIFE

3	MAX LAGER'S AMERICAN GRILL AND BREWERY	11	TRADER VIC'S
		23	THE MARK ULTRALOUNGE

🎭 ARTS AND LEISURE

7	NATIONAL BLACK ARTS FESTIVAL	29	THE APEX MUSEUM
9	IMAGINE IT! THE CHILDREN'S MUSEUM OF ATLANTA	33	MARCIA WOOD GALLERY
		37	EYEDRUM ART AND MUSIC GALLERY
13	ATLANTA FALCONS	42	ATLANTA PRESERVATION CENTER WALKING TOURS OF HISTORIC ATLANTA
14	ATLANTA HAWKS		
14	ATLANTA THRASHERS		
19	TABERNACLE		
24	THEATRICAL OUTFIT	44	WREN'S NEST HOUSE MUSEUM
27	ATLANTA GHOSTS AND LEGENDS TOUR	45	ATLANTA BRAVES

🛍 SHOPS

30	SWEET AUBURN CURB MARKET

🏨 HOTELS

1	TWELVE HOTEL CENTENNIAL PARK	15	OMNI HOTEL AT CNN CENTER
4	EMBASSY SUITES ATLANTA AT CENTENNIAL OLYMPIC PARK	17	GLENN HOTEL
		21	WESTIN PEACHTREE PLAZA
10	ATLANTA MARRIOTT MARQUIS	25	ELLIS HOTEL

0   500 yds

0   500 m

DISTANCE ACROSS MAP
Approximate: 4.1 mi or 6.6 km

✪ SIGHTS
15 ⊂ HIGH MUSEUM OF ART
18 ⊂ ATLANTA BOTANICAL GARDEN
32 ⊂ PIEDMONT PARK
46 MARGARET MITCHELL HOUSE AND MUSEUM
65 ⊂ FOX THEATRE

ⓡ RESTAURANTS
1 FAT MATT'S RIB SHACK
8 AGNES AND MURIEL'S
11 GEISHA HOUSE
14 ⊂ NAN THAI FINE DINING
16 TABLE 1280
20 ⊂ BACCHANALIA
20 JCT KITCHEN & BAR
26 PASTA DA PULCINELLA
29 ⊂ SOUTH CITY KITCHEN
41 OCTANE COFFEE BAR & LOUNGE
42 EINSTEIN'S
44 DRESSED
45 ECCO
48 LITTLE AZIO
56 APRÈS DIEM
58 SILVER MIDTOWN GRILL
61 LAS PALMERAS
63 ⊂ THE VARSITY
70 ⊂ MARY MAC'S TEA ROOM

ⓝ NIGHTLIFE
12 LOBBY AT TWELVE
24 THE BAR AT TROIS
27 TWISTED TACO
28 LEOPARD LOUNGE
30 ⊂ OPERA
34 AMSTERDAM CAFÉ
35 ⊂ LOCA LUNA
36 RED LIGHT CAFÉ
37 BELLISSIMA LOUNGE
38 NORTHSIDE TAVERN
53 GILBERT'S MEDITERRANEAN CAFÉ
54 ⊂ BLAKE'S ON THE PARK
55 ⊂ PARK TAVERN
59 HALO
64 APACHE CAFÉ
66 ⊂ CHURCHILL GROUNDS
67 ⊂ BAZZAAR URBAN BAR

ⓐ ARTS AND LEISURE
2 THE BILL LOWE GALLERY
3 RHODES HALL
4 WILLIAM BREMAN JEWISH HERITAGE MUSEUM
5 CENTER FOR PUPPETRY ARTS
6 ATLANTA BALLET
10 TEN PIN ALLEY
17 ⊂ ALLIANCE THEATRE
17 ATLANTA SYMPHONY ORCHESTRA
39 ⊂ ACTOR'S EXPRESS
43 SKATE ESCAPE
47 YES HOME
49 ⊂ BLUE MEDSPA
50 TWELVE BOUTIQUE AND FLOWERS
57 MIDTOWN ART CINEMA
62 THE ATLANTA CONTEMPORARY ART CENTER
51 HELMET
52 ⊂ OUTWRITE BOOKSTORE AND COFFEEHOUSE

ⓢ SHOPS
7 INTAGLIA HOME COLLECTION
9 BOY NEXT DOOR
19 BELVEDERE
21 ⊂ STAR PROVISIONS
21 SID MASHBURN
21 SPROUT
22 FAB'RIK
31 GREEN MARKET FOR PIEDMONT PARK
33 PIEDMONT BARK
40 LUXE ATLANTA

ⓗ HOTELS
13 TWELVE HOTEL ATLANTIC STATION
23 FOUR SEASONS HOTEL
25 ⊂ W ATLANTA MIDTOWN
60 SHELLMONT INN
68 HOTEL INDIGO
69 GEORGIAN TERRACE HOTEL
71 ATLANTA INTERNATIONAL HOSTEL

© AVALON TRAVEL

[Map of Midtown Atlanta showing neighborhoods including ATLANTIC STATION, BLANDTOWN, WEST MIDTOWN, BELLWOOD, GEORGIA TECH, Georgia Institute of Technology, with streets and numbered location markers. SEE MAP 1.]

SEE MAP 3

WIMBLEDON RD NE

ROCK SPRINGS RD NE

PIEDMONT RD NE

HUNTINGTON RD NE

PEACHTREE RD NE

19

85

13

Ansley
Golf Course

MORNINGSIDE

SHERWOOD
FOREST

DONCASTER DR NE

MORNINGSIDE DR

SHERWOOD RD NE

2 A

ROBIN HOOD RD NE

BEVERLY RD NE

7 S

MONROE DR NE

CUMBERLAND RD NE

3 A

THE PRADO NE

Eubanks
Park

AVERY DR NE

8 R

YORKSHIRE RD NE

4 A
5 A

ANSLEY
PARK

17TH ST NE

WESTMINSTER DR NE

9 S

HILLPINE DR NE

A
6

14TH ST NE

PEACHTREE ST NE

PEACHTREE CIR NE

W PEACHTREE ST NW

R
14

19

High
Museum
of Art

R
15 16 17

Arts
Center M

16TH ST NW

15TH ST NE

Winn
Park

PIEDMONT AVE NE

18

Atlanta Botanical
Garden

Piedmont

SEE MAP 4

35 36 37
33 34 N N N
S N

AMSTERDAM AVE NE

FOWLER ST NW

SPRING ST NW

24 N

25 H

ORME CIR NE

Piedmont
Park

14TH ST NE

22 R

23 N

13TH ST NE
26 R   29   30
N   N   N
27   28

31 S

32

Piedmont
Lake

PARK DR NE

VIRGINIA
HIGHLAND

CRESTHILL AVE NE

TECHWOOD DR NW

WILLIAMS ST NW

SPRING ST NW

PEACHTREE WALK

12TH ST NE

42 R   43 A

Park

55 N

11TH ST NE

Margaret Mitchell
House and Museum

10TH ST NW

49 S   50 F

11TH ST NE

10TH ST NE

VIRGINIA AVE NE

46

PEACHTREE PL NE

51 N   52 N

9TH ST NE

TAFT AVE NE

66 R   57 A

44 R   M
Midtown

8TH ST NW

45 R

47 R

48 H

JUNIPER ST NE

8TH ST NE

MIDTOWN

58 R

MONROE DR NE

75
85

5TH ST NW

59 N

W PEACHTREE ST NW

PEACHTREE ST NE

CYPRESS ST NE

8TH ST NE

5TH ST NE

60 R

PIEDMONT AVE NE

JUNE AVE NE

ARGONNE AVE NE

DURANT PL NE

6TH ST NE

5TH ST NE

61 R

CHARLES ALLEN DR NE

DURAND WAY NE

63 R

NORTH AVE NW

78

64 N

SPRING ST NW

W PEACHTREE ST NW

65 66
Fox Theatre N
67

68 H
69 H

North Avenue
M

3RD ST NE

PONCE DE LEON AVE NE

70 R

71 H

78

TECHWOOD DR NW

NORTH AVE NE

0   500 yds
0   500 m

DISTANCE ACROSS MAP
Approximate: 3.4 mi or 5.5 km

KINGSWOOD

WEST PACES FERRY/NORTHSIDE

Georgia Governor's Mansion

CASTLEWOOD

WYNGATE

BRANDON

Georgia Memorial Park

COLLIER HILLS

Bobby Jones Golf Course

Crest Lawn Memorial Cemetery

Underwood Hills Park

SEE MAP 2

© AVALON TRAVEL

✪ SIGHTS
3 GEORGIA GOVERNOR'S MANSION
16 ◖ ATLANTA HISTORY CENTER

◖ RESTAURANTS
1 OK CAFE
2 JOËL
6 BLUEPOINTE
11 RU SAN'S TOWER PLACE
14 THE TACO STAND
15 SOUPER JENNY
17 CHOPS LOBSTER BAR
18 NAVA
20 BONE'S
21 FOGO DE CHÃO CHURRASCARIA
23 ARIA
26 ROASTERS
30 GEORGIA GRILLE
31 RESTAURANT EUGENE
34 CAFE SUNFLOWER
36 ◖ TAQUERIA DEL SOL
37 THE COLONNADE
38 R. THOMAS DELUXE GRILL

◖ NIGHTLIFE
4 THE TAVERN AT PHIPPS
8 DANTE'S DOWN THE HATCH
22 SAMBUCA

◖ ARTS AND LEISURE
29 BOBBY JONES GOLF COURSE
32 BITSY GRANT TENNIS CENTER
33 MUSEUM OF CONTEMPORARY ART OF GEORGIA
33 TULA ART CENTER

◖ SHOPS
5 JEFFREY ATLANTA
5 PHIPPS PLAZA
9 ◖ LENOX SQUARE MALL
19 SUGARCOAT
25 OXFORD COMICS & GAMES
28 RICHARD'S VARIETY STORE
35 POSTER HUT

◖ HOTELS
7 RITZ-CARLTON BUCKHEAD
10 WESTIN BUCKHEAD ATLANTA
12 GRAND HYATT ATLANTA
13 ◖ INTERCONTINENTAL BUCKHEAD
24 BEVERLY HILLS INN
27 COUNTRY INN AND SUITES BUCKHEAD

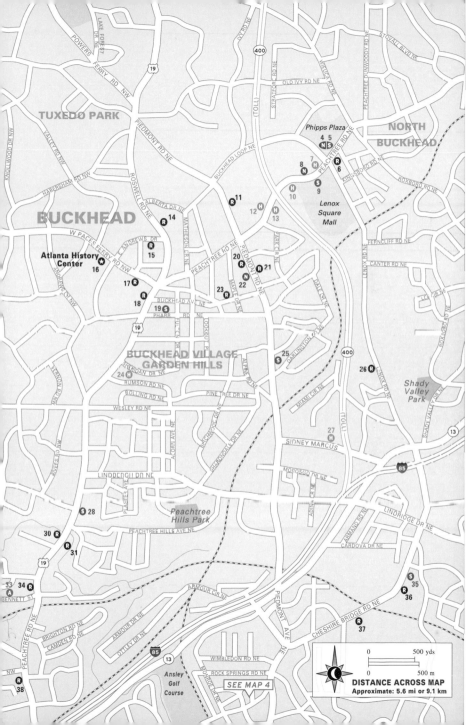

MAP 4

VIRGINIA-HIGHLAND

MAP 4

VIRGINIA-HIGHLAND

ⓡ RESTAURANTS

1	FLOATAWAY CAFÉ	16	MURPHY'S	27	EATS
6	DOC CHEY'S NOODLE HOUSE	17	PAOLO'S GELATO	32	LA FONDA LATINA
14	LA TAVOLA TRATTORIA	20	HARRY AND SONS		
		23	ATKINS PARK		

ⓝ NIGHTLIFE

15	HIGHLAND TAP	21	DARK HORSE TAVERN	31	ⓒ CLERMONT LOUNGE
18	BLIND WILLIE'S	29	MJQ CONCOURSE	33	EL BAR
19	LIMERICK JUNCTION IRISH PUB	30	THE LOCAL	35	RIGHTEOUS ROOM

ⓐ ARTS AND LEISURE

3	LULLWATER PARK	28	URBAN BODY FITNESS	36	FERNBANK MUSEUM OF NATURAL HISTORY
4	ⓒ MICHAEL C. CARLOS MUSEUM OF EMORY UNIVERSITY	34	PLAZA THEATRE	36	FERNBANK MUSEUM'S IMAX THEATRE

ⓢ SHOPS

7	THE FICKLE MANOR	10	MORNINGSIDE FARMERS MARKET	22	KEY LIME PIE SALON AND WELLNESS SPA
8	ALON'S	12	HIGHLAND PET SUPPLY	24	KNITCH
9	PROVIDENCE	13	MITZI & ROMANO	25	ⓒ BILL HALLMAN MEN

ⓗ HOTELS

2	EMORY CONFERENCE CENTER HOTEL	11	VIRGINIA HIGHLAND BED AND BREAKFAST	26	GASLIGHT INN BED & BREAKFAST
5	UNIVERSITY INN AT EMORY				

DISTANCE ACROSS MAP
Approximate: 4.6 mi or 7.4 km

SIGHTS
4 JIMMY CARTER PRESIDENTIAL LIBRARY AND MUSEUM

RESTAURANTS
2 TWO URBAN LICKS
5 SOUL VEGETARIAN
9 JAVAVINO
10 HIGHLAND BAKERY
12 FRITTI
18 THE VORTEX BAR AND GRILL
27 THUMBS UP DINER
28 RATHBUN'S
32 SHAUN'S
34 SON'S PLACE
35 FRONT PAGE NEWS
36 RADIAL
38 THE FLYING BISCUIT CAFE
40 SUN IN MY BELLY
41 CARROLL STREET CAFÉ
42 AGAVE
43 GRANT CENTRAL PIZZA

NIGHTLIFE
1 THE MASQUERADE
8 MANUEL'S TAVERN
17 STAR COMMUNITY BAR
44 EASTSIDE LOUNGE
45 THE EARL
46 MY SISTER'S ROOM
47 MARY'S

ARTS AND LEISURE
3 FREEDOM PARK
7 YOUNG BLOOD GALLERY AND BOUTIQUE
11 DAD'S GARAGE THEATRE
13 HORIZON THEATRE COMPANY
14 VARIETY PLAYHOUSE
26 CANDLER PARK GOLF COURSE
33 INMAN PARK FESTIVAL
37 JAI SHANTI YOGA

SHOPS
15 A CAPPELLA BOOKS
16 JUNKMAN'S DAUGHTER
19 ABBADABBA'S
20 WAX 'N FACTS
21 PSYCHO SISTERS CONSIGNMENT
22 THE CLOTHING WAREHOUSE
23 CHARIS BOOKS AND MORE
24 CRIMINAL RECORDS
25 STEFAN'S VINTAGE CLOTHING
39 SALON RED & SPA
43 TRADERS NEIGHBORHOOD STORE

HOTELS
6 HIGHLAND INN
29 SUGAR MAGNOLIA BED & BREAKFAST
30 1890 KING-KEITH HOUSE BED AND BREAKFAST
31 INMAN PARK BED & BREAKFAST

DISTANCE ACROSS MAP
Approximate: 4 mi or 6.4 km

0   500 yds
0   500 m

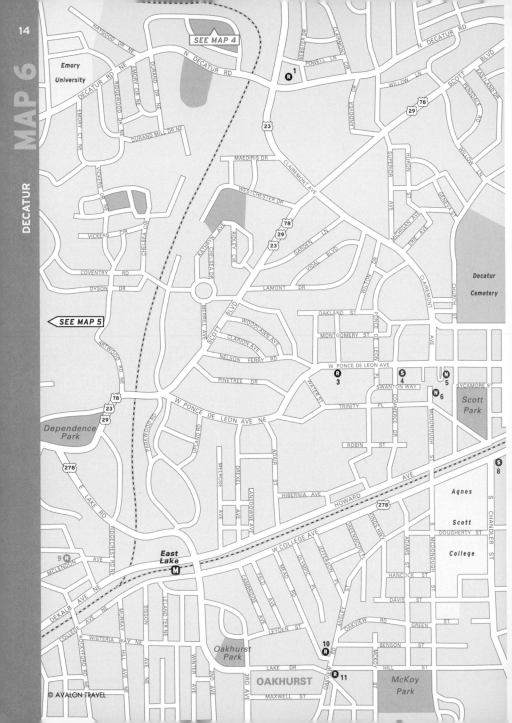

0   400 yds

0   400 m

DISTANCE ACROSS MAP
Approximate: 3.4 mi or 5.5 km

To ⓗ7 Mileybright
Farmhouse
Bed & Breakfast

Avondale

AVONDALE

DECATUR

Avondale
Park

ⓡ RESTAURANTS

1	MEXICO CITY GOURMET	10	MATADOR CANTINA
3	WATERSHED	11	UNIVERSAL JOINT

ⓝ NIGHTLIFE

5	BRICK STORE PUB	6 ⓒ	EDDIE'S ATTIC

ⓢ SHOPS

2	YOUR DEKALB FARMERS MARKET	4	DRESSCODES
		8	WIGGLE

ⓗ HOTELS

7	MILEYBRIGHT FARMHOUSE BED & BREAKFAST	9	LAUREL HILL BED & BREAKFAST

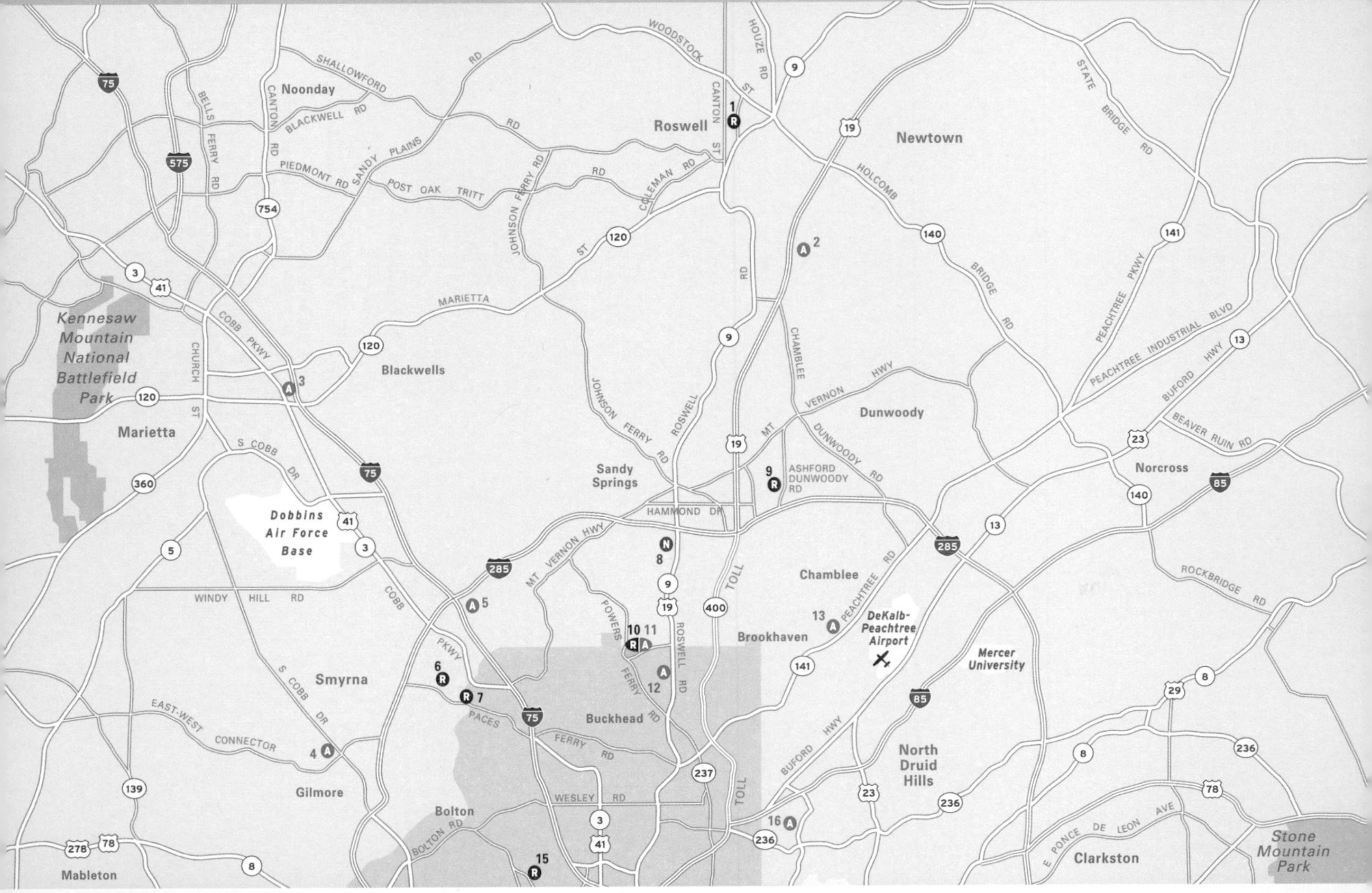

MAP 7

GREATER ATLANTA

Stone Mountain Park

Clarkston

Mercer University

North Druid Hills

DeKalb-Peachtree Airport

Chamblee

Brookhaven

Ashford Dunwoody RD

Dunwoody

Newtown

Norcross

PEACHTREE INDUSTRIAL BLVD
BUFORD HWY
BEAVER RUIN RD
ROCKBRIDGE RD

PEACHTREE PKWY

STATE BRIDGE RD

BRIDGE RD

HOLCOMB

HOUZE RD

CANTON ST

WOODSTOCK

Roswell

COLEMAN RD

ROSWELL

JOHNSON FERRY RD

Sandy Springs

HAMMOND DR

Roswell RD

Buckhead

FERRY RD

WESLEY RD

BOLTON RD

Bolton

POWERS FERRY RD

MT VERNON HWY

MARIETTA

Blackwells

Marietta

CHURCH ST

Kennesaw Mountain National Battlefield Park

COBB PKWY

S COBB DR

Dobbins Air Force Base

WINDY HILL RD

S COBB DR

EAST WEST CONNECTOR

Smyrna

Gilmore

Mableton

Noonday

SHALLOWFORD RD
BLACKWELL RD
SANDY PLAINS RD
PIEDMONT RD
POST OAK TRITT RD

CANTON RD

BELLS FERRY RD

TOLL

PACES

COBB

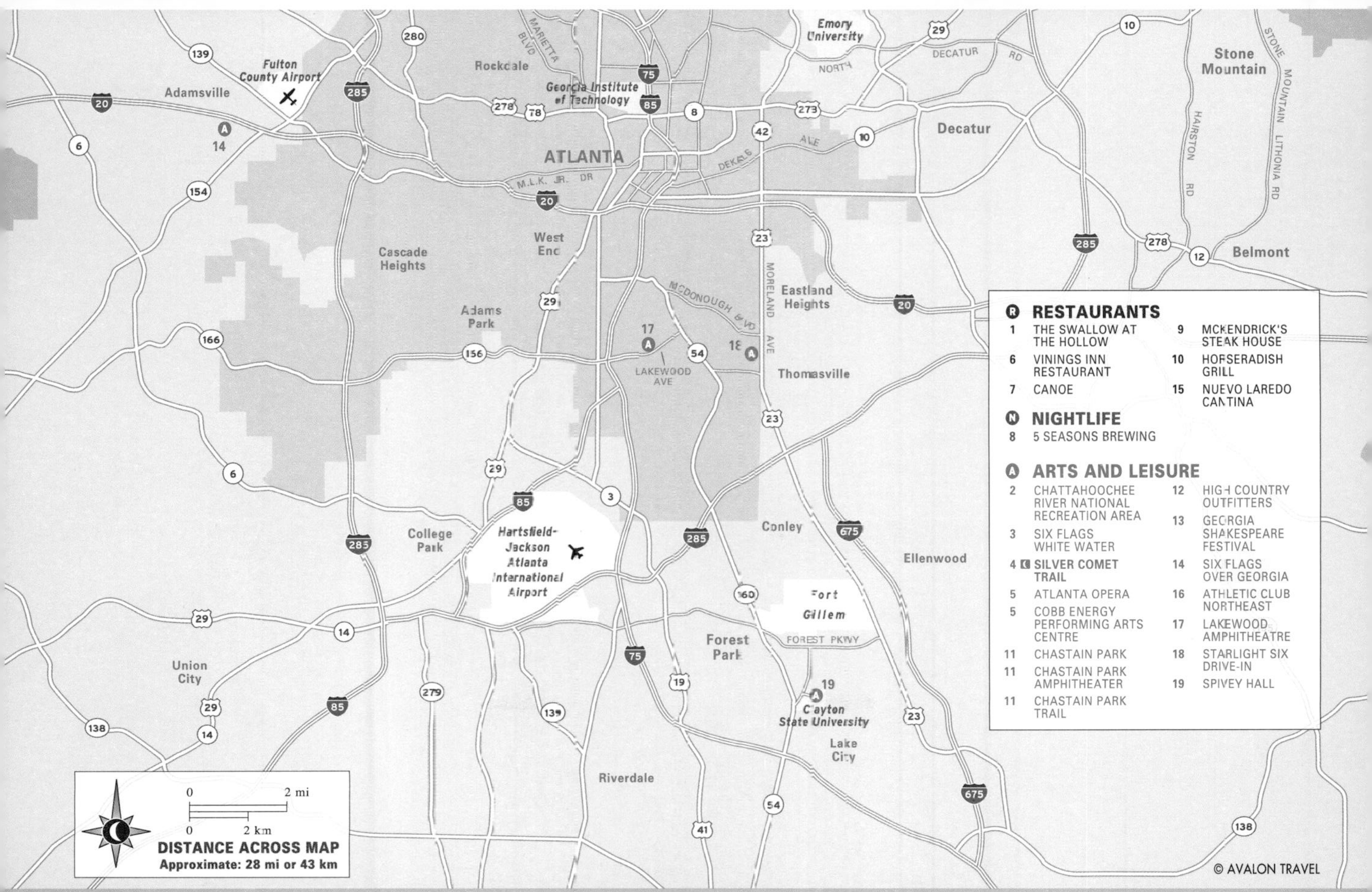
RESTAURANTS
1 THE SWALLOW AT THE HOLLOW
6 VININGS INN RESTAURANT
7 CANOE
9 MCKENDRICK'S STEAK HOUSE
10 HORSERADISH GRILL
15 NUEVO LAREDO CANTINA
NIGHTLIFE
8 5 SEASONS BREWING
ARTS AND LEISURE
2 CHATTAHOOCHEE RIVER NATIONAL RECREATION AREA
3 SIX FLAGS WHITE WATER
4 SILVER COMET TRAIL
5 ATLANTA OPERA
5 COBB ENERGY PERFORMING ARTS CENTRE
11 CHASTAIN PARK
11 CHASTAIN PARK AMPHITHEATER
11 CHASTAIN PARK TRAIL
12 HIGH COUNTRY OUTFITTERS
13 GEORGIA SHAKESPEARE FESTIVAL
14 SIX FLAGS OVER GEORGIA
16 ATHLETIC CLUB NORTHEAST
17 LAKEWOOD AMPHITHEATRE
18 STARLIGHT SIX DRIVE-IN
19 SPIVEY HALL
ATLANTA
Emory University
Georgia Institute of Technology
Stone Mountain
Decatur
Belmont
Rockdale
Adamsville
Fulton County Airport
Cascade Heights
West End
Adams Park
Eastland Heights
Thomasville
Conley
Ellenwood
Fort Gillem
Forest Park
Clayton State University
Lake City
College Park
Hartsfield-Jackson Atlanta International Airport
Riverdale
Union City
STONE MOUNTAIN LITHONIA RD
HAIRSTON RD
DECATUR RD
NORTH AVE
DEKALB AVE
MARIETTA BLVD
M.L.K. JR. DR
MORELAND AVE
MCDONOUGH BLVD
LAKEWOOD AVE
FOREST PKWY
0 2 mi
0 2 km
DISTANCE ACROSS MAP
Approximate: 28 mi or 43 km
© AVALON TRAVEL

Discover Atlanta

When seen from above, Atlanta looks like an anomaly — an improbable cluster of skyscrapers cradled in a blanket of green. But this is a place comfortable with contradictions, a big city that never outgrew its small-town charms and an urban center flirting with a forest. Dubbed the "city of trees," Atlanta has recently felt more like the city of cranes: An unprecedented building boom is transforming the inner city and has ushered in a new era of hometown enthusiasm.

Vestiges of the Old South still remain — the famous hospitality, the appetite for sweet tea, and an eye-popping explosion of dogwood blossoms every spring — but you just might stumble across the "Dirty South" hip-hop scene mixed among the magnolias. As you walk the streets of Midtown, marvel at the sparkling new high-rises, developments that have brought new residents, restaurants, shops, and public spaces. Hit the bars in Virginia-Highland or along Crescent Avenue and you'll discover an Atlanta that savors both excitement and comfort, a town of fine dining, friendly neighbors, and ferocious nightlife.

Sure, the old standards are still popular. Kids still splash in Centennial Olympic Park's fountain, and shoppers still flood Lenox Square Mall in glitzy Buckhead. But such favorites have been augmented by newcomers like the stunning Georgia Aquarium or the sudden arrival of Atlantic Station — virtually a town of its own.

In 2005, officials unveiled the city's new slogan, "Atlanta: Every day is an opening day." It may not be literally true, nor will it ever replace the city's many other nicknames, but the motto sums up the spirit of the times in Atlanta, a vigorous, contradictory, and fascinating American success story.

Planning Your Trip

▶ WHERE TO GO

Downtown

Countless first-time visitors to Atlanta never venture beyond Downtown, which is home to CNN Center, the Georgia Aquarium, the King Center, and a nexus of other attractions. Downtown also features some of the city's largest hotels. As the heart of Atlanta's business district, Downtown can feel deserted after 6 P.M. Look to nearby Castleberry Hill, an up-and-coming arts enclave, or eclectic Cabbagetown for excitement after dark.

Midtown

Midtown is often called Atlanta's home of the arts, thanks to institutions like the High Museum of Art, Symphony Hall, and Alliance Theatre. It's also a desirable residential neighborhood with a vibrant blend of restaurants, shops, and nightlife. The area around Piedmont Park was once known as the city's main gayborhood, but an influx of newcomers has made Midtown anything but homogenous. Across the interstate, West Midtown is a white-hot pocket of new growth, including the brand-new Atlantic Station shopping district.

Buckhead

Conventional wisdom used to say that Buckhead was the place where old money lives and new money parties, but the area's rep as a nightclub destination has all but dried up. What remains is a genteel, upscale neighborhood filled with resplendent Southern mansions, high-end boutiques, and some of the city's most elite restaurants. The Atlanta History Center keeps Atlantans in touch with their roots, while Lenox Square Mall and Phipps Plaza tend to their shopping needs.

the Georgia Aquarium

Virginia-Highland

The tree-lined avenues of Virginia-Highland are certainly quaint and homey, but the clusters of shops along North Highland Avenue are the jewels in the neighborhood's crown. It's a busy blend of amiable restaurants, yuppie watering holes, chic clothing shops, and home-accessory stores. Nearby Emory University features the prestigious Michael C. Carlos Museum, though more visitors flock to Fernbank Museum of Natural History, home to dinosaur skeletons and the city's only IMAX theater.

Little Five Points and East Atlanta

Little Five Points has long been Atlanta's default stomping ground for all things alternative—a funky crossroads where pink mohawks mix with tie-dye and tattoo parlors thrive alongside thrift stores. Next door, the more elegant neighborhood of Inman Park has seen a burst of new life, with a rash of trendy restaurants popping up along Highland Avenue. Farther south, East Atlanta has also undergone a dramatic renaissance. The area now has a lively mix of cute shops and grungy bars.

Decatur

The city of Decatur is technically older than Atlanta, but it proudly defends its character as a cozy and compact bedroom community. Located 15 minutes east of Downtown and with a population of only 18,000, Decatur is best known for its gorgeous town square, which features dozens of great restaurants, coffee shops, bookstores, and bars. Eddie's Attic, one of the most well-respected acoustic music venues in the Southeast, is also here.

► WHEN TO GO

Because of its temperate climate, Atlanta's tourism season lasts virtually all year. Spring arrives early here, with short sleeves coming out sometimes as early as March. A phenomenal fit of blossoms and new foliage erupts in April and May, along with some of the best festivals.

The summer's warmth lingers well into autumn, with beautiful breezy days in October. Temperatures can dip below freezing in December or January, but cold snaps don't tend to stick here.

Perhaps the only time to avoid Atlanta is in the hottest part of the summer—late July and August—when the combination of temperatures in the 90s and the infamous humidity make outdoor activities less enjoyable. The upside is that Atlantans love their air-conditioning, making even the dog days of summer desirable to some.

springtime in Atlanta

Explore Atlanta

▶ THE TWO-DAY BEST OF ATLANTA

An ideal visit to Atlanta could easily last a week, with mornings spent touring museums and historic sites and lazy afternoons sipping sweet tea. But you can take in the best of the ATL in just a couple of days. To be centrally located, stay in Downtown or Midtown.

the Swan House at the Atlanta History Center

Day 1

▶ Begin with a visit to Centennial Olympic Park. Enjoy the Fountain of Rings and the monuments to Olympic athletes, but devote most of your morning to exploring either the Georgia Aquarium or the World of Coca-Cola, which will require 2–3 hours each. Next, take in the hour-long Inside CNN Tour; purchase tickets online to save time at all of the major attractions.

▶ Grab lunch at the Sun Dial Restaurant, a rotating restaurant with breathtaking views.

▶ Head to the Sweet Auburn District and dedicate an hour or two to the Martin Luther King Jr. National Historic Site. If time permits, visit Ebenezer Baptist Church.

▶ For dinner, head to Virginia-Highland and check out one of the many fine restaurants along North Highland Avenue, north of Ponce de Leon.

▶ The neighborhood has plenty of bar-hopping options, including Atkins Park and Dark Horse Tavern.

Day 2

▶ Eat a classic down-home breakfast at Mary Mac's Tea Room, then continue your immersion in Southern culture at the Atlanta History Center in Buckhead. If time permits, check out the splendid 1928 Swan House, which gives a glimpse into how upper-crust Atlantans lived in the Jazz Age.

▶ Buckhead has no lack of great lunch options. For quick and easy, hit Souper Jenny or check out the eye candy at R. Thomas Deluxe Grill.

▶ Spend your afternoon exploring the High Museum of Art in Midtown, which can easily take 3–4 hours, or visit the nearby Center for Puppetry Arts. If time allows, take a quick tour of the Margaret Mitchell House, which includes a *Gone With the Wind* museum.

TOP 10 FOR KIDS

- Gasp at the giant whale sharks at the **Georgia Aquarium,** the largest indoor aquarium in the world (p. 28).

- Watch an IMAX film or marvel at the dinosaur skeletons at **Fernbank Museum of Natural History** (p. 91).

- Rub elbows with an actual Muppet at the **Center for Puppetry Arts** – or build your own (p. 90).

- Visit the 23 Western lowland gorillas who roam a naturalistic habitat at **Zoo Atlanta** (p. 35).

- Get wet in the Fountain of Rings at **Centennial Olympic Park** (p. 27).

- Hear a storyteller relate the mischievous adventures of Br'er Rabbit at the **Wren's Nest House Museum** (p. 93).

- Brave the enormous Goliath roller coaster at **Six Flags Over Georgia** (p. 110).

- Take the **Summit Skyride** to the top of Stone Mountain (p. 155).

- Watch the **Atlanta Braves** play a home game at Turner Field (p. 111).

Fernbank Museum of Natural History

▶ You'll be tempted to eat dinner in Midtown, which has dozens of great restaurants, but you'll see more of Atlanta if you trek east. Try extravagant Two Urban Licks in Poncey-Highland, or check out the famous Flying Biscuit in Candler Park for affordable Southern fare.

▶ With a little advance planning you can score tickets to a performance at the Fox Theatre, an eye-popping 1920s movie palace that hosts traveling Broadway musicals and concerts. Or check out the Alliance Theatre to end your Atlanta journey on a cultural high.

FOOD TO PLEASE THE SOUL

The term "soul food" may not have been coined here, but Atlanta is a mecca for fans of deep-fried, down-home Southern vittles.

FRIED CHICKEN

Forget the colonel – you'll find some of the most finger-lickin' fried chicken in town at **Son's Place** (p. 67). It's an old family recipe that's been passed down from a previous much-loved chicken joint, Deacon Burton's.

For a more gourmet take on fried chicken, check out chef Scott Peacock's famous interpretation at **Watershed** (p. 68). The coveted dish is only available after 5:30 P.M. on Tuesdays, and it's known to run out early.

FRIED GREEN TOMATOES

Thanks to Fannie Flagg, fried green tomatoes are synonymous with Southern cooking. Perhaps no place in town prepares the decadent appetizer better than **South City Kitchen** (p. 54). This Midtown institution is Southern with an upscale twist: the fried green tomatoes come with goat cheese and sweet red-pepper coulis.

Agnes and Muriel's (p. 50) puts a different spin on the classic dish, featuring a fried-green-tomato BLT that's served with melted mozzarella and red-pepper sauce.

SOUL STANDARDS

Paschal's (p. 48) is a bona fide culinary landmark. Known for its hospitality, this a great place to discover soul food standards such as collard greens, black-eyed peas, steamed cabbage, candied yams, and grits.

While soul food gets a bad rap for not being an overly healthy option, **Soul Vegetarian** (p. 68) delivers clever updates on classic dishes, such as the vegan mac and cheese or a country-fried tofu. Almost all the items are vegetarian- or vegan-friendly and served without trans fats or preservatives – in other words, it's soul food sans guilt.

a plateful of soul at Paschal's

SIGHTS

From its inception, Atlanta has been hitched to the twin notions of commerce and transportation. Founded as a railroad terminus in 1847, the town flourished as a crossroads for business. The area's love affair with transportation blossomed in the 20th century as civic boosters helped make Atlanta a major hub for air travel. Today, Hartsfield-Jackson Atlanta International Airport is often cited as the busiest in the world, with upwards of 2,500 daily flights. Three major interstates also converge in the beating heart of the city—though as anyone who's ever spent a sweaty afternoon stuck on the Downtown Connector can attest, this isn't always a good thing.

The city for decades has been known as a coveted destination for conventions, many of which take place Downtown in and around the Georgia World Congress Center. But recent years have seen a rise in visitors traveling to Atlanta not for business but for pleasure. As a legacy of the 1996 Olympic Games, Downtown has boosted its credentials as a tourist center thanks to attractions around Centennial Olympic Park, including the new World of Coca-Cola museum, CNN Center, and the world's largest indoor aquarium. Nearby, the Martin Luther King Jr. National Historic Site draws more than 600,000 visitors per year, many of whom come for January's King Week

© TRAY BUTLER

HIGHLIGHTS

LOOK FOR 【 TO FIND RECOMMENDED SIGHTS.

【 **Best Fountain:** The playful Fountain of Rings in **Centennial Olympic Park** remains one of Atlanta's most photographed landmarks — and a great place to cool off on steamy summer afternoons (page 27).

【 **Best Animal Life:** Home to approximately 80,000 animals representing 500 species, the eight-million-gallon **Georgia Aquarium** is the largest indoor aquarium in the world (page 28).

【 **Best Behind-the-Scenes Tour:** Spend an hour exploring one of the world's most influential news organizations via the **Inside CNN Tour.** The interactive tour gives a thrilling backstage view of live television news in the making (page 30).

【 **Best Monument:** Countless visitors come to Atlanta each year solely to visit the **Martin Luther King Jr. National Historic Site,** an impressive and fitting tribute to the slain civil rights leader. The site includes a must-see visitor center and museum (page 31).

【 **Best Hidden Gem:** The quiet **Atlanta Botanical Garden** offers 30 acres of verdant splendor. Don't miss the lovely Fuqua Conservatory, which includes the largest collection of orchid species on permanent display in the country (page 36).

【 **Most Beautiful Theater:** Built in 1929 as both an opulent movie palace and a Shriners mosque, the luxurious **Fox Theatre** today hosts a lively mix of touring Broadway musicals, concerts, and a fun summer film series (page 36).

【 **Best Art Museum:** The **High Museum of Art** more than doubled its size in 2005 with a sweeping new addition by famed Italian ar-

© 2009 KEVIN C. ROSE/ATLANTAPHOTOS.COM

the Fox Theatre

chitect Renzo Piano. His three elegant buildings now complement Richard Meier's iconic ivory cake on the hill (page 37).

【 **Best Park:** Sometimes compared to New York City's Central Park, the 189-acre **Piedmont Park** in Midtown is one of the city's favorite gathering spots, home to dozens of events throughout the year and a seductive slice of nature in the middle of the metropolis (page 39).

【 **Best History Lesson:** Tucked in a pocket of Buckhead best known for over-the-top mansions, the extensive **Atlanta History Center** covers city history from its founding through the modern era. Its rambling campus includes the graceful Swan House, a restored Jazz Age gem (page 41).

celebration or National Black History Month events in February.

Though it's possible to visit the city and never leave the urban grid of Downtown, which includes many of the most famous sights, any serious explorer should make it a priority to experience other neighborhoods. Midtown, in particular, has benefited from a huge influx of development since the late 1990s; its crown jewel is still the stunning High Museum of Art, which underwent a dramatic renovation and expansion in 2005. The area is also known for other prestigious cultural institutions such as the Woodruff Arts Center (which includes the Alliance Theatre and the Atlanta Symphony Orchestra) and the majestic Fox Theatre. Piedmont Park remains a major draw in the neighborhood, as does the Atlanta Botanical Garden.

Atlanta's other key sights tend to be more scattered, with no single neighborhood offering the same concentration of attractions as Downtown or Midtown. Which isn't to say you shouldn't make an effort to see the splendid Atlanta History Center in Buckhead, which includes an unrivaled museum of local artifacts, or the fascinating Jimmy Carter Library and Museum near Little Five Points. To get the best handle on this place, be prepared to cover a lot of ground and venture between several spread-out neighborhoods even in the course of a day. Atlanta, the transportation hub, is a city that's worth all the commuting.

Downtown   Map 1

ATLANTA CYCLORAMA AND CIVIL WAR MUSEUM
800 Cherokee Ave. SE. 404/658-7625. www.atlantacyclorama.org
HOURS: Tues.-Sat. 9 A.M.-4:30 P.M., Sun. 12:30-3:30 P.M.
COST: $8 adult, $6 child, $7 senior

Atlanta has no deficiency of attractions aimed at Civil War enthusiasts, but you need not be an armchair historian to appreciate the curious beauty of the Atlanta Cyclorama. This giant cylindrical oil painting stretches 42 feet high and 358 feet in circumference and depicts the Battle of Atlanta waged on July 22, 1864. Such enormous works of art were in high vogue during the late 19th century, but few have been preserved as meticulously as this one, which was completed in the 1880s by a team of Milwaukee artists. Billed as the world's largest oil painting, the spectacle is augmented by three-dimensional figures and a realistic terrain that stretches 30 feet in the foreground, giving visitors the illusion of being surrounded by the battle. The accompanying Civil War Museum features the steam locomotive Texas, known as the key engine in the Great Locomotive Chase of 1862. The Cyclorama is in Grant Park; Zoo Atlanta sits next door.

⬛ CENTENNIAL OLYMPIC PARK
Centennial Olympic Park Dr. and Luckie St., 404/222-7275, www.centennialpark.com
HOURS: Daily 7 A.M.-11 P.M.

First-time visitors often flock to Centennial Olympic Park as a starting point for exploring Atlanta—which isn't a bad strategy for getting an initial taste of Downtown's diverse attractions. The 21-acre park, built to accommodate 1996's Centennial Olympic Village, is a well-groomed green space in the thick of the tourist district, with easy access to the World

SAVE MONEY WITH CITYPASS

If you're planning to hit several of the city's most popular tourist spots, CityPass represents a real value. The pocket-size booklet includes admission to the Georgia Aquarium, the World of Coca-Cola, Zoo Atlanta, and the Inside CNN Tour, and two additional "option tickets." (Visitors choose either the Fernbank Museum of Natural History or the Atlanta Botanical Garden, and the High Museum of Art or the Atlanta History Center.) The pass is valid for nine days starting on the first day the booklet is used. Pass-holders can skip the lines at some attractions, and the booklet also contains site information, directions, best times to visit, a map, and suggestions for shopping and eating. It includes a coupon for two-for-one admission for Atlanta Preservation Historical Walking Tours and discounts at Lenox Square and Phipps Plaza shopping malls. The pass is available online (www.citypass.com) or at the ticket offices of any of the participating attractions. The cost for adults is $69 (a $120 value) and $49 for kids.

of Coca-Cola, the Georgia Aquarium, CNN Center, Philips Arena, and the Georgia World Congress Center.

The park features several monuments dedicated to Olympic ideals as well as a memorial to the two people killed during the 1996 bombing. Visitors are likely to spend much of their time marveling at the playful **Fountain of Rings,** which blasts jets of water into the air from the central plaza. The fountain teems with toddlers during warm months, though the plaza is cleared four times a day for synchronized water-dancing shows, complete with music and lighting effects. December finds the park's towering Olympic torch–shaped lampposts dripping with strings of lights and decorations for the holiday season. Atlanta's only outdoor ice skating rink operates in the park from November through early January.

It's easily one of the city's grandest public spaces, but Centennial Olympic Park still seems to be finding its footing as a premier gathering ground for locals. The crowds do show up for outdoor concerts and film screenings. As with much of Downtown, the park draws a share of homeless people, including a few aggressive panhandlers, but a visible police presence and the private downtown Ambassador Force help keep the area safe.

◖ GEORGIA AQUARIUM

225 Baker St., 404/581-4000,
www.georgiaaquarium.org

HOURS: Sun.-Fri. 10 A.M.-5 P.M., Sat. 9 A.M.-6 P.M.

COST: $26 adult, $19.50 child, $21.50 senior

Leave it to can-do Atlanta, stranded 250 miles from the ocean, to overcompensate for its landlocked limitations by building one of the most ambitious fish tanks ever seen.

The attraction came about through an unprecedented $250 million gift to the city from Bernie Marcus, cofounder of Atlanta-based The Home Depot, who envisioned a world-class aquarium and conservation center like those he and his wife, Billi, had visited elsewhere. The aquarium hosted its five millionth visitor within the first two years of opening in late 2005. Despite its popularity, not everything has been smooth sailing for the enormous ship-shaped facility. An unfortunate string of animal deaths led to early controversy, followed by a major staff shake-up in 2008.

Still, the Georgia Aquarium can only be

© TRAY EUTLER

The eight-million-gallon Georgia Aquarium has quickly emerged as one of Atlanta's must-see attractions.

called a stunning success. Its star residents include four fully grown whale sharks, the largest fish in the world. The aquarium boasts being the only facility outside of Asia featuring whale sharks, which can be surveyed from below via an always-crowded underwater viewing tunnel with a moving sidewalk. The graceful, alien-faced Beluga whales also draw big crowds, as do the playful sea otters. Other highlights include the large collections of grouper, stingrays, hammerhead sharks, California sea lions, and African black-footed penguins, as well as hundreds of freshwater fish.

Adventurous guests can slide their fingers over stingrays and horseshoe crabs in the touch pools; *really* adventurous guests can pay $290 to reserve one of the six spots per day to scuba dive among the whale sharks.

Hours for the aquarium vary during holiday weekends and special events—which are often—so check the website for specifics.

GEORGIA CAPITOL MUSEUM
2 Martin Luther King Dr., Ste. 820, 404/656-2846,
www.sos.georgia.gov/state_capitol
HOURS: Mon.-Fri. 8 A.M.-5 P.M.
COST: Free

Completed in 1889, the regal Georgia State Capitol is one of the state's most recognizable landmarks. Its noble 75-foot dome is plated in Georgia gold, which was mined in Dahlonega, and has a neoclassical structural style said to mimic the U.S. Capitol in Washington, D.C. The vital nerve center of the state's government is housed here, including the governor's office and both chambers of the General Assembly. The Georgia Capitol Museum, founded in 1895, features exhibitions detailing the cultural heritage of Georgia, including artifacts from the state's earliest history, Native-American exhibitions, portraits of famous Georgians, and a discussion about the construction of the building itself. But no visit to the Capitol should end with the

SIGHTS

museum alone. Check out the Georgia Capitol Flag collection housed in the Hall of Valor on the 1st floor, and take some time to admire the works of art inside the high Victorian rotunda. Free guided tours are available Monday–Friday at 10 and 11 A.M. and 1, 2, and 3 P.M. It's possible to see the Georgia General Assembly during their annual session which begins the second Monday in January and continues for 40 working days.

HISTORIC OAKLAND CEMETERY

248 Oakland Ave., 404/688-2107,

www.oaklandcemetery.com

HOURS: Daily dawn-dusk

Although it sits just a stone's throw from Downtown, Oakland Cemetery feels like a hundred years away from the buzz of the metropolis. This rambling 88-acre graveyard is one of the few sites in the city dating from before the Civil War. Founded in 1850, it was the spot from which Confederate Gen. John B. Hood watched the Battle of Atlanta, and where

nearly 7,000 Confederate—and Union—soldiers are buried today.

Famous Atlantans including *Gone With the Wind* author Margaret Mitchell, golf champion Bobby Jones, and former Atlanta mayor Maynard Jackson are buried in Oakland Cemetery. The graveyard contains sections devoted to Jewish, black, and pauper graves, which were separated from other areas. Despite its macabre ambience, the cemetery today is a frequent destination not only for history buffs, but also for joggers, dog-walkers, and even picnickers seeking respite from the bustle of the city. Don't miss its fun slate of Halloween-themed activities.

(INSIDE CNN TOUR

190 Marietta St. NW, 404/827-2300,

www.cnn.com/studiotour

HOURS: Daily 9 A.M.–5 P.M.

COST: $12 adult, $9 child, $11 senior

Blame the 24-hour news cycle on Atlanta's own Ted Turner, who in 1980 launched the Cable

With a luxury hotel, shops, and restaurants, CNN Center is more than just the headquarters of the news organization.

© 2009 KEVIN C. ROSE/ATLANTAPHOTOS.COM

News Network and forever changed the pace and character of broadcast journalism. Though many of CNN's banner shows and personalities now operate out of New York or Washington, D.C., Atlanta's **CNN Center** remains the company's headquarters.

The Inside CNN Tour takes visitors on a behind-the-scenes journey through the newsrooms of CNN, CNN Headline News, and CNN International. Guests start by ascending what's billed as the world's longest freestanding escalator and begin the tour with an interactive exhibit detailing CNN's founding and early history. A viewing chamber gives an overhead look at reporters and anchors in action, along with an absorbing narrative on how live news programs come together in real time.

Once the tour is over, mill around CNN Center for the many souvenir shops and the large mall-style food court. The building connects to the Omni Hotel, Philips Arena, and the CNN Center MARTA station.

◖ MARTIN LUTHER KING JR. NATIONAL HISTORIC SITE

450 Auburn Ave., 404/331-5190, www.nps.gov/malu
HOURS: Daily 9 A.M.–5 P.M., until 6 P.M. June-Aug.
COST: Free

More than just a memorial to a man who changed the course of the 20th century, the Martin Luther King Jr. National Historic Site provides a thorough and poignant history lesson on the civil rights movement. Administered by the National Park Service since 1980, a vast preservation district surrounds the **King Birth Home, Historic Ebenezer Baptist Church,** the **King Center,** and the tombs of both King and his late wife, Coretta Scott King.

Any outing should start at the National Park Service Visitor Center, which offers a series of engaging and interactive exhibits on King's life and a stark retelling of the history of racial segregation in America. On display is the wooden mule wagon that carried King's body during his 1968 funeral procession, with extensive

Visitor Center at the Martin Luther King Jr. National Historic Site

MARTIN LUTHER KING JR.'S ATLANTA

On January 15, 1929, a son was born to Rev. Michael Luther King in the family home at 501 Auburn Avenue. (The Baptist minister would later change both his own name and the name of his second child from Michael to Martin in homage to Martin Luther.) Young Martin attended Atlanta's segregated public schools and graduated from Morehouse College in Atlanta and Crozer Theological Seminary in Pennsylvania. While completing a fellowship at Boston University, he met and married Coretta Scott. The couple settled in Montgomery, Alabama, in 1954, and the reverend's career took off. A year later, Rosa Parks made headlines when she refused to give up her seat on a city bus. King was instrumental in organizing a bus boycott, which lasted 382 days. In December 1956, the U.S. Supreme Court declared bus segregation unconstitutional, but the battle hit King hard: His home was bombed, he was arrested, and he was stabbed during an appearance in Harlem. Still, the 27-year-old emerged as a national leader in the battle for civil rights.

In the years that followed, King maintained a busy schedule of speaking engagements, activism, and protests, honing the message of non-violent social change inspired by Mahatma Gandhi. He and his family came home to Atlanta in 1960 and King became co-pastor of Ebenezer Baptist Church with his father. Three years later, in August 1963, 250,000 protes-tors joined the March on Washington, where King delivered his famous "I have a dream" speech. *Time* magazine named him Man of the Year, and the following year King was awarded the Nobel Peace Prize.

By 1968, King had spread his message of social justice to millions, and he surprised some of his supporters by speaking out against the Vietnam War. He traveled to Memphis, Tennessee, to rally striking sanitation workers, and was there fatally gunned down on his motel balcony. He died on April 4, 1968. President Lyndon B. Johnson declared a national day of mourning.

Thousands of visitors venture to Atlanta each year to pay tribute to King's legacy. Since 1980 the National Park Service has maintained the Martin Luther King Jr. National Historic Site, which includes the graves of both King and his wife, the historic Ebenezer Baptist Church, the King Birth Home, and Historic Fire Station No. 6. To the west, the site borders the Sweet Auburn Historic District, a once-vital African-American neighborhood from the turn of the 20th century.

THE KING BIRTH HOME

Built in 1895, this Queen Anne–style dwelling housed several generations of the King family – often all at once. For the first dozen years of his life, Martin Luther King Jr. shared the house with his grandparents, parents, brother,

photography from the turbulent era. The large free visitors parking lot is accessible from John Wesley Dobbs Avenue.

UNDERGROUND ATLANTA

50 Upper Alabama St., 404/523-2311, www.underground-atlanta.com

HOURS: Mon.-Sat. 10 A.M.-9 P.M., Sun. 11 A.M.-7 P.M. (bar and restaurant hours vary)

Atlanta may be the Phoenix City, always fixated on self-reinvention, but the number of incarnations we've seen of Underground Atlanta is getting to be ridiculous. The bizarre, subterranean entertainment district was born essentially by accident in the 1920s, when the city built a system of viaducts to raise traffic flow above its tangled railroad tracks. Businesses moved up to the 2nd or 3rd floors of their buildings, leaving their former storefronts below for storage—or occasional use as speakeasies during Prohibition days. In the late 1960s, the abandoned five-block area

sisters, a great aunt, and an uncle. The King Birth Home (501 Auburn Ave., 404/331-6922, www.nps.gov/malu, daily 10 A.M.-5 P.M.) has been refurbished to reflect the aesthetics of the 1930s. Visitors who want to tour the King Birth Home should plan to arrive early at the National Park Service Visitor Center (450 Auburn Ave.); tours are free but tend to fill up fast since they're limited to 15 people. The half-hour tours are led by park rangers.

HISTORIC FIRE STATION NO. 6

Atlanta's oldest standing fire station was built in 1894 and served the Sweet Auburn neighborhood until 1991. It underwent a thorough renovation in 1995 and today the two-story redbrick Romanesque Revival building houses a museum (39 Boulevard, 404/331-5190, www.nps.gov/malu, daily 10 A.M.-5 P.M., free) detailing the desegregation of Atlanta's fire department and features a 1927 American LaFrance fire engine. Two of the original brass sliding poles also remain.

HISTORIC EBENEZER BAPTIST CHURCH

Martin Luther King Jr.'s father and grandfather presided at this Auburn Avenue landmark, which was completed in 1922. King was baptized here as a child and ordained after giving a trial sermon here at the age of 19. His funeral was held here in 1968. In 1974, violence erupted in the church when a gunman shot and killed King's mother, Alberta Christine Williams King, along with another deacon. The church's congregation moved in 1999 to the massive new Horizon Sanctuary across the street, and plans were later unveiled to renovate Historic Ebenezer Baptist Church (407 Auburn Ave., 404/688-7263, www.historicebenezer.org, Mon.-Sat. 10 A.M.-5 P.M.).

SWEET AUBURN HISTORIC DISTRICT

Designated as a National Historic Landmark in 1976, the Sweet Auburn Historic District stretches from Courtland Street to the Downtown Connector. The six-square-block area was once an essential enclave for the city's African-American movers and shakers, a place where black businesses and cultural life flourished. Atlanta's first black-owned office building rose here, as did the city's first black-owned newspaper. The Royal Peacock Club hosted acts like Ray Charles, James Brown, and Aretha Franklin. Sadly, a visit to Sweet Auburn today reveals a neighborhood still troubled by inner-city blight. You can cover the area in less than an hour. Worth visiting is the **APEX Museum** (135 Auburn Ave., 404/521-2739, www.apexmuseum.org, Tues.-Sat. 10 A.M.-5 P.M., Sun. 1-5 P.M., $4 adult, $3 child and senior), which includes historical information about the neighborhood's role in Atlanta history.

below Alabama Street was rediscovered and gained new life as a historic site and groovy nightlife district.

The experiment didn't last, and by the early '80s Underground was again shuttered. It sprang to life once more in 1989 as a far more sanitized shopping mall aimed at tourists. The 1990 arrival of the World of Coca-Cola next door increased the site's foot traffic, though it was filled with suburban-style chain stores and souvenir stands. The complex suffered a reputation—perhaps undeserved—for being unsafe after dark, and by the end of the decade had again fallen into financial turmoil. In 2004 the city attempted to return Underground to its '70s nightlife roots, granting a new crop of nightclubs in Kenny's Alley special permission to stay open later than bars elsewhere in the city, but even that effort wasn't an immediate success. These days Underground Atlanta still draws plenty of tourists and convention-goers by day. Several of the clubs from the

2004 reboot have closed, and a new batch of hot spots, many aimed at a primarily African-American clientele, have cast their lot with Kenny's Alley, hoping that the phoenix will once again rise from the ashes.

Explorers with time to kill Downtown or a burning desire to buy cheesy tchotchkes might take a fast stroll through Underground, a better taste of Atlanta architecture from yesteryear is a few blocks north in the Fairlie-Poplar Historic District, which is decidedly less touristy and more authentic.

WORLD OF COCA-COLA

121 Baker St., 404/676-5151,
www.worldofcoca-cola.com

HOURS: Mon.-Sat. 9 A.M.-6 P.M., Sun. 10 A.M.-6 P.M.

COST: $15 adult, $9 child, $13 senior

There's something very Willy Wonka about the new World of Coca-Cola. The soft-drink giant's museum-meets-infomercial lures visitors into a candy-coated, sometimes surreal otherworld where the docents are called "ambassadors" and vintage advertisements are labeled "artifacts." After 17 years at Underground Atlanta, the museum relocated in 2007 to a fancy new $96 million facility next to the Georgia Aquarium and within deliberate eyeshot of Coca-Cola's global headquarters.

Visitors begin with a quick (and mandatory) animated film introducing "The Happiness Factory," then they're ushered into the museum's light-filled atrium where they can choose exhibitions ranging from a 4-D theater (a 3-D movie with moving seats) to an exhaustive collection of Coca-Cola memorabilia. A working production line offers a behind-the-scenes peek at how glass bottling plants work; guests are later given free eight-ounce bottles of Coke filled on-site.

Though the experience can feel like a long and relentless commercial, the World of Coca-Cola does have moments even for nonbelievers. One gallery features cola-inspired paintings

the World of Coca-Cola

and sculptures by Georgia artists Howard Finster and Steve Penley, while a side exhibit details the controversial—but ultimately ingenious—"New Coke" marketing debacle of 1985. Best of all, the tour ends with a tasting room, where caffeinated guests can sample exotic beverage brands from five continents. Now there's a pause that refreshes.

The museum is a 10-minute walk from either the Peachtree Center or CNN Center MARTA stations. Parking in the Pemberton Place garage is $10.

ZOO ATLANTA

800 Cherokee Ave. SE, 404/624-5822, www.zooatlanta.org
HOURS: Daily 9:30 A.M.–5:30 P.M. (ticket booths close at 4:30 P.M.)
COST: $18.99 adult, $13.99 child, $14.99 senior

With a history in Grant Park dating all the way back to 1889, Zoo Atlanta is one of the city's trademark attractions, adored by schoolchildren for countless generations and endured by just as many adults. After an ugly period during the 1980s when the facility lost national accreditation due to substandard animal housing, the zoo bounced back with unbridled vigor and a sweeping renovation. Most of the more than 800 animals living here today roam freely in lush, naturalistic habitats, no longer confined to cramped glass cages or dirty cement ditches.

For decades, Zoo Atlanta was synonymous with its mascot, Willie B., a giant silverback gorilla named for former Atlanta mayor William B. Hartsfield. Though Willie B. passed away in 2000, his descendants now play among the 23 other Western lowland gorillas in the zoo's striking African rain forest area. Devotees can also pay their respects to the much-loved ape at his 700-pound bronze statue and memorial garden. More recently, the mascot mantle has been passed to the resident giant pandas, Lun Lun and Yang Yang, who gave birth to

© TRAY BUTLER

Zoo Atlanta

their first cub, Mei Lan ("Atlanta Beauty"), in 2006, and their second cub, Xi Lan ("Atlanta's Joy"), in 2008. The panda habitat is by far the zoo's most polished and up-to-date exhibition; surrounding areas can feel neglected by comparison. The pandas are due to be returned to China, though zoo officials are hopeful to extend their visit. Other highlights of Zoo Atlanta include the African lions, komodo dragons, "living treehouse" aviary, and an Australian-themed Outback Station, with a petting zoo and extensive playground for tykes. The Atlanta Cyclorama and Civil War Museum sits next door.

Midtown   Map 2

⟨ ATLANTA BOTANICAL GARDEN

1345 Piedmont Ave., 404/876-5859,
www.atlantabotanicalgarden.org
HOURS: Apr.-Oct. Tues.-Sun. 9 A.M.-7 P.M. (Thurs. until 10 P.M. May-Oct.), Nov.-Mar. Tues.-Sun. 9 A.M.-5 P.M.
COST: $12 adult, $9 child and senior

With persistent growth in the past three decades, the Atlanta Botanical Garden has quietly blossomed into one of Midtown's greatest treasures—a lush oasis hidden in plain sight. It used to be easy to jog around its fences inside Piedmont Park and never notice the expansive 30-acre garden and conservation center contained within. But a recent renovation has aimed to heal any such psychological disconnect by relocating the garden's main entrance and incorporating a new visitors center on the park side of the garden.

Old favorites such as the breathtaking **Fuqua Conservatory** haven't been changed. The impressive orchid center still hosts a stunning collection of rare specimens from around the world, while the moist, jungle-like atmosphere of the conservatory can feel more like a trip to a zoo than a garden. A new 600-foot elevated canopy walk towers over the **Southern Seasons Garden,** offering a rare up-close peek at the treetops of the **Storza Woods.** A new garden of edible plants is slated to sprout where the parking lot used to be.

Harried travelers seeking a quiet afternoon break can catch a moment of meditation in the peaceful **Japanese Garden** or explore the secluded trails winding throughout the forest. The **Children's Garden** keeps young visitors occupied, while a summer concert series, seasonal art exhibitions, and evening cocktail parties (May–Sept. Thurs. 6–10 P.M.) have helped boost the garden's profile. Definitely a must-see, and not just for plant lovers.

⟨ FOX THEATRE

660 Peachtree St., 404/881-2100, www.foxtheatre.org
HOURS: Tours Mon., Wed., Thurs. 10 A.M., Sat. 10 A.M. and 11 A.M. (conducted by the Atlanta Preservation Center, 404/688-3353, www.preserveatlanta.com)
COST: $10 adult, $5 child and senior

The "Fabulous Fox" defies easy characterization: It's an enormous and opulent 1920s movie house, a richly ornamented Moorish palace with a fetish for Egyptian accents, and an adored local monument whose history sowed the seeds for Atlanta's modern preservation movement.

Built as the Yaarab Temple Shrine Mosque, its original owners realized their lavish vision by securing financial aid from movie magnate William Fox, who agreed to lease its main auditorium as a movie hall. The 4,000-seat theater,

PHANTOMS OF THE FOX

As any visitor to the magnificent Fox Theatre will attest, the cavernous old film palace just about drips with history. You can almost hear the murmurs of moviegoers from yesteryear when you climb the luxuriantly carpeted stairs to the upper balconies or descend into one of the echoing lounges below the lobby. And after seven decades of continuous use as an active entertainment venue, the theater has also accumulated a couple of ghost stories.

One famous local legend says that the face of a Confederate soldier can be seen staring out of certain 2nd-floor windows. It's a curious choice of a specter, though, considering that the venue wasn't built until 1929. Another tale that seems more rooted in actual history focuses on the basement, supposedly haunted by a Depression-era coal handler who once slept on a cot next to the furnace. Apparently he never got the message that the place had switched to central heat.

Urban folktales aside, at least one story of an unusual figure dwelling on the fringes of the Fox Theatre is certifiably true. For more than 20 years, former technical director Joe Patten has lived on-site in the Fox's "secret" private residence, a well-appointed 3,600-square-foot apartment opposite the Egyptian Ballroom. Patten was granted the privilege of living at the Fox rent-free for the duration of his life, thanks to his vast efforts to save the building from demolition. Sometimes jokingly referred to as "the Phantom of the Fox," Patten enjoys unprecedented access to all areas of the theater, from the onion-shaped domes to the bowels of backstage.

---

replete with onion domes, minarets, and an interior sky full of sparkling stars, opened a few weeks after 1929's stock-market meltdown, leading to a decade of economic hardship and eventual bankruptcy. The Fox bounced back in the 1940s and became one of the city's premier cinemas and concert halls, wowing moviegoers with its 3,622-pipe Möller organ—the second-largest theater organ in the world. The early 1970s found the theater again in decline, leading to a proposal by Southern Bell to demolish the property. A grassroots "Save the Fox" campaign successfully halted the wrecking ball and landed the building a National Historic Landmark designation in 1976.

Today the Fox boasts one of the city's most varied cultural calendars, with touring Broadway shows, annual performances of Atlanta Ballet's *Nutcracker,* and a well-attended summer film series featuring a pre-show sing-along with the refurbished "Mighty Mo" organ. Walking tours of the facility, offered by the Atlanta Preservation Center, last around 90 minutes and explore the inspiration behind the Egyptian Ballroom, Spanish Room, and Grand Salon.

◖ HIGH MUSEUM OF ART

1280 Peachtree St., 404/733-4400, www.high.org

HOURS: Tues.-Sat. 10 A.M.-5 P.M. (Thurs. until 8 P.M.), Sun. noon-5 P.M.

COST: $18 adult, $11 child, $15 senior

When Renzo Piano agreed to design the High Museum's unprecedented $124 million expansion, the Italian "starchitect" took on an inimitable challenge: How to add three new buildings to Richard Meier's 1983 minimalist masterpiece while still maintaining the integrity of the site. Luckily for Atlanta, Piano's creation not only complements the gleaming white Meier building, but elegantly relocates the museum's center of gravity to a central campus that unites the High with the affiliated Woodruff Arts Center.

© TRAY BUTLER

High Museum of Art

The 2005 expansion doubled the museum's size to 312,000 square feet, with light-filled skyway galleries and a sleekly understated aesthetic that lets the 11,000 works of art hold center stage. The new **Wieland Pavilion** houses the modern and contemporary collections, while the Meier building (now the **Stent Family Wing**) holds the permanent and folk art collections, including one of the most impressive exhibitions of self-taught artists in the country. Georgia folk artists Howard Finster, Nellie Mae Rowe, and Ulysses Davis feature prominently. Other highlights of the permanent collection include works by masters ranging from Degas, Monet, and Rodin to more modern figures such as Chuck Close, Dorothea Lange, and Georgia O'Keeffe.

Recent years have found the High hosting a notable roster of touring exhibitions, including an ongoing partnership with the Louvre, Lorenzo Ghiberti's "The Gates of Paradise," and a well-received showing of Annie Leibovitz photographs. Visitors are typically drawn first to the touring exhibitions on the upper floors of the Wieland Pavilion, but should make a point of seeing the grand rotunda of the Meier building next door. Across the courtyard, the **Anne Cox Chambers Wing** exhibits special collections in a striking glass-enclosed lobby with two upper floors of gallery space. Next door, the upscale tapas restaurant Table 1280 has become a destination in its own right, though reservations are usually required. For snacks, pop by the High Café on the ground floor of the Stent Family Wing.

Limited street parking can be found on 15th, 16th, and 17th Streets, but your best bet is to pay at one of the nearby parking decks. The Arts Center MARTA station is also close by.

MARGARET MITCHELL HOUSE AND MUSEUM

990 Peachtree St., 404/249-7015, www.gwtw.org
HOURS: Mon.-Sat. 9:30 A.M.-5 P.M., Sun. noon-5 P.M.
COST: $12 adult, $5 child, $9 senior

A famous snippet of Atlanta folklore notes that Margaret Mitchell showed little love for the tiny one-bedroom apartment she and husband John Marsh shared from 1925 to 1932; she even dubbed the place "the dump." But while convalescing in the shotgun-style flat, Mitchell passed her days by writing the bulk of *Gone With the Wind*—a novel that would eventually sell more copies worldwide than any other book except the Bible.

It would take another 50 years for the former Crescent Apartments to become a certified local landmark, and early efforts at its preservation met hot resistance. Arsonists struck the dilapidated Tudor Revival building in 1994 and 1996, though neither fire significantly damaged Mitchell's unit. The Margaret Mitchell House and Museum finally opened in 1996, thanks to a grant from the Daimler-Benz corporation, and has since become part of the Atlanta History Center.

The docent-led tour begins in the adjacent visitors center, which explores Mitchell's early life and features a collection of her letters, and continues through apartment No. 1, furnished similarly to when Mitchell lived there. Visitors should also check out the **Gone With the Wind Movie Museum,** located behind the house in a refurbished bank building; it includes the front door of Tara plantation from the film set, as well as storyboards and the portrait of Scarlett O'Hara from the Butler mansion. The Midtown MARTA station is one block away.

◖ PIEDMONT PARK

10th St. and Piedmont Ave., www.piedmontpark.org
HOURS: Daily 6 A.M.-11 P.M.

An ebullient green playground in the heart of the city, the 189-acre Piedmont Park remains a

© TRAY BUTLER

Sun lovers, dog walkers, and in-line skaters escape to Piedmont Park year-round.

wildly popular gathering spot for nature-craving Atlantans. Joggers, inline skaters, and bicyclists dot the paved paths, while the grassy slopes of **Oak Hill** are packed with sunbathers and picnic blankets in the warmer months—which is most of the year in the temperate South. The park also offers tennis courts, ball fields, a swimming pool (renovated in 2008), a dog park, and volleyball courts.

Originally a private fairground and racetrack purchased by the Gentlemen's Driving Club in 1887, the land now known as Piedmont Park underwent major transformation to host the Cotton States and International Exposition of 1895, which drew 800,000 visitors from around the world. In 1904, the city of Atlanta purchased the park and extended its city limits to encompass the new acreage. Eight years later, the Olmsted Brothers (sons of Central Park architect Frederick Law Olmsted) unveiled a master plan for the park, which wasn't implemented at the time but did shape its growth for the next century.

Today, visitors can still spot remnants of the Cotton States Exposition, including the peaceful **Lake Clara Meer** and a few stone balustrades that once supported steps to the main building. Extensive renovations since the late 1990s have updated and rejuvenated

the park, adding new jogging paths, lookout points, restrooms, and the perennially busy dog park north of the Meadow. A controversial plan to build a parking deck near the Atlanta Botanical Garden finally moved forward in 2008, part of a $72 million project to add 53 acres of previously untapped forest to the green space.

To access Piedmont Park's **Active Oval,** which includes jogging paths, playfields, and picnic tables, enter at 14th Street and Piedmont Avenue. Nearby, the unique and colorful **Noguchi Playscape,** designed by world-famous sculptor Isamu Noguchi in 1976, is a favorite destination for families. The southern edge of the park, including Oak Hill and the Meadow, opens along 10th Street from Myrtle Street to Monroe Drive. Though fishing is allowed in Lake Clara Meer, boating and swimming are not.

Many of the city's most beloved and well-attended annual events traditionally take place in Piedmont Park, including the Dogwood Festival in April, the Atlanta Pride Festival in June, and the ending of the Peachtree Road Race in July. However, Georgia's persistent drought has forced some of the larger events to temporarily relocate. Double-check the park's website for its calendar of events.

Buckhead Map 3

◖ ATLANTA HISTORY CENTER

130 W. Paces Ferry Rd., 404/814-4000,
www.atlantahistorycenter.com

HOURS: Mon.-Sat. 10 A.M.-5:30 P.M., Sun.
noon-5:30 P.M.

COST: $15 adult, $10 child, $12 senior

The holdings of the Atlanta History Center reach far beyond the exhaustive display of regional relics in its museum. The center's verdant 33-acre campus also includes an extensive research library, a restored antebellum farmhouse (complete with livestock), and an opulent Jazz Age mansion. Visitors should start with the Atlanta History Museum, which tells the city's story in a series of well-curated, comprehensive exhibitions. The permanent display of Civil War artifacts boasts 1,400 objects ranging from uniforms to firearms, while "Metropolitan Frontiers" takes guests on an absorbing chronological tour of Atlanta from its earliest settlers through modern times. (Don't

miss the creepy female Ku Klux Klan outfit on display near the exhibition's midpoint, or the collection of vintage downtown neon signs.)

In 2006, the History Center unveiled a sparkly new permanent exhibition devoted to the 1996 Olympic Games. Atlanta had never bid for the Olympics before, and no city in history had ever won the games on its first bid. The state-of-the-art exhibition offers a timeline of how the Olympic bidding effort came about, as well as a deep look at the city's hosting challenge, and a fun collection of Olympic memorabilia.

Beyond the museum, don't miss **Swan House,** former residence of the aristocratic Inman family, heirs to a vast cotton fortune. Completed in 1928 and designed by noted Georgia architect Philip Trammell Shutze, the lavish estate has been lovingly restored to give a glimpse into how upper-crust Atlantans lived during the 1930s and '40s, with many

© TRAY BUTLER

Swan House

original furnishings still in place. Nearby, **Tullie Smith Farm** turns back the clock to 1845 via a humble yeoman-style farmhouse. The house originally sat east of the city and survived the 1864 burning of Atlanta. It was moved to the History Center campus in 1969. Costumed interpreters lead tours of the farm and act out daily chores typical of 19th-century rural Georgia, including blacksmithing, candle making, quilting, and weaving.

Because both Swan House and Tullie Smith Farm are open only during tours given at certain times, a visit to the Atlanta History Center might easily require three or four hours. A café in the basement of the museum makes for a good refueling station between tours.

GEORGIA GOVERNOR'S MANSION

391 W. Paces Ferry Rd., 404/261-1776, www.mansion.georgia.gov
HOURS: Tues.-Thurs. 10-11:30 A.M.

It's certainly not the most luxurious home along glitzy West Paces Ferry Road, nor is it the most ostentatious. But the Greek Revival–style Governor's Mansion has been the official residence of Georgia's first family since 1968. Located on 18 acres of forest in one of the city's most prestigious ZIP codes, the 24,000-square-foot mansion was designed by noted Georgia architect Thomas Bradbury and features 30 luxurious rooms spread out over three floors. The home's first occupant was Governor Lester Maddox, an outspoken segregationist. Later occupants have included Jimmy Carter, Zell Miller, and Sonny Perdue.

The free self-guided tour of the mansion takes about 45 minutes and includes a wealth of information about the home's museum-quality furnishings and fine antiques. Docents are stationed in each room to answer questions. Don't miss the signed first edition of Margaret Mitchell's *Gone With the Wind* on display in the library.

Little Five Points and East Atlanta   Map 5

JIMMY CARTER PRESIDENTIAL LIBRARY AND MUSEUM

441 Freedom Pkwy., 404/865-7100, www.jimmycarterlibrary.org
HOURS: Mon.-Sat. 9 A.M.-4:45 P.M., Sun. noon-4:45 P.M.
COST: $8 adult, $6 senior (children are free)

It's easy enough to drive through heavily wooded Freedom Park and never notice the Jimmy Carter Presidential Library and Museum. Closer inspection reveals a vast cluster of buildings that encompasses not only a museum and research library but also the Carter Center, a not-for-profit organization devoted to advancing human rights. The 69,750-square-foot library hosts a vast exhibition exploring the life of America's 39th president, from his childhood in rural Plains, Georgia, to his meteoric rise into national politics.

The museum includes an amusing replica of the Oval Office presented as it was during the Carter presidency, as well as many relics from his campaigns. First Lady Rosalynn Carter's inaugural gown is on display along with gifts the Carters received from various heads of state and a comprehensive look at the Carters' humanitarian efforts since leaving the White House. The archives contain almost 27 million pages of Carter's White House materials, including documents, letters, and 500,000 photographs.

RESTAURANTS

Atlantans love to eat. Visitors here are sometimes surprised to discover such an animated—and ever-changing—restaurant scene, a playground for foodies and a boon for budget-minded gourmands. The city's quota of celebrity chefs has exploded in recent years, as has our number of celebrity-driven restaurants. Southern cooking has enjoyed a renaissance in the new millennium, but don't be surprised if a place described as "Southern" features dishes that are anything but traditional. The city has also long enjoyed a vibrant assortment of international fare.

For years, Buckhead held sway as the center of Atlanta's culinary universe, home to at least a dozen of the finest upscale restaurants in town.

Though the well-heeled 'hood still features many amazing and in-demand options, there's been a noticeable movement southward for some of the most exciting newcomers. Shiny new rows of restaurants have popped up in places both obvious and peculiar: on Juniper Street in Midtown, within Atlantic Station, along Highland Avenue in the Old Fourth Ward, and in up-and-coming West Midtown—to name only a few.

Unlike other major cities, Atlanta isn't necessarily a place where each neighborhood is identified with one major food type. Rather, areas with lively restaurants tend to have a blend of options. Virginia-Highland, for example, offers some of the tastiest Asian places around,

HIGHLIGHTS

LOOK FOR **(** TO FIND RECOMMENDED RESTAURANTS.

(**Most Romantic Setting:** French **American Brasserie** has the seductive atmosphere of a café on the Seine. Be prepared to fall in love (page 47).

(**Best Thai Cuisine:** Although the city has plenty of delicious casual Thai joints, **Nan Thai Fine Dining** ups the ante on sophistication and palate (page 49).

(**Most Buzzed-About Restaurant:** With a list of awards and accolades to make any chef-owner blush, **Bacchanalia** remains one of the Southeast's critical darlings (page 50).

(**Best Local Landmark:** Atlanta's been chowing down on the greasy chili dogs at **The Varsity** since 1928 (page 53).

(**Best Classic Southern Dining:** Mary **Mac's Tea Room** is a portrait of local gentility, and a fine choice for comfort food (page 54).

(**Best Contemporary Southern Eatery:** Crescent Avenue mainstay **South City Kitchen** has been a go-to destination for Lowcountry brilliance since 1993 (page 54).

(**Best Tacos:** If you can endure the impossibly long lines, you'll enjoy **Taqueria del Sol**'s creative spin on Mexican street fare (page 58).

(**Best Special-Occasion Restaurant:** **Rathbun's** pulls off the neat trick of creating

© TRAY BUTLER

civilized, sensual dining in an unexpected industrial setting (page 65).

(**Best Be-Seen Dining Room:** The cavernous **Two Urban Licks** is a feast for the eyes, and a great echo chamber for people-watching (page 66).

(**Best Breakfast:** Thumbs Up Diner does breakfast classics right, but also gets points for its healthy options (page 67).

PRICE KEY

$ Most entrées less than $10
$$ Most entrées $10-20
$$$ Most entrées more than $20

Atlanta has a food scene that could fill several volumes of guidebooks. Today's has-been tofu house can quickly morph into tomorrow's white-hot tapas joint. The landscape changes fast, and the crowds here can be fickle. The restaurants listed in this chapter represent a blend of the city's most-loved landmarks, buzzed-about staples, and promising newcomers. But don't be afraid to set out on your own quest to discover Atlanta's next big tastemakers.

but also noteworthy pub grub and some mind-blowing Italian.

As a city with more than 8,000 restaurants (nearly 500 of which are Zagat-rated),

Downtown Map 1

Downtown has long catered to the convention market, whose middle-of-the road tastes are reflected on many menus, but it has also sprouted a new batch of be-seen eateries and high-concept dining. The area has no lack of chain establishments, especially around **Peachtree Center**, though it's still best known for a few of the more longstanding hotel restaurants. For more creative dining options, leave the central business district and venture to **Cabbagetown, Castleberry Hill**, or **Grant Park**.

BARBECUE

DADDY D'Z ❸

264 Memorial Dr., 404/222 0206, www.daddydz.com

HOURS: Mon.-Thurs. 11 A.M.-10 P.M., Fri.-Sat. 11 A.M.-12:30 A.M., Sun. noon-9:30 P.M.

Daddy D'z has the feel of a laid-back juke joint where the waiters know your name, but the clientele ranges from Cabbagetown bohemians and Grant Park old-timers to Downtown execs rushing through their lunch breaks. Renowned especially for its sumptuous spare ribs, the menu swims in authentic Southern barbecue served in big daddy–sized portions. The chicken dishes and pulled pork are particular hits. Blues bands perform Friday and Saturday nights.

ROLLING BONES BARBECUE ❸❸

377 Edgewood Ave., 404/222-2324, www.rollingbonesbbq.com

HOURS: Mon.-Thurs. 11 A.M.-9 P.M., Fri. 11 A.M.-10 P.M., Sun. 12:30-8 P.M.

Rolling Bones often gets mentioned as one of Atlanta's best barbecue spots, an accolade that owes just as much to the decor as the dinner menu. Housed in a 1940s gas station that's

been spruced up as a retro-kitschy meat-and-three diner, the popular Edgewood hangout serves traditional Texas Pit Barbecue, with meats that are slow-cooked over mesquite and treated with chef Bill Collins's signature sauces. The menu follows all the usual rules of barbecue joints—ribs, brisket, and pork—but also lists the peculiar option of barbecue tacos.

BRUNCH

RIA'S BLUEBIRD ❸

421 Memorial Dr., 404/521-3737, www.riasbluebird.com

HOURS: Daily 8 A.M.-3 P.M.

What was once a dingy drive-thru liquor store across from Oakland Cemetery has morphed into one of the city's most talked-about brunch spots. Ria Pell, former chef for Floataway Café and Dish, opened Ria's Bluebird in 2001 and is still minding the nest. The cozy, light-drenched diner quickly drew a following for its clever updates on classic Southern dishes and breakfast standards. The wait time on weekends can be mind-boggling—unless you're an early bird who can beat the crowds.

CONTEMPORARY AND NEW AMERICAN

CITY GRILL ❸❸❸

50 Hurt Plaza, 404/524-2489, www.citygrillatlanta.com

HOURS: Mon.-Fri. 11:30 A.M.-2 P.M. and 5-10 P.M., Sat. 5-10 P.M.

A luxurious downtown destination for business-class dining, City Grill is also known as a familiar spot for formal wedding receptions and upscale events. Everything about the restaurant, located in the old 1912 Federal Reserve Bank, says "majesty," from the marble columns to the opulent crystal chandeliers. The menu changes daily and features nouveau American dishes with a penchant for regional organic flavors. Its wine list has been cited as one of the best in town. An unexpected perk for those who are staying nearby but don't want to face the dress code: City Grill delivers.

SUN DIAL RESTAURANT, BAR & VIEW ●●●

210 Peachtree St., 404/935-4279, www.sundialrestaurant.com

HOURS: Mon.-Fri. 11:30 A.M.-2:30 P.M. and 6-11 P.M., Sat. 11:30 A.M.-2:30 P.M. and 5:30-11 P.M., Sun. 11:30 A.M.-2:30 P.M.; view open daily 10 A.M. until closing

COST: (for viewing only) $5 adult, $3 child

Perched 73 stories above the city at the top of the Westin Peachtree Plaza Hotel, the longstanding Sun Dial Restaurant has been a perennial tourist destination for more than three decades. The tri-level complex features a revolving restaurant, cocktail lounge, and observation deck, all with gasp-inducing 360-degree views of Atlanta and its landscape. The menu of contemporary American fare, including dishes such as shrimp and grits or braised beef short ribs, falls on the pricey side; your best bet is to go for drinks or a light lunch. Evening meals require proper dinner attire, including jackets for men.

TED'S MONTANA GRILL ●●

133 Luckie St., 404/521-9796, www.tedsmontanagrill.com/GAAtlanta2.html

HOURS: Sun.-Thurs. 11 A.M.-10 P.M., Fri.-Sat. 11 A.M.-11 P.M.

Ted Turner's experiment in selling bison burgers now has locations from Massachusetts to (duh) Montana, but the corporate headquarters of Ted's Montana Grill is here on Luckie Street. The restaurant, which shares a building with the media mogul's Atlanta penthouse, may not be as sprawling as some of its suburban siblings,

Ted's Montana Grill

but it has a quaint and classic atmosphere that suits the traditional menu just fine. You can choose between beef and bison for most of the entrées, which include tasty burgers and timeless blue-plate specials like meatloaf and slow-roasted pork. The bison pot roast is a particular delight. It may be a chain, but there are far worse places to end up Downtown.

THRIVE ●●●

101 Marietta St., 404/389-1000, www.thriveatl.com

HOURS: Mon.-Fri. 11:30 A.M.-2:30 P.M. and 5:30-11 P.M., Sat.-Sun. 5:30-11 P.M.; bar: Thurs.-Sat. 11 P.M.-2 A.M.

So maybe it's trying a little too hard to be cool, but Thrive still gets points for effort. If nothing else, the restaurant has injected a flashy, West Coast attitude into a once-sleepy downtown office building. The impeccably modern dining room was designed with a pouty fashionista crowd in mind, which is exactly the scene that erupts after 11 P.M. on weekends when the restaurant morphs into martini lounge. The Asian-

American fusion menu defies easy explanation, ranging from upscale burgers and chicken dishes to a full sushi bar. Plus, Thrive offers free valet parking—which is unheard-of in these parts.

FRENCH

◖ FRENCH AMERICAN BRASSERIE $$$

30 Ivan Allen Jr. Blvd., 404/266-1440, www.fabatlanta.com

HOURS: Mon.-Thurs. 11:30 A.M.-10 P.M., Fri.-Sat. 11:30 A.M.-11 P.M.

Fans of Brasserie Le Coze were devastated when the French favorite closed due to renovations at Lenox Square Mall. Rather than relocating, owner Fabrice Vergez opted to tweak the concept and create the new French American Brasserie in a grand 15,000-square-foot space Downtown. The festive four-story restaurant feels both classy and authentic, like enjoying dinner in a quiet corner of the Moulin Rouge (if such a corner ever existed). The menu features French standards like escargot, coq au vin, and duck confit, and retains many favorites from the Brasserie Le Coze days. Don't miss the chic rooftop deck; as the restaurant's sign says, it's "FAB."

MEXICAN

NO MAS! CANTINA $$

180 Walker St., 404/574-5678, www.nomascantina.com

HOURS: Sun.-Thurs. 11:30 A.M.-10 P.M., Fri.-Sat. 11:30 A.M.-11 P.M.

It would be a risky concept in almost any neighborhood: an authentic Mexican cantina mixed with an upscale furniture gallery and home accessories store. But No Mas! Cantina has emerged as one of the restaurant scene's greatest recent success stories—even in up-and-coming Castleberry Hill. What was once a 15,000-square-foot warehouse space has

been dramatically revamped as a jovial two-story hacienda serving creative Mexican fare. If you fall in love with the restaurant's Margarita glasses or a handblown glass light fixture, pop in next door to **No Mas! Productions** (404/215-9769, Mon.-Thurs. 10 A.M.-7 P.M., Fri.-Sat. 10 A.M.-9 P.M., Sun. noon-5 P.M.), where all the furniture of the cantina is on sale along with a vast collection of handcrafted home accessories imported from Mexico. Free valet parking behind the restaurant.

PIZZA

GRANT CENTRAL PIZZA $

451 Cherokee Ave., 404/523-8900

HOURS: Mon.-Sat. 11 A.M.-10 P.M., Sun. noon-10 P.M.

The quintessential neighborhood pizza joint, Grant Central Pizza offers a neat and easy peek into the casual dining habits of intown residents. The New York–style pizza has a dedicated local fan base, though the restaurant also serves great calzones, salads, and a few pasta dishes. Depending on the night, the place can either be teeming with small children (apparently it's a popular choice for hip neighborhood parents) or have a more bar-like atmosphere, with drinkers almost outnumbering eaters. The building itself is also noteworthy, a charming former grocery store converted into an urban gathering spot.

SLICE $

259 Peters St., 404/588-1820, www.sliceatlanta.com

HOURS: Mon.-Thurs. 11:30 A.M.-midnight, Fri. 11 A.M.-3 A.M., Sat. noon-3 A.M., Sun. noon-midnight

Since opening in 2006, Slice has been all about the scene, all about the atmosphere, and all about its ability to attract a flashy urban crowd to an otherwise unassuming storefront in Castleberry Hill. Given the focus on fashion over flavor, it should come as no surprise that

RESTAURANTS

the pizza here takes a backseat to the bling. The space itself is immaculate, with a dramatic central bar and a loft-like aesthetic, and probably works better as an upscale martini lounge than pizza parlor—which isn't a bad thing.

SEAFOOD

SIX FEET UNDER $$

437 Memorial Dr., 404/523-6664,
www.sixfeetunderatlanta.com

HOURS: Mon.-Thurs. 11 A.M.-1 A.M., Fri.-Sat. 11 A.M.-2 A.M., Sun. 11 A.M.-midnight

So (morbidly) named because of its proximity to Oakland Cemetery, Six Feet Under serves an exhaustive selection of seafood in a hipster-ready pub environment. The menu doesn't shy away from deep-fried decadence, with the catfish and shrimp baskets being some of the best you'll find in town. In 2008 the restaurant moved down the street to The Jane, a huge and eye-popping mixed-use redevelopment. Six Feet Under's **Westside location** (685 11th St., 404/810-0040) features an amazing rooftop deck with a worth-seeing view of the skyline.

SOUL FOOD

PASCHAL'S $$

180B Northside Dr., 404/525-2023,
www.paschalsrestaurant.com/castleberryhill.htm

HOURS: Mon.-Thurs. 8 A.M.-10 P.M., Fri.-Sat. 8 A.M.-11 P.M., Sun. 11 A.M.-9 P.M.

Perhaps no Atlanta restaurant can brag about its unique place in local history quite the same way as Paschal's, now located in Castleberry Hill after various previous incarnations. The soul food staple founded more than 50 years ago by James and Robert Paschal became a hot gathering spot for the likes of Martin Luther King Jr., Andrew Young, Hosea Williams, and John Lewis, activists who jokingly called the restaurant the "unofficial headquarters" of the Civil Rights movement. These days the spacious Northside Drive location has less of a politically charged atmosphere and feels more like a sociable hotel breakfast buffet. Known for scrumptious fried chicken, authentic Southern sides, and live jazz brunches on weekends, Paschal's still attracts plenty of tourists curious about its Civil Rights history and eager to sample homegrown soul food for the first time.

Midtown   Map 2

The **Crescent Avenue** corridor, Midtown's most celebrated restaurant row, remains a hot spot for both chic bistros and cheeky martini lounges. But that's only part of the story in this rapidly evolving neighborhood. **West Midtown,** especially around the intersection of 14th Street and Howell Mill Road, is home to a growing selection of trendy restaurants and better-than-average cheap eats. **Juniper Street** between Ponce de Leon and 10th Street has also seen some interesting activity on the food front. Look for an eager—and ever-changing—cast of newcomers in the street-level spaces of the new condo and office towers along **Peachtree Street,** starting around 5th Street and continuing north to 14th Street.

ASIAN

GEISHA HOUSE $$

1380 Atlantic Dr., 404/872-3903,
www.dolcegroup.com/geisha

HOURS: Sun.-Thurs. 5-10:30 P.M., Fri.-Sat. 5-11:30 P.M.

An actual Geisha would take major umbrage at being called anything other than an entertainer, but Geisha House doesn't hesitate to talk about sex. Billed as a "five-star sushi restaurant set in a surreal, high-class brothel," the sleek West Coast export exudes attitude, making it popular with the see-and-be-seen crowd that fills Atlantic Station on weekends. Though sushi purists may give the menu mixed reviews—or balk at the L.A.-priced cocktails—the food remains reliable enough to serve as set decoration for the outstanding people-watching. Dress to impress.

🅒 NAN THAI FINE DINING ⑤⑤⑤

1350 Spring St., 404/870-9933,
www.nanfinedining.com
HOURS: Mon.-Thurs. 11:30 A.M.-2:30 P.M. and 5:30-10 P.M., Fri. 11:30 A.M.-2:30 P.M. and 5:30-11 P.M., Sat. 5-11 P.M., Sun. 5-10 P.M.

For years, Charlie and Nan Niyomkul's Tamarind was celebrated as one of the city's finest Thai restaurants, inspiring the kind of customer loyalty most chefs only dream of. The couple captured lightning in a curry bottle a second time with Nan, an elegant big sister to Tamarind that decidedly upped the ante on Thai in Atlanta. Entrées tend to be appropriately exotic without straying too far from familiar seafood-and-short-rib territory. Plus, the service is frightfully attentive. It's worth the trip alone just to check out the extravagant restrooms, which feel more like day spas.

BARBECUE

FAT MATT'S RIB SHACK ⑤

1811 Piedmont Ave., 404/607-1622,
www.fatmattsribshack.com
HOURS: Mon.-Thurs. 11:30 A.M.-11:30 P.M., Fri.-Sat. 11:30 A.M.-12:30 A.M., Sun. 1-11:30 P.M.

Be prepared to stand in line at this bare-bones and cherished barbecue joint, known not only for its mouth-watering ribs but also for the blues bands that play nightly. The menu keeps it simple—choose either ribs, chopped pork, or chicken—but be sure to sample the rum baked beans and other Southern sides. Getting a table after the music cranks up can take a minor miracle, and forget about carrying on a conversation. But with ribs this tasty, who needs to talk?

COFFEEHOUSES

APRÈS DIEM ⑤⑤

931 Monroe Dr., 404/872-3333, www.apresdiem.com
HOURS: Mon.-Thurs. 11:30 A.M.-midnight, Fri. 11:30 A.M.-2 A.M., Sat. 11 A.M.-2 A.M., Sun. 11 A.M.-midnight

Is Après Diem a cozy coffee bar that serves tasty French-inspired sandwiches, a casually chic lounge with a robust liqueur list, or a late-night watering hole with a massive dessert display? Try all of the above. Though the menu offers a mixed bag of international influences (from Argentinian Beef Tenderloin to Penne Albuféra) and there's a booming brunch crowd, the Midtown staple is most often mentioned as an after-dinner destination, where a casual intown crowd sinks into the huge couches and ruminates over iced cappuccinos for hours. The location in a busy strip mall seems quirky at first, but nothing about Après Diem makes for easy classification.

OCTANE COFFEE BAR & LOUNGE ⑤

1009-B Marietta St., 404/815-9886,
www.octanecoffee.com
HOURS: Mon.-Thurs. 7 A.M.-midnight, Fri. 7 A.M.-1 A.M., Sat. 8 A.M.-1 A.M., Sun. 8 A.M.-10 P.M.

In a city overrun with corporate coffeehouses (what American city isn't?), Octane brews a strong case for keeping your caffeine habit local. An early pioneer into its particular corner of rapidly changing West Midtown, the hip and artsy espresso bar quickly drew a devoted crowd of laptop-bearing college students lured by the free Wi-Fi and superior drink menu. The trendier-than-thou baristas can be borderline surly, but the unpredictable service is tempered by tasty sandwiches and an extensive list of Belgian beers.

CONTEMPORARY AND NEW AMERICAN

AGNES AND MURIEL'S $$

1514 Monroe Dr., 404/814-9103, www.mominthekitchen.com

HOURS: Tues. 11 A.M.-6 P.M., Wed.-Thurs. 11 A.M.-9 P.M., Fri. 11 A.M.-11 P.M., Sat. 10 A.M.-11 P.M., Sun. 10 A.M.-6 P.M.

Named for the moms of its two founders, colorful Agnes and Muriel's serves up a welcome return to the comfort food baby-boomers remember fondly from their formidable years. Though the renovated two-story Midtown bungalow retains plenty of yard-sale-inspired kitsch, the decor has gradually moved away from 1950's camp and more toward a casual and genuine Southern graciousness. It's busiest during weekend brunch times, with folks lining up outside to sample the amazing buttermilk pancakes—made from scratch and swimming in blueberries—or the mushroom feta omelets. Don't miss the fried green tomatoes, available either as an appetizer (your best bet) or on a sandwich.

BACCHANALIA $$$

1198 Howell Mill Rd., 404/365-0410, www.starprovisions.com

HOURS: Mon.-Sat. 6-10 P.M.

The good news: Atlanta's most raved-about restaurant actually *deserves* all the fanfare. The bad news: Thanks to the buzz, landing a decent reservation requires the patience of Job. Since 1993, chef-owners Anne Quatrano and Clifford Harrison have frequently refined their contemporary American concept, carving a niche as the city's quintessential gathering

Diners enter Bacchanalia through its sister gourmet market, Star Provisions.

RESTAURANTS

spot for foodies. The seasonal prix-fixe menu offers only organic ingredients, many of which are grown on the owners' farm. Specials change daily, but a few old favorites like the crab fritters always get rave reviews. Hint: Skip the line by ordering à la carte at the bar.

DRESSED ⑤

950 W. Peachtree St., Ste. 240, 404/347-3434, www.dressedsalads.com

HOURS: Mon.-Sat. 11 A.M.-9 P.M.

The concept is deliciously simple: Come to the counter and build your own salad, or else choose one of the suggested recipes. If you'd like, you can make your salad into a wrap. Grab an Arnold Palmer from the big pit of ice, pay up, and you're out the door. Dressed is a chic—and healthy—alternative to greasy fast food, with delectable greens and a great assortment of toppings served in a crisp, minimally designed dining room that feels inspired by *2001: A Space Odyssey*. There's also a **Buckhead location** (3280 Peachtree Rd., 404/781-2800, Mon.–Sat. 11 A.M.–9 P.M., Sun. 11 A.M.–3 P.M.).

EINSTEIN'S ⑤⑤

1077 Juniper St., 404/876-7925, www.einsteinsatlanta.com

HOURS: Mon.-Thurs. 11 A.M.-11 P.M., Fri. 11 A.M.-midnight, Sat. 10 A.M.-midnight, Sun. 10 A.M.-11 P.M.

The words "brunch" and "Einstein's" have been almost synonymous in Midtown for years now, though you could also add "patio" to that list. It's true that Einstein's has one of the most attractive outdoor dining areas in town—and also one of the most popular. But there's more to this local institution than its Sunday-morning crowd. A series of major renovations have vastly recast the restaurant's interior (actually a collection of three linked

1920s bungalows) into a warm and cozy lodge-like atmosphere with an active bar. The menu of slightly inventive comfort food, pasta, and sandwiches is hardly the draw here: It's all about being seen—preferably on the patio.

CUBAN

LAS PALMERAS ⑤

368 5th St., 404/872-0846

HOURS: Wed.-Fri. 11:30 A.M.-3 P.M. and 5:30-9:30 P.M., Sat. noon-9:30 P.M.

The antithesis of touristy, longtime Midtown favorite Las Palmeras serves authentic home-style Cuban in an unexpected hole-in-the-wall location. Attached to a nondescript bodega on a residential street, the intimate restaurant might never be noticed if not for the busy patio out front. Sumptuous pork and chicken dishes come with reliable black beans and some of the city's best fried plantains, all at prices that'll warm your heart. Though sometimes teeming with families from the neighborhood, Las Palmeras also makes for a suitably romantic dinner destination, as long as you can snag a seat on the patio.

DINERS

SILVER MIDTOWN GRILL ⑤

900 Monroe Dr., 404/817-9827

HOURS: Mon.-Fri. 6:30 A.M.-9 P.M., Sat.-Sun. 9 A.M.-3 P.M.

Longtime Atlantans cried foul in 2006 when one of their favorite greasy spoons, the venerable Silver Grill, abruptly shut down after a jaw-dropping 58-year run. A year later, the diner returned to life under new ownership, with a similar menu and familiar faces from the former waitstaff. (One septuagenarian waitress has been slinging fried chicken there for more than 50 years.) Though the Grill will never win any awards for culinary greatness, its

RESTAURANTS

WHAT'LL YA HAVE, WHAT'LL YA HAVE?

After more than 70 years of business and six locations across the state, The Varsity has grown into something far bigger than just another hamburger joint: It's a genuine Atlanta institution. The restaurant boasts that it whips up two miles of hot dogs, a ton of onions, 2,500 pounds of potatoes, 5,000 fried pies, and 300 gallons of chili each day.

A visit to the "world's largest drive-in" can be intimidating for a first-timer. The counter workers – though friendly – bark at customers, "What'll ya have?" in a booming baritone, and the scene reeks of chaos to the uninitiated. It's helpful to know the lingo before you order. Here are some of the more colorful menu terms:

- Naked Dog: plain hot dog

- Heavy Weight: hot dog with extra chili

- Yellow Dog: naked dog with mustard

- Red Dog: naked dog with ketchup

- Naked Dog Walking: plain hot dog to go

- Glorified Steak: hamburger with mayo, lettuce, and tomato

- Mary Brown Steak: hamburger with no bun

- Bag of Rags: potato chips

- Squirt One: The Varsity's signature orange beverage

© TRAY BUTLER

The Varsity

meat-and-three blue plates always come with a heaping side of genuine Southern hospitality, as authentic as it gets.

◖ THE VARSITY ❺

61 North Ave., 404/881-1706, www.thevarsity.com

HOURS: Sun.-Thurs. 10 A.M.-11:30 P.M., Fri.-Sat. 10 A.M.-12:30 A.M.

Atlanta without The Varsity would be like summer without sunshine. The bona fide homegrown institution boasts its own catch phrases ("What'll ya have?"), costumes (red paper hats free for customers), and colorful names (ask about the "naked dog walking"). What started in 1928 as a carhop for Georgia Tech students has grown into a sprawling lunch counter serving comfort food to a melting pot of locals, with a deep fried menu sure to inspire pangs of guilt for today's health-conscious diners. The formula must work: The Varsity claims to serve 17,000 hot dogs a day, and up to 50,000 on Tech football days.

ITALIAN

LITTLE AZIO ❺

903 Peachtree St., 404/876-7711, www.littleazio.com

HOURS: Sun.-Thurs. 11 A.M.-11 P.M., Fri.-Sat. 11 A.M.-midnight

There's no shortage of fast, cheap pasta counters around Midtown, but Little Azio may be the most reliable. A spinoff from Azio Downtown, this rapidly growing local chain keeps regulars coming back for the straightforward Italian dishes served in a casual, stylish environment. Though the 12-inch thin-crust pizzas seldom disappoint (try the Margarita), venture into the pasta menu for more adventurous fare—particularly the often-featured tortellini special. Other locations in **Berkeley Heights** (1700 Northside Dr., 404/917-1717, Sun.–Thurs. 11 A.M.–10 P.M., Fri.–Sat. 11 A.M.–11 P.M.)

and **Decatur** (340 W. Ponce de Leon Ave., 404/373-4225, Sun.–Thurs. 11:30 A.M.–9 P.M., Fri.–Sat. 11:30 A.M.–10 P.M.) offer the same menu, but Midtown wows with its valet parking and large, busy patio.

PASTA DA PULCINELLA ❺❺

1123 Peachtree Walk, 404/876-1114, www.pastadapulcinella.com

HOURS: Mon.-Thurs. 5:30-10 P.M., Fri.-Sat. 5:30-11 P.M., Sun. 5:30-9 P.M.

Crescent Avenue teems with fashionable restaurants packed on weekend nights, but for a quieter, more graceful experience, wander one street over for the nearly hidden Pasta Da Pulcinella. Elegant without being pretentious, the quaint, converted bungalow serves some of the most inventive pasta dishes you'll find in town, including the dazzling Granny Smith apple ravioli—all at prices that won't break the bank. The menu may not be exhaustive, but a candlelit meal on the breezy front porch makes for an unforgettable night.

MEDITERRANEAN

ECCO ❺❺❺

40 7th St., 404/347-9555, www.ecco-atlanta.com

HOURS: Mon.-Thurs. 5:30-11 P.M., Fri.-Sat. 5:30-midnight, Sun. 5:30-10:30 P.M.

Named one of America's best new restaurants in 2006 by *Esquire,* Ecco sprouted from a family of much-loved local eateries (including La Tavola Trattoria and South City Kitchen). It's labeled "Mediterranean," though a broader "European" label better fits the menu, which changes seasonally. Ecco delivers sophistication set in a *Sex and the City*–ready dining room. Try the mind-blowing fried goat cheese appetizers (gooey spheres of goodness seasoned with honey and black pepper) and, if offered, the chili-braised pork. (Note: Use extra caution when walking this corner of Midtown late at night; it remains a throwback to the neighborhood's grimier days.)

SOUTHERN

JCT KITCHEN & BAR 💲💲

1198 Howell Mill Rd., Ste. 18, 404/355-2252,

www.jctkitchen.com

HOURS: Mon.-Thurs. 11:30 A.M.-2:30 P.M. and 5-10 P.M., Fri.-Sat. 11 A.M.-2:30 P.M. and 5-11 P.M., Sun. 5-9 P.M.

JCT Kitchen & Bar has defied conventional wisdom and transformed what was once a cursed corner of the Westside Urban Market into a thriving business. Promoted as "Southern farmstead cooking," the menu tweaks many expected down-home favorites, arriving at combinations like crispy duck leg confit served with sheep's milk ricotta dumplings, or divine wood-grilled pork tenderloin paired with blue cheese potatoes. The fried chicken is some of the best in town, the servers some of the most gracious. Try the flavored sweet tea and grab a Lemonhead on your way out.

🌙 MARY MAC'S TEA ROOM 💲💲

224 Ponce de Leon Ave., 404/876-1800,

www.marymacs.com

HOURS: Daily 11 A.M.-9 P.M.

Finding quality food from the Old South can be a tall order here in the capital of the New South. Mary Mac's Tea Room, though, has been offering the same genteel, down-home goodness since 1945, earning the nickname "Atlanta's Dining Room." As evidenced by the autographed photos lining the walls, *every* famous Georgian has eaten there. The restaurant remains a packed brunch destination both for the retired Sunday School set and hungover college students entertaining

parents for the weekend. The menu, heavy on fried items, has expanded in recent years to include more healthy fare and vegetarian-friendly options.

🌙 SOUTH CITY KITCHEN 💲💲💲

1144 Crescent Ave., 404/873-7358,

www.southcitykitchen.com

HOURS: Mon.-Thurs. 11:30 A.M.-3:30 P.M. and 5-10:30 P.M., Fri.-Sat. 5-11 P.M., Sun. 11 A.M.-3:30 P.M. and 5-10 P.M.

In the row of restaurants and bars along Crescent Avenue, South City Kitchen may not be the flashiest, but it's certainly one of the most reliable and satisfying. Located in a renovated bungalow with a lovely front patio, the restaurant whispers an understated Southern gentility. That same attitude shines through on the menu of contemporary Southern fare—with an urbane twist—heavy on Lowcountry favorites like she-crab soup, shrimp and grits, or buttermilk fried chicken. The main dining room seems almost always packed and is especially full around the bar, so ask for a table outside, weather permitting. Sunday brunch here can be less of a meal and more of a party, with lots of visiting between tables and diners who hang around, nursing drinks for hours. South City also has a location in **Vinings** (1675 Cumberland Pkwy., 770/435-0700, Mon.–Thurs. 5–10 P.M., Fri.–Sat. 5–11 P.M., Sun. 10 A.M.–3 P.M. and 5–10 P.M.).

TAPAS

TABLE 1280 💲💲💲

1280 Peachtree St., 404/897-1280,

www.table1280.com

HOURS: Tues.-Wed. 11 A.M.-2:30 P.M. and 5-8 P.M., Thurs.-Sat. 11 A.M.-3 P.M. and 5-8 P.M., Sun. 11 A.M.-3 P.M.

Perhaps no restaurant in town can rival the architectural chops of Table 1280, which was unveiled as part of the vast expansion of the High Museum of Art by the internationally acclaimed Renzo Piano. It quickly became one of the hottest tables in town, which had just as much to do with the menu as with the design. Guests choose between two vaguely different dining experiences: The restaurant features full-service American brasserie-inspired fare, or the Tapas Lounge offers up small plates of upscale, seasonal ingredients. Table 1280 is wedged in the new courtyard between the High Museum and the Woodruff Arts Center, but it's not a terribly convenient choice for grabbing a bite after browsing the art. Reservations usually need to be booked several days in advance.

Buckhead   Map 3

Buckhead's reputation for doing glitzy, over-the-top dining isn't going away anytime soon, even as more cutting-edge restaurants have opened in other parts of town. Metro Atlanta's wealthiest neighborhood still has plenty of classic favorites to choose from, largely upscale Italian and French places that will keep a certain luxury-loving segment of the population coming back for more for years to come. The heart of the restaurant scene has traditionally been near the intersection of **East Paces Ferry and Peachtree Roads,** though there are also some notable options near Lenox Square Mall. For cheaper, less stuffy fare, venture southeast to **Cheshire Bridge Road.**

ASIAN

RU SAN'S TOWER PLACE 💲💲
3365 Piedmont Rd., 404/239-9557
HOURS: Daily 11:30 A.M.-midnight

If you like your sushi served in a sedate, meditative environment, where gentle fountains tinkle in the background and a demure attendant promptly refills your *ochoko,* then Ru San's is absolutely not the place for you. If you're looking more for a Sake-fueled college party, where blasting music shakes your table and the chefs yell at each other from behind the bar, then you just might join the legions of locals who swear by Ru San's. The sushi itself is serviceable without being stellar; the multi-page menu might be daunting for beginners. Ru San's **Midtown location** (1529 Piedmont Rd., 404/875-7042, daily 11:30 A.M.–midnight) tends to be a few notches quieter—but is sometimes just as raucous.

BRAZILIAN

FOGO DE CHÃO CHURRASCARIA 💲💲💲
3101 Piedmont Rd., 404/266-9988,
www.fogodechao.com
HOURS: Mon.-Thurs. 11:30 A.M.-2 P.M. and 5-10 P.M., Fri. 11:30 A.M.-2 P.M. and 5-10:30 P.M., Sat. 4:30 10:30 P.M., Sun. 4:30 9:30 P.M.

Part of an international chain of steak houses, Fogo de Chão brings something unique to Atlanta: an authentic all-you-can-eat Brazilian *churrasco.* Guests entering the restaurant first encounter slabs of beef roasting in the front window, then receive a card used to signal when they're ready for a parade of meats to be brought to the table: Green means "Sim por favor" ("Yes, please"), while red signals "Não obrigado" ("No thanks"). Beware: The food comes quickly and it can be hard to keep saying no (remember to turn your card over to red when you've had your fill, otherwise the servers will just keep coming around with food). Vegetarians are directed toward the salad bar, but really should steer clear of this carnivore's paradise altogether.

BRUNCH

OK CAFE $

1284 W. Paces Ferry Rd., 404/233-2888,
www.okcafe.com

HOURS: Sun.-Thurs. 7 A.M.-11 P.M., Fri.-Sat.
11 A.M.-midnight, Sun. 11 A.M.-2 P.M.

Opened in 1987, OK Cafe claims to serve
more customers than any other full-service
restaurant in Georgia. And judging from the
crowds that gather outside on weekend mornings, you might think it was the only brunch
spot in all of Buckhead. The family-friendly
diner menu is heavy on hot sandwiches,
omelets, and comfort food, which suits the
retro-inspired roadhouse atmosphere just fine.
Beyond its brunch business, the café also has
a great take-away station and is open later
than most restaurants in this mostly residential area.

CONTEMPORARY AND NEW AMERICAN

ARIA $$$

490 E. Paces Ferry Rd., 404/233-7673,
www.aria-atl.com

HOURS: Mon.-Sat. 6-10 P.M.

This buzz-worthy Buckhead gem has been
pushing the envelope on New American fare
since 2000, hyping what head chef (and owner)
Gerry Klaskala calls his own unusual take on
the "slow food" movement. The "slow" here
seems to refer mainly to process, with meats
that are braised, roasted, and simmered to per-
fection, along with a pleasantly unpredictable
menu of seafood entrées inspired by Klaskala's
years in coastal Savannah. The dining room
itself is intimate, minimally decorated, and
barely lit—making the place perfect for a romantic evening, as long as you don't mind taking things slow.

BLUEPOINTE $$$

3455 Peachtree Rd., 404/237-9070,
www.buckheadrestaurants.com/bp.html

HOURS: Mon.-Thurs. 11:30 A.M.-2:30 P.M. and
5:30-11 P.M., Fri. 11:30 A.M.-2:30 P.M. and 5:30-11 P.M.,
Sat. 5:30-11 P.M., Sun. 5:30-10 P.M.

The keyword at Bluepointe is "drama," as sig-
nified by the glowing two-story liquor wall behind the central bar and the suggestive giant
red room divider with a peek-a-boo hole in the
center. Thankfully, the upscale eatery's menu
tones down the drama and still manages to be
plenty titillating, offering modern American
with a dash of Asian attitude. Standout
dishes include the peanut-crusted grouper in
Masaman curry, or the mouth-watering soy-
seasoned butterfish on coconut sticky rice. The
creative sushi menu also deserves accolades.
Its location in the striking Pinnacle Building
brings in a busy business dinner crowd.

RESTAURANT EUGENE $$$

2277 Peachtree Rd., 404/355-0321,
www.restauranteugene.com

HOURS: Sun.-Thurs. 5:30-10 P.M., Fri.-Sat. 5:30-11 P.M.

Owner Linton Hopkins competed against a
Who's Who of Atlanta culinary talent in 2006
to earn the top prize on the Food Network's
Iron Chef—but you'd never know it from a visit
to his gracious Restaurant Eugene, an exercise
in restraint and quiet charm. The menu changes
with the seasons, but Hopkins seems to know
how to strike the right balance between man-
nerly Southern influences and elegant, upscale
classics. He also goes to astounding lengths to
include local ingredients in his dishes, a goal
that is sometimes reflected in the menu's eye-
popping prices. Budget-conscious gourmands
should check out the Sunday Supper, a steal of
a prix-fixe meal at around $30 a head.

© TRAY BUTLER

Bluepointe

SOUPER JENNY ⑤

56 E. Andrews Dr., 404/239-9023,
www.souperjennyatl.com

HOURS: Mon.-Wed. 11 A.M.-5 P.M., Thurs. 11 A.M.-10 P.M.,
Fri. 11 A.M.-5 P.M., Sat. 11 A.M. 4 P.M., Sun. 10 A.M. 2 P.M.

When she's not busy heating up some of the most mouth-watering soups in Atlanta, Jenny Levison is a popular actress on local stages. Her welcoming Buckhead café is usually staffed by a host of thespian professionals— but don't expect a song and dance while you wait for your turkey chili. The place is one of the neighborhood's most in-demand lunch spots, with a line that curves out the door. Souper Jenny usually serves six hot soups each day, including vegetarian and vegan options, as well as sandwiches and salads. If you can't make it for lunch, Thursday is grilled-cheese night. The last hour of each day is take-out only.

FRENCH

JOËL ⑤⑤⑤

3290 Northside Pkwy., 404/233-3500,
www.joelrestaurant.com

HOURS: Tues.-Fri. 11:30 A.M.-2 P.M. and 5.30-10 P.M.,
Sat. 5:30-10 P.M.

The brainchild of local celebrity chef Joël Antunes, this graceful Buckhead gem under went a much-needed renovation in 2007. In 2008 Antunes moved to New York, but the French-fusion restaurant seems to have taken its founder's departure in stride, with subtle but appropriate tweaks to the Mediterranean-influenced menu under a new head chef. The modern, minimalist interior works much better after its renovation, which reduced the size of the dining room and introduced hushed earth tones careful not to overshadow the culinary creations on display. Be prepared to peruse one of the most extensive wine lists in the city.

RESTAURANTS

RESTAURANTS

MEXICAN

THE TACO STAND ⑤

3279 Roswell Rd., 404/995-0307,
www.thetacostand.com

HOURS: Sun.-Tues. 11 A.M.-midnight, Wed.-Sat.
11 A.M.-2 A.M.

Finding good cheap eats in hoity-toity
Buckhead can be a real challenge, unless you're
willing to settle for fast food. The Taco Stand
is a noteworthy exception to the rule, with
budget-friendly burritos and tacos served in
a casual sports-bar environment. It's the only
Atlanta offshoot of a wildly successful family of
Mexican joints in Athens, Georgia, and retains
plenty of the original college-town flavor. The
Buckhead location features a menu that's arguably more mature and often hosts impromptu
University of Georgia alumni gatherings, especially on football-game Saturdays.

TAQUERIA DEL SOL ⑤

2165 Cheshire Bridge Rd., 404/321-1118,
www.taqueriadelsol.com

HOURS: Mon.-Thurs. 11 A.M.-2 P.M. and 5:30-9 P.M.,
Fri. 11 A.M.-2 P.M. and 5:30-10 P.M., Sat. 5:30-10 P.M.

Technically speaking, the **West Midtown
location** (1200-B Howell Mill Rd.,
404/352-5811, Mon.–Thurs. 11 A.M.–2 P.M. and
5:30–9 P.M., Fri. 11 A.M.–2 P.M. and 5:30–10 P.M.,
Sat. noon–3 P.M. and 5:30–10 P.M.) was the
original Taqueria del Sol—but the experiment
in creative, cross-cultural tacos began here on
Cheshire Bridge with the former Sundown Café.
The restaurant's owners stumbled upon a white-
hot concept with their spin-off cantina, serving
authentic Mexican street tacos and creative blue-
plate specials in a crisp, urban setting, and eventually ditched the Sundown name in favor of
the more popular brand. Be prepared for lines
that snake out into the parking lot, although the
wait time can easily be tempered with one of

© TRAY BUTLER

TDS's signature margaritas. There is a third location in **Decatur** (359 W. Ponce de Leon Ave.,
404/377-7668, Mon.–Thurs. 11 A.M.–2 P.M. and
5:30–9 P.M., Fri. 11 A.M.–2 P.M. and 5:30–10 P.M.,
Sat. noon–3 P.M. and 5:30–10 P.M.).

SEAFOOD

CHOPS LOBSTER BAR ⑤⑤⑤

70 W. Paces Ferry Rd., 404/262-2675,
www.buckheadrestaurants.com/chops.html

HOURS: Mon.-Thurs. 11:30 A.M.-2:30 P.M.
and 5:30-11 P.M., Fri. 11:30 A.M.-2:30 P.M. and
5:30 P.M.-midnight, Sat. 5:30 P.M.-midnight, Sun.
5:30-10 P.M.

Chops was once known as one of Atlanta's most
exclusive (and pricey) steak houses. These days
the clientele has drifted down-market some, with
more curious suburbanites filling the art deco
dining room, but the menu remains a study in
exorbitance. Downstairs, the more cozy Lobster
Bar features not only seafood but steaks from the
Chops menu (which also offers all items from the

Lobster Bar menu). Business attire is suggested, but the dress code is not enforced as strictly as when the restaurant opened in 1989.

SOUTHERN

THE COLONNADE ⑤⑤

1879 Cheshire Bridge Rd., 404/874-5642

HOURS: Mon.-Thurs. 5–9 P.M., Fri. 5–10 P.M., Sat. 11 A.M.–2 P.M. and 5–10 P.M., Sun. 11 A.M.–9 P.M.

The polar opposite of pretentious, the Colonnade feels like it fell into a time warp during the Carter administration and has barely changed since. Its clientele is equally peculiar, known around town as "all gays or grays," though that characterization is far from exhaustive. What's true is that the Colonnade serves some of the most authentic—and unapologetic—Southern food in town, from greasy fried chicken to collard greens and frog legs. It's the kind of home cooking you'd expect to find at a rural Georgia church basement, and almost nowhere else. Have a drink at the bar, if you dare: The cocktails are known as some of the stiffest around, even here on seedy Cheshire Bridge Road.

ROASTERS ⑤

2770 Lenox Rd., 404/237-1122, www.roastersfresh.com

HOURS: Mon.-Thurs. 11 A.M.–10 P.M., Fri.-Sat. 11 A.M.–10:30 P.M., Sun. 11 A.M.–10 P.M.

The success of this much-loved Buckhead staple is obvious when you consider its northward expansion, with new locations popping up in the outer suburbs. Roasters has made a name for itself by serving dependable comfort food to a diverse clientele, ranging from families from the surrounding neighborhood and shoppers en route from Lenox Square Mall to imports from Midtown and Brookhaven who swear that the rotisserie chicken is worth the drive. It's also a tremendous value, with a meat-and-three with fresh veggies—as well as rolls and cornbread—costing far less than most of the trendy restaurants in the area.

SOUTHWESTERN

GEORGIA GRILLE ⑤⑤⑤

2290 Peachtree Rd., 404/352-3517, www.georgiagrille.com

HOURS: Tues.-Thurs. 6–10 P.M., Fri.-Sat. 6–11 P.M., Sun. 5:30–10 P.M.

The name comes from Georgia O'Keeffe, not the state, which explains a lot about the Southwestern-inspired menu. Georgia Grille has been a word-of-mouth favorite in Buckhead for almost two decades—a real feat considering the tiny restaurant's nearly invisible location in the corner of an unassuming strip mall. Inside, the living room–like space is split between a main dining room and a smaller bar, with eclectic Southwestern artifacts adorning the walls (including a very O'Keeffe cow's skull). The food is both creative and familiar, with twists on traditional Tex-Mex dishes such as lobster enchiladas, "Cowboy" shrimp, and some truly potent margaritas.

NAVA ⑤⑤⑤

3060 Peachtree Rd., 404/240-1984, www.buckheadrestaurants.com/nava.html

HOURS: Mon.-Fri. 11:30 A.M.–2:30 P.M. and 5:30-11 P.M., Sat. 5–11 P.M., Sun. 5:30-10 P.M.

Given the sweeping changes happening in Buckhead Village, it's comforting to know that a staple like Nava is still alive and thriving. The multilevel temple to all things Southwestern has been a smart choice since it opened back in 1995, offering upscale Native-American-influenced Tex-Mex in a festive adobe-themed dining room. The menu drips with chili powder, jalapeños, white corn, and salsa, but there's plenty of options even for spice skeptics. The

RESTAURANTS

prickly pear margarita has a local reputation and well-deserved following.

STEAK HOUSES

BONE'S ⑤⑤⑤

3130 Piedmont Rd., 404/237-2663,
www.bonesrestaurant.com

HOURS: Mon.-Fri. 11:30 A.M.-2:30 P.M. and 5:30-10 P.M., Sat. 5-11 P.M., Sun. 5:30-10 P.M.

After three decades of business, Bone's has racked up no shortage of accolades, including being named as one of the best steak houses in America by *USA Today* and the *New York Times*. The elite steak house is known as a gathering spot for local power brokers and retains the posture of an exclusive gentlemen's club from a bygone era. The service is impeccable and the steaks are, even after all these years, still worth the hype. The menu includes prime cuts of beef, Maine lobster, and a variety of seafood options, along with a respect for Southern favorites.

VEGETARIAN

CAFE SUNFLOWER ⑤⑤

2140 Peachtree Rd., 404/352-8859,
www.cafesunflower.com

HOURS: Mon.-Thurs. 11:30 A.M.-2:30 P.M. and 5-9:30 P.M., Fri. 11:30 A.M.-2:30 P.M. and 5-10 P.M., Sat. noon-2:30 P.M. and 5-10 P.M.

The influences vary wildly at Cafe Sunflower, from Asian spring rolls and edamame to soy chili burritos, but the one constant is a complete devotion to vegetarian dishes. Located in a busy Buckhead strip mall, the inconspicuous diner has a relaxed, sunny ambience and a cheery staff. The black bean quesadilla is to die for, though customers craving meat might settle for one of the many faux chicken options. There's also a **Sandy Springs location** (5975 Roswell Rd., 404/265-1675, Mon.–Thurs. 11:30 A.M.–2:30 P.M. and 5–9 P.M., Fri. 11:30 A.M.–2:30 P.M. and 5–9:30 P.M., Sat. noon–2:30 P.M. and 5–9:30 P.M.).

R. THOMAS DELUXE GRILL ⑤⑤

1812 Peachtree St., 404/872-2942,
www.rthomasdeluxegrill.com

HOURS: Open 24 hours, 7 days a week

Richard Thomas must be feeling pretty proud of himself these days, having predicted the current organic food craze more than 20 years ago. His funky, San Francisco–inspired R. Thomas Deluxe Grill has prided itself on promoting healthy and sustainable diet choices since its opening in 1985. The menu is heavy on vegetarian and vegan-friendly dishes (like the walnut sunflower loaf or the veggie sloppy joe), though it also includes free-range chicken and beef options for the carnivores in the crowd. The restaurant itself is an eclectic roadside attraction, with multicolored windmills and a collection of tropical parrots on display. Even better, it's one of the only restaurants in town that's open all night, making for a truly off-the-wall destination after the bars have shut down.

Virginia-Highland

Map 4

You could spend weeks sampling all the food along **North Highland Avenue,** starting around East Rock Springs Road and working your way south, and never try the same place. You'd also come across some of Atlanta's most-loved restaurants. This busy street alone has dozens of delectable favorites representing a huge range of cuisines, from sushi to Southern, and many are budget-friendly places. For even cheaper favorites, check out **Ponce de Leon Avenue** between Monroe Drive and North Highland Avenue, a favorite stomping ground of college students and thrifty locals.

Highland bars and restaurants, Harry and Sons is practically hidden in plain sight. The inconspicuous plate-glass entrance hardly hints at the commotion inside, let alone the busy back patio—one of the best in the neighborhood. The menu sticks to Thai and Chinese favorites like curry chicken or Thai noodle dishes, but also includes a full selection of sushi options—also some of the best in the neighborhood. The exposed-brick dining room is tastefully adorned with contemporary artwork, giving it the feel of a college-town coffee shop. But really, you should ask for the patio.

RESTAURANTS

ASIAN

DOC CHEY'S NOODLE HOUSE ❸

1424 N. Highland Ave., 404/888-0777,
www.doccheys.com

HOURS: Daily 11:30 A.M. 10 P.M.

The concept has been copied plenty in Atlanta, but never topped: Cheap, tasty, and Americanized noodle dishes served fast. Doc Chey's has been a Morningside landmark for more than a decade and has since expanded into Athens and the Carolinas. The bargain prices and enormous portions draw crowds of young people, as well as yuppies from the neighborhood. Its large outdoor patio overlooks nothing special but manages to be romantic and convivial during the warmer months.

HARRY AND SONS ❸❸

820 N. Highland Ave., 404/873-2009,
www.harryandsonsrestaurant.com

HOURS: Mon.-Thurs. 11:30 A.M.-2:30 P.M. and 5:30-10:30 P.M., Fri. 11:30 A.M.-2:30 P.M. and 5:30-11:30 P.M., Sat. noon-2:30 P.M. and 5:30-11:30 P.M., Sun. noon-2:30 P.M. and 5:30-10:30 P.M.

Tucked in a bustling pocket of Virginia-

BRUNCH

MURPHY'S ❸❸

997 Virginia Ave., 404/872-0904,
www.murphysvh.com

HOURS: Mon. Thurs. 11 A.M. 10 P.M., Fri. 11 A.M. midnight, Sat. 8 A.M.-11 P.M., Sun. 8 A.M.-10 P.M.

Somehow Atlanta never got the hint that having just a handful of quality brunch options causes major headaches on weekends. Which is only good news for Murphy's, one of the most in-demand brunch spots in Virginia-Highland. The wait time for a table on a Sunday morning can be ludicrous, especially after 11 A.M., but luckily the place is known for its killer Bloody Marys to help you cope with the delay. The restaurant itself has the tasteful ambience of a French bistro, but without the attitude.

DESSERT

PAOLO'S GELATO ❸

1025 Virginia Ave., 404/607-0055,
www.paolosgelato.com

HOURS: Tues.-Fri. noon-3 P.M. and 6-10 P.M., Sat. noon-10 P.M., Sun. noon-9 P.M.

Paolo's is one of the only dessert spots in town

offering authentic Italian gelato, with a rotating selection of more than 50 flavors. Proprietor Paolo, whose smiling face figures prominently in all the marketing goods, brings gelato-making expertise from his homeland of Italy and is often on hand to educate customers in the closet-sized shop. It sits on one of the busiest corners of Virginia-Highland and does a brisk after-dinner business. It's cash only, so be prepared.

ITALIAN
EATS $
600 Ponce de Leon Ave., 404/888-9149,
www.eatsonponce.net
HOURS: Daily 11 A.M.-10 P.M.

After 15 years of slinging cheap pasta to an eclectic crowd, Eats deserves a spot as a genuine ATL institution, up there with The Varsity and Margaret Mitchell. The bare-bones spaghetti shack has a rough-around-the-edges charm, with a fleet of pierced employees who seem to be killing time between punk rock gigs serving a peculiar cross section of locals: from college students to cops to yuppies. Diners choose either the pasta counter, serving simple noodle dishes with a choice of sauces and toppings, or the chicken counter, known for its spicy Jerk Chicken and Southern sides like collard greens and baked sweet potatoes.

FLOATAWAY CAFÉ $$$
1123 Zonolite Rd., Ste. 15, 404/892-1414,
www.starprovisions.com
HOURS: Tues.-Sat. 6-10 P.M.

Floataway Café is the dreamy younger sister of one of the most talked-about restaurants in town, Bacchanalia. But if there's any sibling rivalry between the two, it's hard to detect at the small wistful bistro that has a style and attitude all its own. Located in a renovated warehouse on a scary-looking industrial side street north of Morningside, Floataway might get more fanfare

if it were in a more visible spot. Still, the place is often packed and a trip there feels like finding a hidden treasure. The menu, which changes daily, features seasonal cuisine created with country French, Mediterranean, and Italian influences.

LA TAVOLA TRATTORIA $$
992 Virginia Ave., 404/873-5430,
www.latavolatrattoria.com
HOURS: Mon.-Thurs. 5:30-10 P.M., Fri.-Sat. 5:30-11 P.M.,
Sun. 11 A.M.-3 P.M. and 5:30-10 P.M.

La Tavola ("the table" in Italian), a charming and chatty trattoria on a busy intersection, is about as close as Virginia-Highland comes to Little Italy. The small restaurant somehow feels larger as it fills up; there's a warm jubilance that seems to suit the menu of pasta and seafood favorites (baked manicotti, veal scaloppine) just fine. The food itself might not set off fireworks, but La Tavola does boast an impressive wine list and gracious staff. It's the perfect spot for a second date.

LATIN
LA FONDA LATINA $
923 Ponce de Leon Ave., 404/607-0665,
www.fellinisatlanta.com/lafonda.html
HOURS: Mon.-Thurs. 11 A.M.-11 P.M., Fri.-Sat.
11:30 A.M.-midnight, Sun. noon-11 P.M.

Mexican, Cuban, and Latin-American dishes all collide at La Fonda, a bargain staple that has a tendency to polarize patrons—which is to say people seem to either love it or hate it. Detractors will say that the "Latin" label is too generous, that it's really just a Mexican joint with a broad menu, pointing to the fact that they bring out chips and salsa when you sit. But the loyalists will swear that La Fonda offers consistently fresh and tasty quesadillas, Cuban sandwiches, and seafood paella (which is, admittedly, not very authentic, but still downright yummy). The Ponce de Leon location has a breezy second-story patio that's perfect for summer nights; there are also locations in **Candler Park** (1639 McLendon Ave., 404/378-5200) and **Buckhead** (2813 Peachtree Rd., 404/816-8311) with the same hours.

SOUTHERN

ATKINS PARK ⑤⑤

794 N. Highland Ave., 404/876-7249,

www.atkinspark.com

HOURS: Mon.-Sat. 11 A.M.-3 A.M., Sun. 11 A.M.-midnight

This Virginia-Highland landmark often gets mentioned for its bar credentials, mainly because of its designation as Atlanta's oldest continuously licensed tavern, open since 1922. But the drinking crowd that fills the place later on is only half the story. Atkins Park also serves really great comfort food several notches above the usual pub fare. The fried chicken is a guilty pleasure served just the way Grandma made it, with mac and cheese and green beans. The wild Georgia shrimp and grits could make a great gateway dish for dubious Northerners who've never tried grits before. Just be sure to wrap up dinner before the jukebox cranks up and the tipsy masses start stumbling in.

Little Five Points and East Atlanta — Map 5

Bohemian Little Five Points is better known as a destination for thrift stores or dive bars than fine dining—but the quality of some of the cheap eats here really can't be beat (nor can the people-watching). Nearby **Old Fourth Ward** has seen a major building boom along Highland and Edgewood Avenues, with some outstanding new trendy restaurants popping up. East Atlanta, like Little Five, might better be known for its music venues than bistros, but even the indie-rock kids gotta eat sometime.

BRUNCH

THE FLYING BISCUIT CAFE ⑤⑤

1655 McLendon Ave., 404/687-8888,

www.flyingbiscuit.com

HOURS: Sun.-Thurs. 7 A.M.-10 P.M., Fri.-Sat. 7 A.M.-10:30 P.M.

Busy? Always. Raved about? Often. Worth the fuss? Well, mostly. After more than 15 years in business, the Flying Biscuit continues to receive accolades and still draws a long line of folks during weekend brunch hours. The original Candler Park location is a colorful urban enclave, with sunflowers painted on the walls and an endearing girly-girl personality. The food can be less creative than the setting, but does include some standouts among the regular breakfast fare such as a delicious turkey meatloaf and pudge (mashed potatoes with sun-dried tomatoes, basil, and olive oil) and, of course, the signature biscuits. Hint: Beat the crowds by going there for dinner or a late lunch: Breakfast is served all day. There are less zany locations in **Midtown** (1001 Piedmont Ave., 404/874-8887, daily 7 A.M.–10 P.M.) and **Buckhead** (3280 Peachtree Rd., 404/477-0013, daily 6:30 A.M.–10 P.M.).

HIGHLAND BAKERY ⑤

655 Highland Ave., 404/586-0772,

www.highlandbakery.com

HOURS: Mon.-Fri. 7 A.M.-4 P.M., Sat.-Sun. 8 A.M.-4 P.M.

Part of the major crop of new restaurants and business that has blossomed in the Old Fourth Ward district along Highland Avenue, Highland Bakery is known as much for its

RESTAURANTS

RESTAURANTS WITH STAR POWER

Atlanta may not have the same mega-kilowatt celebrity culture of L.A. or New York, but it is a city where well-known actors and musicians have an odd tendency to open restaurants. In many keeps, the stars keep their involvement with the establishment partly under wraps. The Indigo Girls' Emily Saliers maintained a low profile as an early investor in the **Flying Biscuit Cafe** (1655 McLendon Ave., 404/687-8888, www.flyingbiscuit.com) in Candler Park, and is co-owner of much-loved **Watershed** (406 W. Ponce de Leon Ave., 404/378-4900, www.watershedrestaurant.com) in Decatur. Ashton Kutcher and pals from *That '70s Show* are famously linked to **Geisha House** (1380 Atlantic Dr., 404/872-3903, www.dolcegroup.com/geisha), **Dolce** (261 19th St., 404/872-3902, www.dolcegroup.com), and **Ten Pin Alley** (261 19th St., 404/872-3364, www.dolcegroup.com/tenpinalley), but don't expect to spot them partying in Atlantic Station anytime soon.

Other celebrities have taken an altogether different approach to the restaurant biz. Soul legend Gladys Knight put her star power front and center with **Gladys Knight and Ron Winans Chicken & Waffles** (529 Peachtree St., 404/874-9393), a café cofounded by late gospel singer Ron Winans. The downtown destination serves up the soul food staple of fried chicken and buttery waffles (as the name would imply) and other Southern favorites.

Hip-hop mogul Sean Combs put an unusual spin on soul food for his upscale Buckhead restaurant **Justin's** (2200 Peachtree Rd., 404/603-5353, www.justinsrestaurant.com), opting for health-conscious and Caribbean-inspired cuisine. Combs, who named the restaurant after his son, has said that the menu is an homage to the food his late grandmother loved.

Another chart-topping rapper, Atlanta native Ludacris, drew fast fanfare when he opened **Straits** (793 Juniper St., 404/877-1283, www.straitsrestaurants.com), a high-concept bistro that blends Singaporean cuisine with Georgian influences. The glitzy Midtown restaurant reportedly set its owners back $2.7 million, arriving in 2008 in the former Spice location on Juniper Street.

---

exquisite whole-grain breads as for its extensive brunch menu. The setting is a converted redbrick warehouse that just oozes character and warmth; the staff is attentive and polite, if often a little harried. The bakery grinds its flour on-site daily using a unique Austrian Stone Mill. Though busiest during breakfast hours, the bakery also offers a choice selection of sandwiches and salads for lunch.

RADIAL $

1530 DeKalb Ave., 404/659-6594, www.radial.us

HOURS: Mon.-Fri. 7:30 A.M.-3:30 P.M.,

Sat.-Sun. 8:30 A.M.-3:30 P.M.

Radial is the kind of place where you can sip some organic fair-trade coffee and listen in as the twentysomething couple at the table next to you dish about the art show they saw the

night before. Radial retains the up-to-date and urban energy of a joint that's cool without striving, ripe for discovery but not hungry for fame. True, the busy weekend brunch crowds might show that the discovery happened long ago, but it's still relatively easier to get a table here than many other intown brunch destinations. The food tends to be smart and eclectic remakes of breakfast classics (such as biscuits and vegetarian gravy, or organic buckwheat pancakes).

CAJUN

FRONT PAGE NEWS $$

351 Moreland Ave., 404/475-7777,

www.frontpageatlanta.com

HOURS: Mon.-Wed. 11 A.M.-11 P.M., Thurs.

11 A.M.-midnight, Fri.-Sat. 11 A.M.-1 A.M., Sun. 10 A.M.-11 P.M.

Although the original **Midtown location** (1104

Crescent Ave., 404/897-3500) remains as popular as ever, the newer Little Five Points incarnation of Front Page News has a couple of distinct advantages. Located in a gorgeous 100-year-old warehouse, the restaurant features an irresistible patio and a cavernous dining room (which, admittedly, can get noisy on busy nights). Billed as a New Orleans–style tavern, the restaurant taps into a playful French Quarter energy, with a menu influenced, but not overwhelmed, by Creole favorites. Sunday's Live Jazz Brunch is immensely popular, as is the signature Build Your Own Bloody Mary Bar.

COFFEEHOUSES

JAVAVINO $

579 N. Highland Ave., 404/577-8673, www.javavino.com

HOURS: Mon. 6:30-11 A.M., Tues.-Thurs. 6:30 A.M.-10 P.M., Fri. 6:30 A.M.-midnight, Sat. 8 A.M.-midnight, Sun. 8 A.M.-8 P.M.

There are plenty of quality coffeehouses near Poncey-Highland, but JavaVino gets extra credit for its unique concept, adding wine to the mix. The intimate espresso house serves a wide range of coffees and wines from around the world. The house coffee is truly a family affair: Co-owner Heddy Kühl's coffee-growing relatives in Nicaragua hand-pick the beans, and the roast is made in-house at JavaVino. Beyond the caffeine and spirits, JavaVino also serves desserts, cheese plates, and a few sandwiches.

CONTEMPORARY AND NEW AMERICAN

CARROLL STREET CAFÉ $$

208 Carroll St., 404/577-2700, www.apresdiem.com

HOURS: Sun.-Thurs. 8 A.M.-midnight, Fri.-Sat. 8 A.M.-1 A.M.

Part of the same family as Après Diem in Midtown, Carroll Street Café beams with bohemian personality, a reflection of its location in the heart of gentrifying Cabbagetown. The featured paintings are all by local artists and change monthly, and a folksy ambience overflows into both the staff and the food. Healthy salads, serviceable sandwiches, and pasta dishes fill the menu, though things get more complicated at dinner when more steaks and seafood show up. It's probably best to visit during lunch on a sunny day when you can snag one of the few tables on the sidewalk, offering an intriguing view of the up-and-coming neighborhood.

◖ RATHBUN'S $$$

112 Krog St., 404/524-8280, www.rathbunsrestaurant.com

HOURS: Mon.-Thurs. 5-10:30 P.M., Fri.-Sat. 5-11:30 P.M.

Kevin Rathbun has emerged in recent years as one of Atlanta's most in-demand celebrity chefs, with a slew of television appearances and a winning turn (along with his brother, Kent) on the Food Network's *Iron Chef.* The trendy Old Fourth Ward restaurant that bears his name is a study in contrasts: an ultramodern space carved out of an industrial urban complex, and an upscale dining experience that's also curiously casual. Rathbun clearly had a lot of fun putting together the playful menu, which goes from Hamachi tartare to Carolina Mountain Red Trout without missing a beat. The chef's empire includes nearby **Kevin Rathbun Steak** (154 Krog St., 404/524-5600, Mon.–Thurs. 5:30–10:30 P.M., Fri.–Sat. 5:30–11:30 P.M.), which is, as the name implies, a steak house.

SHAUN'S $$$

1029 Edgewood Ave., 404/577-4358, www.shaunsrestaurant.com

HOURS: Wed.-Thurs. 5-10 P.M., Fri.-Sat. 5-11 P.M., Sun. 11 A.M.-2 P.M. and 5-10 P.M.

After heading up the kitchens at several high-concept eateries around town, chef Shaun Doty has gone for the opposite of glitzy with his quaint Inman Park restaurant. Not that Shaun's lacks excitement, but it's more of a refined classic American bistro, with entrées like Carolina shrimp and grits or Berkshire pork schnitzel. The intimate main room has the cozy vibe of a private home—albeit with sexy Italian light fixtures, painted brick walls, and gallery-fresh artwork. A massive farm table dominates the dining room, but don't miss the outdoor patio.

SUN IN MY BELLY $$

2161 College Ave., 404/370-1088,
www.suninmybelly.com
HOURS: Mon.-Sat. 8 A.M.-8 P.M., Sun. 9 A.M.-9 P.M.

Located in an idiosyncratic former hardware store from the 1940s, Sun in My Belly is a popular Atlanta catering company first and a neighborhood nosh spot second. Modeled after a relaxed European café, the restaurant is probably best enjoyed for a lingering Sunday brunch. The first Sunday of each month features live jazz performances during brunch. Oddly enough, the restaurant might be most famous for its bacon, a decadent but delicious side that comes glazed in honey. The menu also includes a persuasive selection of sandwiches (try the balsamic grilled veggies with goat cheese) and seasonal entrées ranging from traditional meatloaf to adobe-spiced pork tenderloin. Foodies will appreciate the above-average attention paid to even the most microscopic details.

TWO URBAN LICKS $$$

820 Ralph McGill Blvd., 404/522-4622,
www.twourbanlicks.com
HOURS: Mon.-Thurs. 5:30 P.M.-midnight,
Fri.-Sat. 5:30 P.M.-1 A.M., Sun. 5:30-10:30 P.M.

An exhilarating sense of (barely) controlled chaos permeates the air at Two Urban Licks— and there's a lot of air to fill in this cavernous former warehouse. With sky-high ceilings, hushed lighting, and an exposed kitchen that fills the center of the dining room, the buzzed-about restaurant doesn't skimp on atmosphere or extravagance; its unique 26-foot wine wall holds 42 stainless-steel barrels of wine, while elsewhere a towering rotisserie cooks up an army's worth of poultry. Given all the theatrics of the dining room, you might worry that the food is an afterthought—luckily this is not the case. Heavy on small plates, the menu features New American fare that's inventive without being too intimidating, including its famous ribs and a couple of inspired beef dishes. But really Two Urban Licks is the kind of place for sharing and socializing—a boisterous, be-seen nightspot that also features a lovely courtyard.

THE VORTEX BAR AND GRILL $

438 Moreland Ave., 404/688-1828,
www.thevortexbarandgrill.com
HOURS: Sun.-Thurs. 11 A.M.-midnight,
Fri.-Sat. 11 A.M.-3 A.M.

Given that its main entrance is a two-story wild-eyed skull, the Vortex isn't exactly the kind of place known for subtlety. It's a snarling burger joint whose clientele tends to be more mixed (and middle class) than the tattoo-inspired wall art might suggest, a hangout where regular dudes mix it up with weekend Harley enthusiasts and Little Five Points slacker types. The star of the kitchen is the half-pound hamburger dressed up in a wide variety of incarnations, including a veggie version and the bizarre Elvis Burger (king-sized with peanut butter and bacon). The menu warns, "Don't come in here and start acting like a damned fool," which says plenty about the service. It's an 18-and-up establishment so leave the kids in the car.

© T. TAY BUTLER

The Vortex Bar and Grill

DINERS
THUMBS UP DINER ⑤⑤
573 Edgewood Dr., 404/223-0690,
www.thumbsupdiner.com
HOURS: Mon.-Fri. 7 A.M.-3 P.M., Sat.-Sun. 7 A.M.-4 P.M.

"Relax, it's just eggs," says the motto of the wildly popular Thumbs Up Diner, though the mood on busy Sunday mornings can be anything but relaxed. Folks flock to Thumbs Up for the reliable and somewhat eclectic breakfast menu, which really is one of the most consistently appealing in town. Favorites include the Heap (seasoned spuds with cheddar/jack) and the Belgian waffle (topped with 100 percent pure Vermont maple syrup). Thumbs Up also offers burgers and sandwiches. In 2008 Thumbs Up opened another location near **West Midtown** (826 Marietta St., 404/745-4233, Mon.–Fri. 7 A.M.–3 P.M., Sat.–Sun. 8 A.M.–4 P.M.). The diner accepts cash only.

ITALIAN
FRITTI ⑤⑤
309 N. Highland Ave., 404/880-9559,
www.frittirestaurant.com
HOURS: Mon.-Thurs. 11:30 A.M.-3 P.M. and 5:30-11 P.M., Fri. 11:30 A.M.-3 P.M. and 5:30-midnight, Sat. 11:30 A.M.-2 A.M., Sun. 1-10 P.M.

An apparent craze for fussy thin-crust pizza swept through Atlanta a few years back, and perhaps no place ever did it better than Fritti. The fashionable younger sister of longstanding Italian restaurant Sotto Sotto next door, this stylish Inman Park destination offers 26 varieties of Neapolitan pizzas—pies that have actually been certified by the Verace Pizza Napoletana Association in Naples, Italy, and that are cooked in handmade wood-burning ovens. The festive patio is a sort of yuppie paradise, with plenty of young professionals sipping Chardonnay and folks heading to Dad's Garage Theater nearby.

SOUL FOOD
SON'S PLACE ⑤
100 Hurt St., 404/581-0530,
www.sonsplacerestaurant.com
HOURS: Mon.-Fri. 7 A.M.-3 P.M.

At first glance Son's Place might look like just another cafeteria, serving comfort food staples to a workaday crowd of lunchtime regulars. But the story goes a lot deeper: It's owned by the son of Deacon Burton, whose longtime Inman Park eatery was a beloved local landmark. Son's Place continues the legacy of Burton's famous fried chicken, cooking up what some devotees say is the best in town. The sides are soul food standards, like collard greens, hoe cakes, fatback biscuits, and grilled cornbread. The menu changes daily; cash only.

RESTAURANTS

RESTAURANTS

SOUTHWESTERN

AGAVE $$

242 Boulevard Dr. SE, 404/588-0006,
www.agaverestaurant.com
HOURS: Sun.-Thurs. 5-10 P.M., Fri.-Sat. 5-11 P.M.

The name comes from the plant that produces tequila, so it's no wonder that Agave prides itself on offering 100 kinds of the coveted Mexican liquor. This giddy Cabbagetown cantina opened in 2000 and was fast to attract a following. Located in a historic former general store, the quaint dining room is both upscale and boisterous. The creative Southwestern fare varies from traditional New Mexican dishes (like posole or Hatch Green Chile stew) to more Americanized options ("sunburned" strip steak or tenderloin medallions). Agave also features an extensive wine list and a dedicated parking lot.

VEGETARIAN

SOUL VEGETARIAN $$

652 N. Highland Ave., 404/874-0145,
www.soulvegetarian.com
HOURS: Tues.-Sun. 11 A.M.-10 P.M.

Part of a national chain of organic, vegan, and kosher restaurants, this cozy Poncey-Highland café is a welcome change of pace from the noodle houses and gin joints along North Highland Avenue. The diner gets major points for creativity in its unusual takes on soul food classics, using little or no fat in the preparation of its dishes and, for the most part, steering clear of meat altogether. The resulting entrées can be heavy on soy substitutes and deliver some truly bizarre taste variations, but it's no doubt a healthy alternative to the real thing. Try the signature soy shake.

Decatur   Map 6

Decatur's **downtown square** has enough attractive food options to keep most folks occupied for days on end, with a charming blend of brew houses, ethnic fare, and casually elegant eateries. Nearby **Oakhurst** has in recent years come into its own as a burgeoning restaurant scene, where a smattering of comfortable neighborhood joints double as pubs for locals.

CONTEMPORARY AND NEW AMERICAN

UNIVERSAL JOINT $

906 Oakview Rd., 404/373-6260, www.ujointbar.com
HOURS: Mon.-Thurs. 11:30 A.M.-2 A.M., Fri.-Sat.
11:30 A.M.-3 A.M., Sun. 12:30 P.M.-3 A.M.

Named for a car part, Universal Joint converted a dilapidated gas station into a busy Oakhurst watering hole. The large patio is packed almost year-round, weather permitting. Though it's known to many of its patrons as a bar first, the Joint also serves tasty burgers, sandwiches, and quesadillas that are in a class well above the usual pub fare. The spicy egg rolls—stuffed with chicken, cream cheese, grapes, and jalapeños—are a decadent delight.

WATERSHED $$

406 W. Ponce de Leon Ave., 404/378-4900,
www.watershedrestaurant.com
HOURS: Mon.-Sat. 11 A.M.-10 P.M., Sun. 10 A.M.-3 P.M.

Watershed is famous not only for its co-owner, Emily Saliers of the Indigo Girls, but also for celebrity chef Scott Peacock and his gourmet fried chicken. But there's more to this classy Decatur destination than the star power. The gorgeous dining room itself feels not only impeccably designed but also

© TRAY BUTLER

Decatur's downtown restaurant row

comfortable, a muted spruce-and-white den that's politely artistic. Chef Peacock prepares seasonal Southern cooking for discerning modern palates. His legendary fried chicken is only served on Tuesdays and is known to run out early.

MEXICAN

MATADOR CANTINA $

350 Mead Rd., 404/377-0808,
www.matadorcantina.com
HOURS: Sun.-Wed. 11:30 A.M. 10 P.M., Thurs.
11:30 A.M.-11 P.M., Fri.-Sat. 11:30 A.M.-midnight

Matador may seem like your typical Americanized Mexican cantina. But beyond the usual round-up of combo plates and fajitas, the extensive menu also features a few surprises, with dishes inspired by traditions of the Michoacán region of central Mexico. The unique tacos are a particular treat. This lively Oakhurst hole-in-the-wall also offers an extensive tequila list and is known for hosting a rowdy crowd for the $3 margaritas on Wednesdays.

MEXICO CITY GOURMET $$

2134 N. Decatur Rd., 404/634-1128
HOURS: Mon.-Thurs. 11 A.M.-10 P.M., Fri. 11 A.M.-10:30 P.M.,
Sat. noon-10:30 P.M., Sun. 5-9:30 P.M.

Open since 1982, this is one of those cherished local restaurants that keeps the regulars coming back for more—thus their slogan, "Sooner or later, everyone comes to Mexico City Gourmet." When they do come, what they'll find is suitably authentic fare, with all the usual dishes normally seen on a strip-mall Mexican menu: tacos, quesadillas, fajitas. The "gourmet" in the name might be something of a misnomer: A better word might be "home-style." The restaurant itself, while pleasant, isn't fancy in the least. If nothing else, the place gets points for its enormous menu. Maybe that's why the place has stayed in business so long: You could eat here for years and never have the same thing twice!

Greater Atlanta Map 7

RESTAURANTS

Atlanta's outer suburbs may not have the same density of trendy dining destinations as neighborhoods like Buckhead or Midtown, but that's not to say that everything outside of the Perimeter is a culinary wasteland. The most interesting—and non-corporate—spots tend to pop up around historic small-town centers, such as in quaint **Roswell** or in the crossroads at **Vinings.** Finding fine dining in Greater Atlanta requires a bit more research and potentially a lot more driving, but there are definitely some hidden gems waiting to be unearthed.

BARBECUE

THE SWALLOW AT THE HOLLOW $$

1072 Green St., Roswell, 678/352-1975,
www.theswallowatthehollow.com

HOURS: Wed.-Thurs. 11 A.M.-2:30 P.M. and 5-9 P.M.,
Fri. 11 A.M.-2:30 P.M. and 5-10 P.M., Sat. 11 A.M.-10 P.M.,
Sun. 11 A.M.-9 P.M.

An actual canoe filled with iced beer greets guests at The Swallow at the Hollow, a down-home barbecue joint that doubles as a music

venue. The rustic Roswell restaurant, with wood-paneled walls covered by picture frames, is about as close to an actual honky-tonk as you'll find in the 'burbs, with live country music Friday and Saturday nights. Though it's billed as a barbecue house, the menu includes plenty of Southern favorites and even some vegetarian-friendly dishes. Be prepared for communal seating; on a busy night you might end up rubbing elbows with strangers at one of the larger tables.

CONTEMPORARY AND NEW AMERICAN

CANOE $$$

4199 Paces Ferry Rd., Vinings, 770/432-2663,
www.canoeatl.com

HOURS: Mon.-Thurs. 11:30 A.M.-2:30 P.M. and
5:30-10:30 P.M., Fri. 11:30 A.M.-2:30 P.M. and 5:30-11 P.M.,
Sat. 5:30-11 P.M., Sun. 10:30 A.M.-2:30 P.M. and
5:30-9:30 P.M.

Landlocked Atlanta suffers from a real envy of cities with waterfronts, which makes Canoe all the more outstanding. It's nestled on a quiet

WAFFLE HOUSE AND DWARF HOUSE

The world's first Waffle House opened in Atlanta on Labor Day 1955, though neither Joe Rogers nor Tom Forkner had any sense that their diner would eventually become a Southern icon. Most often found along interstates and known for being open 24 hours a day, seven days a week, Waffle House now operates more than 1,500 locations in 25 states. In 2008 the company reopened its original Avondale Estates café as the **Waffle House Museum** (2719 E. College Ave., 877/992-3353). The 13-stool diner has been stocked with antique equipment, classic Waffle House uniforms, displays of memorabilia, and place

settings with plastic food. The jukebox offers a selection of original Waffle House songs. The museum is open by appointment only on Monday, Wednesday, and Friday.

Another national chain that emerged from Atlanta has taken a different route with its original location. Though it's known today as Chick-fil-A, Truett Cathy's chicken-sandwich empire started as the Dwarf Grill in 1946 in Hapeville, a stone's throw from what is now Hartsfield-Jackson Atlanta International Airport. Now called the **Dwarf House** (461 Central Ave.), the busy restaurant serves the usual Chick-fil-A menu – but with table service.

bank of the Chattahoochee River near Vinings, about 10 minutes outside of Buckhead. Many tables feature prominent views of the water, but the main dining room is plenty comfortable even without a window or patio seat. To complement the setting, Canoe's menu features original and creative seafood along with upscale New American fare. It's definitely worth the trip.

MEXICAN

NUEVO LAREDO CANTINA 💲💲
1495 Chattahoochee Ave., 404/352 9009,
www.nuevolaredocantina.com

HOURS: Mon.-Thurs. 11 A.M.-10 P.M., Fri.-Sat. 11 A.M.-11 P.M.

As you drive to Nuevo Laredo for the first time, someone in the car will probably announce, "This can't be right." But it is. Located on a distant industrial edge of town, the eternally crowded cantina is a place locals would rather no one else find (the line's long enough already). Serving authentic, homey Mexican

fare since 1992, the place is known for its fresh salsas, sauces, and delicious chicken mole. For extra credit, order the Cadillac Margarita Grande which might help you make sense of the oddball downstairs decor.

SOUTHERN

HORSERADISH GRILL 💲💲💲
4320 Powers Ferry Rd., 404/255-7277,
www.horseradishgrill.com

HOURS: Mon.-Thurs. 11:30 A.M.-2:30 P.M. and 5:30-9 P.M., Fri. 11.30 A.M.-2.30 P.M. and 5-10 P.M., Sat. 5-10 P.M., Sun. 11 A.M.-2:30 P.M. and 5-9 P.M.

Atlanta's answer to Tavern on the Green, Horseradish Grill sits a stone's throw from scenic Chastain Park. The converted barn has the feel of a pleasant—if somewhat somber—garden café. The distinctly Southern menu swears by the mantra "What grows together, goes together," and is heavy on Heirloom varieties of local produce, some of which are

Nuevo Laredo Cantina

grown behind the restaurant. Also featured: rosemary wood-grilled lamb chops, an amazing horseradish-crusted grouper, and the curiously named "Carpetbagger filet" (crispy fried oyster and chili hollandaise served with garlic green beans and mashed potatoes).

VININGS INN RESTAURANT $$$

3011 Paces Mill Rd., 770/438-2282, www.viningsinn.com

HOURS: Mon.-Thurs. 5-10 P.M., Fri. 5-10:30 P.M., Sat. 11:30 A.M.-2:30 P.M. and 5-10:30 P.M., Sun. 11:30 A.M.-2:30 P.M. and 5-10 P.M.

The first thing you notice when approaching the Vinings Inn is the building itself, a gently renovated monument of a house that has previously held a post office, antiques store, and apartments. Inside, the setting is white tablecloths and measured gentility. The menu, billed as Southern, includes many regional standards like fried green tomatoes and sweet corn grits, but it could just as easily be categorized as New American, with a few distinct Creole-inspired touches. The **Attic Bar** (above the restaurant) books music acts Tuesday through Saturday and can get quite rowdy.

STEAK HOUSES

MCKENDRICK'S STEAK HOUSE $$$

4505 Ashford Dunwoody Rd., 770/512-8888, www.mckendricks.com

HOURS: Mon.-Thurs. 11:30 A.M.-2:30 P.M. and 5:30-10 P.M., Fri. 11:30 A.M.-2:30 P.M. and 5:30-11 P.M., Sat. 5:30-11 P.M., Sun. 5:30-10 P.M.

Located in the bustling business district around Perimeter Mall, McKendrick's Steak House has been feeding the northern suburbs for more than 25 years. It's a bit less stuffy than most of the business-class steak houses found further south in Buckhead, but the place still has a sophistication worthy of the powerbrokers who dine there. The cuts of beef are appropriately high-end, the waitstaff knowledgeable and attentive. On some nights the crowd can feel a little geriatric, but this is Dunwoody, after all, not Midtown.

NIGHTLIFE

In recent years the keyword for Atlanta nightlife has been "change." For decades, the city had a reputation as having one of the Southeast's spiciest club scenes, with 24-hour dance palaces that were almost always packed and a rowdy, multi-block bar district in Buckhead legendary for its excesses. Since 2004 seismic changes have hit places that go bump in the night, as newly stringent liquor laws and a few outspoken neighborhood associations have led to the demise of many legendary nightlife venues.

However, the party here is far from finished. Rather than wither up and die, Atlanta nightlife has evolved into a different sort of creature. A fresh generation of swank hotel bars and flashy martini lounges has become the stomping ground for the glitterati and the bling scene. Atlanta has long been a city for ballers and the bottle-service bars they love, a legacy that lives on in several velvet-roped lounges.

Meanwhile many restaurants, which enjoy loopholes in the city's nightlife laws, have also reaped the benefits of doubling as gin joints. It's not uncommon for a restaurant's vibe to morph dramatically as the dinner crowd departs and the drinkers drift in. Atlantans have a particular love for brewpubs, an apparent fad that swept through town almost a decade ago and seems to have stuck. More recently the city

HIGHLIGHTS

LOOK FOR ☾ TO FIND RECOMMENDED NIGHTLIFE.

☾ **Best Acoustic Music Venue:** An intimate venue with a long and well-deserved reputation for excellence, **Eddie's Attic** is a Decatur landmark (page 76).

☾ **Best Be-Seen Dance Club:** Housed in a gorgeous former 1920s movie theater, **Opera** has the opulent feel of a European concert hall – with killer house DJs and a huge dance floor (page 78).

☾ **Best Dive Bar:** Definitely not for the squeamish, **Clermont Lounge** is a dingy 1960s-era strip club that's become a hipster heaven (page 79).

☾ **Best Salsa Dancing:** Spontaneous fits of salsa dancing tend to erupt at Midtown's **Loca Luna,** also home to delicious sangria and mojitos (page 81).

☾ **Best Patio:** Perhaps no bar in town has a larger outdoor space than **Park Tavern,** situated on a scenic corner of Piedmont Park (page 83).

☾ **Best Jazz Club:** Located next door to the Fox Theatre, **Churchill Grounds** is a refined local favorite for hot jazz acts (page 84).

☾ **Best Lounge:** Funky **Bazzaar Urban Bar** has atmosphere and attitude (page 85).

☾ **Best Gay Bar:** Open since 1987, **Blake's on the Park** remains one of the city's most popular gathering spots for gay guys of all ages (page 87).

Opera

© TRAY BUTLER

has fallen hard for gastropubs, watering holes with better-than-average bar food.

Despite a few setbacks, Atlanta still teems with raucous music venues, ranging from fanatical emo dive bars to sophisticated jazz joints and folkie favorites. The many blues clubs here attract a particularly devoted clientele. Locals still gather at their beloved neighborhood taverns and scream at the TVs in the city's many sports bars. Gay and lesbian nightlife has been hit particularly hard by the changing times, with a handful of institutions shuttered, but there are still plenty of options.

Many weekends find DJ gigs, concerts, or special after-hours parties raging somewhere in the city; check the listings in *Creative Loafing,* the *Sunday Paper,* or *Southern Voice* to get a handle on what Atlanta's ever-changing nightlife has on offer.

Live Music

APACHE CAFÉ

64 3rd St., 404/876-5436, www.apachecafe.info

HOURS: Mon.-Thurs. 4 P.M.-12:30 A.M., Fri.-Sat. 4 P.M.-2 A.M.

Map 2

Urban music enclave Apache Café features an eclectic calendar of entertainment, from open-mic hip-hop nights to R&B and reggae showcases. Equal parts lounge, restaurant, and art gallery, the café's exposed-brick interior gives it an off-the-radar Greenwich Village feel—an impression bolstered by its location on a dingy, dead-end street near the interstate. The menu is a mixture of soul food dishes with Jamaican influences. Beware: The area nearby can be borderline unsafe at night, so be sure to park in a secure lot.

BLIND WILLIE'S

828 N. Highland Ave., 404/873-2583, www.blindwilliesblues.com

HOURS: Mon.-Sat. 7 P.M.-late

Map 4

Though it sits in a classy row of Virginia-Highland restaurants and bars, Blind Willie's has the atmosphere of a sticky blues joint lifted off some Bourbon Street back alley. Cofounders Eric King and Roger Gregory asked local blues musicians to pitch in with the carpentry and painting to get the club ready for business back when it opened in 1986, so you could say that the place has the blues in its very bones. Expect an always full house on hand to hear touring and regional acts six nights a week. The cover usually hovers around $12 for weekend shows, $3–5 for weeknights. Blind Willie's also serves a light menu inspired by America's three great blues cities, Chicago, Memphis, and New Orleans.

THE EARL

488 Flat Shoals Ave., 404/522-3950, www.badearl.com

HOURS: Mon.-Sat. 11:30 A.M.-2:30 A.M., Sun. noon-midnight

Map 5

This East Atlanta staple is nothing if not reliable: reliably grungy, reliably loud, and reliably crowded. One of the city's best-known spots for the local indie rock scene, the Earl brings in a hard-partying cooler-than-cool crowd that likes to slam back PBRs and scream to be heard, even if a band happens to be playing on stage. The smallish stage in the back room offers clear sightlines and a decent sound system,

NIGHTLIFE

© TRAY BUTLER

Eddie's Attic

but it can get smoky to the point of suffocation. A more roomy lounge up front serves a menu better than bar food, from jerk chicken to a portobello mushroom burger.

C EDDIE'S ATTIC

515-B N. McDonough Rd., Decatur, 404/377-4976, www.eddiesattic.com

HOURS: Mon.-Thurs. 4 P.M.-12:30 A.M., Fri.-Sat. 4 P.M.-2 A.M.

Map 6

Fans waxing poetic about Eddie's Attic have a tendency to describe the welcoming upstairs club in spiritual terms, with talk of musical "pilgrimages" to see this "shrine" to acoustic legends. The humble space itself defies such grandiose language, but you can't argue with its track record. John Mayer, Sugarland, the Indigo Girls, Shawn Mullins, and countless other acts can thank Eddie's for early exposure. The Music Room hosts up to 185 fans in

a smoke-free environment, and it's often filled to capacity. Go here to catch the next big thing before they explode.

THE MASQUERADE

695 North Ave., 404/577-8178, www.masq.com

HOURS: Vary

Map 5

Depending on the night, a trip to the Masquerade can be either heaven or hell—literally. The live-music space, dubbed Heaven, features indie rock, goth, and punk acts in a hall that can accommodate 1,000 fans. Downstairs, the dance club Hell is reserved for DJs spinning everything from electro to old-school hip-hop, along with performances by smaller acts. In between, there's Purgatory, a pub with pool tables. The nightclub compound is housed in a creepy/cool mill building from the early 1900s, and also hosts concerts in its outdoor music space during the summer. Some events at the

Masquerade are 18 and up, so expect an eager college-age crowd.

NORTHSIDE TAVERN

1058 Howell Mill Rd., 404/874-8745,
www.northsidetavern.com
HOURS: Daily noon–2:30 A.M.
`Map 2`

The exterior of Northside Tavern looks like a roadside honky-tonk transplanted from the dusty backwoods of south Georgia. But inside is one of the city's oldest and most respected blues clubs, with a history dating to 1972. The live blues calendar features a standing line-up of local musicians with loyal followings on weeknights, along with touring acts on weekends. Don't miss the wall of fame showing the blues legends who've played Northside through the years.

RED LIGHT CAFÉ

553 Amsterdam Ave., 404/874-7828,
www.redlightcafe.com
HOURS: Sun. and Tues.–Thurs. 6 P.M.–2 A.M.,
Fri.–Sat. 7 P.M.–3 A.M.
`Map 2`

Bluegrass, folk—and hip-hop? The boxy Red Light Café, situated in an unlikely strip mall on the far side of Piedmont Park, gets points for versatility, even if the venue's acoustics and traffic flow sometimes falter. Known for hosting up-and-coming singer-songwriters and diverse group acts, the café also draws crowds to its open-mic nights. The name may imply something naughty, but the venue's interior errs on the side of quirky, with rotating exhibitions of paintings by local artists.

© TRAY BUTLER

Star Community Bar

STAR COMMUNITY BAR

437 Moreland Ave., 404/681-9018,
www.starbar.net
HOURS: Daily 3 P.M.–3 A.M.
`Map 5`

Depending on the day it's either a funky Little Five Points roost for all things rockabilly or else a decadent dance destination for college girls who want to shake their groove thang, but Star Community Bar also hosts an impressive line-up of rock, garage, and punk bands Wednesday through Saturday nights. Its many regulars keep coming back for the $2 PBRs and to admire the impressive shrine to Elvis Presley, a Little Five Points landmark.

Dance Clubs

THE MARK ULTRALOUNGE

79 Poplar St., 678/904-0050,
www.themarkatlanta.com

HOURS: Tues. 10 P.M.-3 A.M., Wed.-Fri. 6 P.M.-3 A.M.,
Sat. 10 P.M.-3 A.M.

COST: Cover charge varies

Map 1

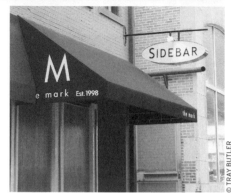

The Mark Ultralounge

Nearly hidden on a sleepy backstreet in the Fairlie-Poplar Historic District, the Mark Ultralounge could almost pass as an exclusive speakeasy. Well-dressed nighthawks and buzzing beauties congregate in this subterranean, design-conscious cocktail den, where the drinks are strong (if a little expensive) and the staff is surprisingly devoid of attitude. The elongated L-shaped basement space also features a dance floor that's really not much larger than the bathrooms. DJs spin everything from '80s alternative to drum 'n' bass, depending upon the night.

MJQ CONCOURSE

758 Ponce de Leon Ave., 404/870-0575,
www.mjqatlanta.com

HOURS: Mon.-Wed. 10 P.M.-4 A.M., Thurs.-Fri.
11 P.M.-4 A.M., Sat. 11 P.M.-3 A.M.

COST: Cover charge varies

Map 4

When a club is described as "underground" it usually means it has an alternative, hipper-than-thou edge, not that it's below street level. But the description fits MJQ Concourse literally and figuratively: Located beneath a plain Poncey-Highland parking lot, the subversive discotheque lures in a racially diverse, hard-partying, and widely mixed crowd for its Brit-pop, hip-hop, and reggae nights. It's also known to host bizarre theme parties (ninjas vs. cowboys?) and features a separate live-music space, dubbed **The Drunken Unicorn** (www .thedrunkenunicorn.net). The only predictable thing about MJQ is its utter unpredictability. If you can't find the front door, you probably shouldn't be looking for it in the first place.

◖ OPERA

1150-B Peachtree St., 404/874-0428,
www.operaatlanta.com

HOURS: Fri.-Sat. 10 P.M.-3 A.M.

COST: Cover charge varies

Map 2

The evolution of Atlanta's nightlife continues at Opera, previous home of the be-seen dance club eleven50. In its latest incarnation as a lavish, vaguely decadent dance den for the fashion-forward bottle-service crowd, the former 1920s movie palace returns to its fussy, opulent roots. With a sensibility lifted from a Parisian concert hall, Opera brings in a rotating lineup of well-known house DJs. Non-dancers can just as easily kick back shots in one of the comfortable areas beyond the dance floor—including a lush outdoor courtyard that shouldn't be missed. Enter on Crescent Avenue.

© TRAY BUTLER

Bars

BRICK STORE PUB

125 E. Court Sq., Decatur, 404/687-0990,
www.brickstorepub.com

HOURS: Mon. 11 A.M.–1 A.M., Tues.–Sat. 11 A.M.–2 A.M.,
Sun. noon–1 A.M.

`Map 6`

Perhaps no place in Atlanta has better Brunswick Stew, but the Brick Store Pub is even more famous for its selection of Belgian beers. The comfortable, cavernous Decatur pub boasts an offering of eight rotating Belgian drafts and more than 120 Belgian (or Belgian styled) bottled beers—in addition to the 17 drafts and 75 bottled beers on its regular menu. A hot spot for Emory and Agnes Scott students, the two-level hangout has the feeling of a bar from the 1930s, though it actually opened in 1997. It's located in a historic building on the Decatur square.

◖ CLERMONT LOUNGE

789 Ponce de Leon Ave., 404/874-4783,
www.clermontlounge.net

HOURS: Mon.–Sat. 1 P.M.–3 A.M.

`Map 4`

"Dive" doesn't begin to describe this legendary Atlanta strip club, which has earned its status as an honest-to-goodness late-night landmark. Open since 1965 in the basement of the Clermont Motor Hotel, the bar is much adored by a certain ironic, hipster clientele who brave the $10 cover and fill the place to capacity on Saturday nights, barely paying attention to the middle-aged ladies wiggling for tips on stage. Blondie, the buxom belle of the bar, has become a local celebrity thanks to her technique for crushing beer cans with her breasts. Truly something you need to see to believe.

DARK HORSE TAVERN

816 N. Highland Ave., 404/873-3607,
www.darkhorseatlanta.com

HOURS: Mon.–Fri. 11 A.M.–3 A.M., Sat. noon–3 A.M.,
Sun. noon–midnight

`Map 4`

A Virginia-Highland mainstay since 1990, this roomy multilevel watering hole seems enormous on an off night (which is rare) and impossibly tiny once the regulars start squeezing in. The crowd piles up three or four deep at the main U shaped bar for a vibe that feels like a college meat market populated by young professionals from the neighborhood. Downstairs, the tavern's live-music room 10 High features karaoke, metal nights, and party bands. A minor round of renovations gave the place a much-needed facelift in 2008, removing the building's exterior stucco to reveal elegant antique brick and improving flow on the outdoor patio.

EL BAR

939 Ponce de Leon Ave., 678/613-3807

HOURS: Wed.–Sat. 10 P.M.–3 A.M.

`Map 4`

You could easily walk past El Bar and never realize you're within spitting distance of one of Atlanta's busiest new gin joints. It's improbably located on the backside of El Azteca, a Mexican restaurant, and barely has room inside to swing a bat at a piñata. Regardless, the space attracts an in-the-know crowd of boisterous hipsters and a full slate of up-and-coming DJs spinning everything from indie rock to old-school hip-hop. Probably not an ideal destination for big groups or the claustrophobic, but it's a great place to start—or end—a memorable night out.

NIGHTLIFE

BYE-BYE, BUCKHEAD VILLAGE

For a place so fixated on becoming "the next great world-class city," as its movers and shakers so often proclaim, Atlanta has taken what feels more like a small-town approach to regulating its nightlife. The city began a major initiative to rein in the club scene not long after the Ray Lewis murder case brought loads of bad press to Buckhead's rowdy bar district in early 2000. Lewis, a linebacker for the Baltimore Ravens, was one of three suspects charged in the late-night murders of two men outside Buckhead's upscale Cobalt Lounge. Though the murder charges against the NFL star were eventually dropped via a plea bargain, the ugly incident added credence to outraged neighborhood groups who had long complained that the nightclubs brought crime and noise pollution to Buckhead.

The Atlanta City Council responded by going after an unlikely culprit: 24-hour nightclubs. Several such "private clubs" had been allowed to stay open and keep pouring thanks to a legal loophole, but a new ordinance in 2001 effectively banned their existence. All-night venues such as Backstreet, the Riviera, and Club 112 challenged the changes, but lost their court case in 2003. The clubs shut down soon after.

Around the same time, local lawmakers rolled back Atlanta bar closing times to 2:30 A.M. This change drew heated criticism from club owners as soon as it was revealed that Underground Atlanta, a city-owned venue, would still be able to serve alcohol until 4 A.M. A few new nightclubs arrived in Underground to take advantage of the later hours, but all eventually closed, thanks partly to Downtown's reputation for being unsafe after dark.

Meanwhile, Buckhead boosters settled on an unusual solution to their late-night woes. Neighborhood activists started covert efforts to convince property owners to stop renting to bars. The campaign was successful, and several once-hot dance clubs shuttered. At the same time, developer Ben Carter began a quiet crusade to buy up buildings in the heart of Buckhead Village's nightlife strip. In 2007, Carter unveiled an $850 million redevelopment plan for the area, which led to the bulldozing of four blocks of prime real estate and the start of construction on an upscale shopping district, Atlanta's answer to Rodeo Drive. The development at Peachtree and Pharr Roads is set to open in 2010 and will include 350,000 square feet of retail space as well as a 225-room hotel and condos. Buckhead's last few nightspots, including longtime favorites Tongue & Groove, Fadó, and the Havana Club, have all relocated.

No single neighborhood inherited Buckhead's former bar scene, though a small handful of new nightspots have sprung up in Midtown, Atlantic Station, and even in Underground. A smattering of watering holes also opened in DeKalb County, where last call comes at 3:55 A.M. One unexpected beneficiary of the city's stringent blue laws seems to be Atlanta's restaurants, which enjoy more liberal regulations, including the ability to serve alcohol on Sundays.

HIGHLAND TAP

1026 N. Highland Ave., 404/875-3673,
www.nnnwcorp.com/highlandtap.html
HOURS: Mon. 4 P.M.-2:30 A.M., Tues.-Sat.
11:30 A.M.-2:30 A.M., Sun. 11:30 A.M.-midnight
Map 4

Although the Highland Tap bills itself as Virginia-Highland's only steak house, the snug subterranean pub keeps getting props as one of the city's best martini bars. Opened in 1989, the restaurant does a reliable and subdued dinner business in the early evening; the mob of upwardly mobile drinkers arrives after midnight for a scene that's loud and flirty. Despite the "tap" in the name, the place isn't known for its wide variety of draft beers. Opt instead for one of the martinis (including a bizarre Sweet Teeni concoction, made with sweet tea) or the better-than-average burger.

LIMERICK JUNCTION IRISH PUB

822 N. Highland Ave., 404/874-7147,
www.limerickjunction.com
HOURS: Mon.-Wed. 5 P.M.-1 A.M., Thurs.-Sat.
5 P.M.-2 A.M., Sun. 5 P.M.-midnight
Map 4

Everything you'd expect from an Irish pub—the Guinness, the Irish folk songs, the Shepherd's Pie—you'll find at Limerick Junction, but the tiny Virginia-Highland taproom also defies easy stereotypes. The free Wi-Fi gives it more of a laptop-friendly Starbucks vibe during happy hour, and the nightly live music lends more to a casual neighborhood pub environment. A mature and often very mixed crowd makes the cozy space feel full almost any night of the week.

THE LOCAL

758 Ponce de Leon Ave., 404/873-5002
HOURS: Mon.-Sat. 5 P.M.-2 A.M., Sun. 5 P.M. midnight
Map 4

Located in a nondescript strip of cheap-eats joints on Ponce de Leon Avenue, The Local

Limerick Junction

is about as no-frills as a nightspot can come: wood-paneled walls, sticky floors, and scruffy waiters. Yet the place has a devoted—borderline maniacal—following that just keeps coming back for more, no doubt hooked on the *Cheers*-like neighborhood vibe and familiarity of the crowd. Known equally for its cheap drinks and famous tater tots, The Local also boasts one of the best barbecue sandwiches in town.

◖ LOCA LUNA

550 Amsterdam Ave., 404/875-4494,
www.loca-luna.com
HOURS: Tues.-Thurs. 5 P.M.-late, Fri.-Sat.
12:30 A.M.-2:30 A.M., Sun. 5-10 P.M.
Map 2

After years of slinging sangria for a rowdy yuppie crowd on 6th Street, Loca Luna up and moved to a marginally more respectable—but equally gaping—space in Amsterdam Walk. Regulars worried that the tapas bar might lose its convivial (read: smashed) atmosphere and begin to focus more on the dinner menu of postage-stamp sized Latin-American and Brazilian dishes, but no such change ever came. Expect ear-splitting merengue and salsa music blasting from the live band and a dance floor filled with hapless gringos swilling mojitos. It's awfully fun, just don't come hungry.

MANUEL'S TAVERN

602 N. Highland Ave., 404/525-3447,
www.manuelstavern.com
HOURS: Mon.-Sat. 11 A.M.-2 A.M., Sun. 11 A.M.-midnight
Map 5

If you're looking for a heated debate about the state of Georgia politics, pull up a stool at Manuel's Tavern. The combination bar and diner is known as a crossroads for politicos and journalists, with lots of actual (and wannabe) movers and shakers in the mix. The laid-back

NIGHTLIFE

neighborhood joint dates back to 1956 and still has the feel of an authentic greasy spoon left over from a less frantic era. Some employees have worked there for more than 30 years and treat their regulars like family. One of the most mixed bars in town, Manuel's has a clientele that transcends race, class, and generation.

RIGHTEOUS ROOM

1051 Ponce de Leon Ave., 404/874-0939
HOURS: Mon.-Thurs. 11:30 A.M.-2 A.M.,
Fri. 11:30 A.M.-3 A.M., Sat. noon-3 A.M., Sun. noon-2 A.M.
`Map 4`

Next door to the nostalgic Plaza Theater, the intimate Righteous Room is a great no-frills place to grab a drink before or after seeing a movie—as long as you're not part of a big group. The narrow bar fills up fast with regulars; early on you'll find less folks drinking and more people eating (the "fatty grilled cheese" is a particular delight), but later the place gets loud and full. As casual as they come, the bar also features rotating art shows by local painters and photographers.

THE TAVERN AT PHIPPS

Phipps Plaza, 3500 Peachtree Rd., 404/814-9640
HOURS: Mon.-Thurs. 11 A.M.-11 P.M.,
Fri.-Sat. 11 A.M.-midnight, Sun. 11 A.M.-10 P.M.
`Map 3`

There's something inherently odd about a restaurant in a shopping mall that attracts a singles scene, but this is Buckhead, after all, so all bets are off. For years The Tavern at Phipps has done a brisk lunch business for power brokers and mall moms, but after happy hour the New Orleans–inspired restaurant gets more of a meat-market feel, with waitresses wearing barely-there skirts and lots of flirty glances exchanged across the bar. It's especially popular with cougars and aspiring trophy wives.

© TRAY BUTLER

The Tavern at Phipps

TRADER VIC'S

255 Courtland St., 404/221-6339,
www.tradervicsatlanta.com
HOURS: Mon.-Sat. 5:30-11 P.M.
`Map 1`

The Tiki revival that swept the nation a few years back has subsided by now, but Trader Vic's shouldn't be worried about a sudden dip in business: The Polynesian-themed Tiki bar and restaurant has been a downtown favorite since 1976. Located in the basement of the Hilton Atlanta, the truly unique dining room feels like a kitschy-fun excursion to the South Pacific, with a dark-bamboo interior and an earnest appreciation for Tahitian accents. The Mai Tai is known as one of the best in the city.

TWISTED TACO

66th 12th St., 404/607-8771, www.twistedtaco.com
HOURS: Mon. 11 A.M.-midnight, Tues.-Thurs.
11 A.M.-2 A.M., Fri. 11 A.M.-3 A.M., Sat. noon-3 A.M.,
Sun. noon-midnight
`Map 2`

Here's what's really twisted: how a suburban-feeling Mexican cantina morphed into a sports bar and singles scene. For years, fashion-forward meat markets dominated the nightlife options around Crescent Avenue, but Twisted Taco turned the formula on its sombrero by welcoming an über-casual, boozy crowd of T-shirt-and-flip-flop-wearing twentysomethings. The decor says Texas saloon, but the crowd says recent Georgia Tech grad.

Brewpubs

5 SEASONS BREWING
5600 Roswell Rd., 404/255-5911,
www.5seasonsbrewing.com
HOURS: Mon.-Thurs. 11 A.M.-midnight,
Fri.-Sat. 11 A.M.-2 A.M., Sun. noon-midnight
Map 7

A Sandy Springs favorite since 2001, 5 Seasons Brewing is known for its authentic handcrafted beers served in a laid-back, gracious environment. Located in an upscale suburban strip mall (which underwent a dramatic renovation in 2008), this massive brew house usually features seven or eight creative drafts brewed in-house, along with a menu that's organic and locally grown when possible. Its suburban locale leads to a yuppie-ish crowd of parents and young professionals. A new location is opening on Marietta Street in West Midtown.

MAX LAGER'S AMERICAN GRILL AND BREWERY
320 Peachtree St., 404/525-4400, www.maxlagers.com
HOURS: Mon.-Sat. 11:30 A.M.-11 P.M., Sun. 4-11 P.M.
Map 1

Downtown is overrun with restaurants that are part of national chains and bars inside swanky hotels, but Max Lager's is an entertaining exception to both rules. The roomy 10,000-square-foot brew house has the atmosphere of a renovated industrial plant, with a loft-like urban bar and dining room. On tap you'll find a handful of German- and Vienna-inspired ales and lagers, including the popular Max Gold pilsner. Most items on the menu are wood-fired, leading to a distinctive dining experience rarely discovered in Downtown.

◖ PARK TAVERN
500 10th St., 404/249-0001, www.parktavern.com
HOURS: Mon.-Fri. 4:30 P.M.-2:30 A.M.,
Sat. 11:30 A.M.-2:30 A.M., Sun. 11:30 A.M.-midnight
Map 2

Bars and restaurants with large, busy patios come a dime a dozen in Atlanta—but not

LOCAL BREWS
Beer lovers should make a point of sampling one of Atlanta's popular homegrown microbrews, or take the time to tour a local brewery. **The Atlanta Brewing Company** (2323 Defoor Hills Rd., 404/355-5558, www.atlantabrewing.com) bills itself as the oldest operational craft brewery in Georgia, open since 1993. Best known for its Red Brick Ale brand, Atlanta Brewing also produces Red Brick Blonde and Peachtree Pale Ale. The brewery hosts a tour and tasting every Wednesday and Friday 6-8 P.M.
　　Sweetwater Brewing Company (195 Ottley Dr., 404/691-2537, www.sweetwaterbrew.com) boasts a 49,000-barrel production of "aggressive, West Coast-style" beers. The award-winning brewery manufactures Sweetwater Blue, Sweetwater IPA, Sweetwater Georgia Brown, and a rotating line of seasonal microbrews. Brewery tours are offered Wednesday, Thursday, and Friday at 5:30 P.M.

NIGHTLIFE

many can match the view at Park Tavern. Overlooking the vast playing fields of Piedmont Park's Meadow, the brewpub's gravel-covered quad buzzes with beer drinkers most weekends of the year. The tavern brews a handful of colorful locally named drafts, including the tangy Druid Hills Pilsner and hops-heavy Park Trail Ale. The brewpub also offers discount drafts on rainy days—their slogan is "When it rains, we pour!"

Jazz Clubs

◖ CHURCHILL GROUNDS

660 Peachtree St., 404/876-3030,
www.churchillgrounds.com
HOURS: Mon.-Fri. 6 P.M.-2 A.M., Sat. noon-2 A.M.
Map 2

Thanks to its proximity to the Fox Theatre, Churchill Grounds attracts a busy pre-show crowd. But the real magic happens later in the night when the intimate nightclub hosts a packed schedule of jazz acts for discerning fans of the genre. The cover charge on weekends can feel like a stretch (sometimes $15, with $10 drink minimum); pop by on a weeknight to beat the crowd and get a better taste of Churchill Grounds' potent sophistication.

DANTE'S DOWN THE HATCH

3380 Peachtree Rd., 404/266-1600,
www.dantesdownthehatch.com
HOURS: Mon.-Sat. 4 P.M.-late, Sun. 5 P.M.-late
Map 3

With a history in Atlanta that dates back more than 30 years, Dante's Down the Hatch is a bizarre, overrated throwback to an earlier era. Make that a couple of earlier eras. The three-story dining room re-creates an 18th-century sailing vessel, complete with a Poop Deck, Captain's Cabin, and an 18,000-gallon moat containing actual crocodiles. The menu recalls the fad of fondue dining from the late '70s, along with strawberry daiquiris served in souvenir glasses. Smooth jazz acts perform six nights a week, with an acoustic guitar player filling in on Mondays. If you like your nightlife touristy, or are longing for the experience of dipping cheese fondue on the set of *Pirates of the Caribbean,* this ship's for you.

SAMBUCA

3102 Piedmont Rd., 404/237-5299,
www.sambucarestaurant.com
HOURS: Sun.-Wed. 4:30-11 P.M.,
Thurs. 4:30 P.M.-midnight, Fri.-Sat. 4:30 P.M.-1 A.M.
Map 3

A mature and sophisticated crowd frequents this jazz café, one of the only nightspots in Buckhead that's been consistently popular during the past few years. The club offers jazz or blues performers playing seven nights a week, along with events sponsored by local smooth jazz radio station WJZZ and occasional torch singers. It's part of a chain of five clubs with other locations in Texas and Nashville; the space, while sleek, does have a slight whiff of suburban sports bar about it.

Lounges

THE BAR AT TROIS

1180 Peachtree St., 404/815-3337, www.trois3.com

HOURS: Mon.-Thurs. 4:30 P.M.-midnight,
Fri.-Sat. 5 P.M.-1 A.M., Sun. 5-10 P.M.

`Map 2`

Architecture buffs thirsty for a peek inside one of Midtown's newest skyscrapers can whet their appetite in style at The Bar at Trois, an urbane lounge on the ground floor of 1180 Peachtree Street. The bar's menu emphasizes sparkling wines and champagnes as well as clever twists on classic cocktails served in a lavish living room–like atmosphere. Plus, it's within easy walking distance of the Crescent Avenue nightlife corridor.

BAZZAAR URBAN BAR

654 Peachtree St., 404/885-7505,
www.bazzaaratlanta.com

HOURS: Tues.-Sat. 6 P.M.-3 A.M.

`Map 2`

One of two bars flanking the Fox Theatre, Bazzaar is the cheeky, young antithesis to the more reserved Churchill Grounds. Modeled after a European martini lounge and decorated with posh Moroccan pillows and accents, the two-story bar feels at once intimate and expansive. Though the venue prides itself on its unpredictable DJ nights and an open-minded vibe, the spirit of inclusion only goes so far unless you've made prior arrangements to reserve one of the VIP seating areas.

EASTSIDE LOUNGE

485 Flat Shoals Ave., 404/522-7841,
www.eastsidelounge.net

HOURS: Mon.-Tues. 9 P.M.-2:30 A.M.,
Wed.-Sat. 5 P.M.-2:30 A.M.

`Map 5`

Nostalgic nightlifers still remember the glory days when this off-the-radar bar was the Fountainhead, a white-hot destination for Atlanta's be-seen twentysomething set. As Eastside Lounge, the space retains plenty of its former occupant's ambience, a dimly lit shotgun-shack loft with a full bar downstairs and exposed brick walls dripping with graffiti-inspired art. Look upstairs for a more private seating area and occasional special events, including art shows. Nightly DJ sets feature everything from Brit pop to electro, and on weekends the upstairs lounge transforms into a dance floor packed elbow to elbow.

GILBERT'S MEDITERRANEAN CAFÉ

219 10th St., 404/872-8012, www.gilbertscafe.com

HOURS: Mon.-Fri. 11:30 A.M.-4 P.M. and 5 P.M.-3 A.M., Sat.
11 A.M.-3 A.M., Sun. 10 A.M.-midnight

`Map 2`

Perhaps brothers Sean and Gilbert Yeremyan never saw it coming, but their polite little Mediterranean bistro has evolved into a hyper-metropolitan cocktail lounge. The dinner and brunch business still takes precedent, even if the food is a little unpredictable, but the real party gets started later on as nearby watering hole Blake's on the Park cranks up. The café has welcomed its mixed gay and straight crowd by hosting occasional flamenco and belly-dancing parties and putting on what may be Midtown's most popular karaoke night (Wed. at 10 P.M.).

HALO

817 W. Peachtree St., 404/962-7333,
www.halolounge.com

HOURS: Mon.-Fri. 4 P.M.-3 A.M., Sat. 6 P.M.-3 A.M.

`Map 2`

The arrival of sleek Halo lounge in the early

2000s raised the stakes on Atlanta nightlife, paving the way for a new generation of ultramodern big-city bars to migrate south from Buckhead into Midtown. These days Halo may not bleed with coolness as it once did, but it remains a trusty watering hole that's still plenty posh and worth a visit. Located in the basement of the historic Biltmore Hotel (refurbished as an office building), the multitiered space is a symphony of cool, industrial surfaces. Crowded nights can make the downstairs bar hard to access, but the place never hurts for eye candy.

LEOPARD LOUNGE

84 12th St., 404/875-7562, www.leopardloungeatl.com
HOURS: Thurs.-Sat. 8 P.M.-3 A.M.
`Map 2`

Countless clubs have braved the tried-and-true Crescent Avenue nightlife corridor, ferocious one month and vacant the next. But the cunning Leopard Lounge has shown remarkable staying power in this competitive lipstick jungle, outlasting most of its rivals by remaining relevant and fresh even 10 years on. A giddy group of beautiful people and buzzing singles sip on potent martinis throughout the multilevel venue, with welcoming fireplaces and a covered patio upstairs. Downstairs, locally loved DJs spin Top 40, hip-hop, and mash-ups for the Den of Sin dance floor. Meow!

LOBBY AT TWELVE

361 17th St., 404/961-7370, www.lobbyattwelve.com
HOURS: Mon.-Thurs. 5:30-11 P.M., Fri.-Sat. 5:30 P.M.-midnight, Sun. 5:30-10 P.M.
`Map 2`

The creators of Lobby at Twelve lose points for uninspired naming (the restaurant/bar is located in the lobby of the Twelve Atlantic Station Hotel, duh) but deserve props for launching what can only be described as a sizzling nightspot for Atlantic Station's flashy urban fashionistas. The atmosphere is an intoxicating jolt of upscale sophistication, though not so fussy as to keep regulars from camping out for hours in the cozy lounge. Bring your A game—but skip the always-backlogged valet parking out front and look for spaces on the street.

Gay and Lesbian

AMSTERDAM CAFÉ

502 Amsterdam Ave., 404/892-2227,
www.myspace.com/amsterdamatlanta
HOURS: Daily 11:30 A.M.-late
`Map 2`

First off, the place is larger inside than it appears from the parking lot—an 8,100-square-foot bar, café, and dance club. Amsterdam draws in a crowd of regular blue-jean guys looking for a more friendly, laid-back atmosphere than some of the glitzier gay watering holes in town. The tricky part might be finding Amsterdam in the first place: It's located on the remote back corner of Amsterdam Walk, far away from the shopping center's more visible businesses. Food is served until 10 P.M. daily.

BELLISSIMA LOUNGE

560-B Amsterdam Ave., 404/917-0220,
www.myspace.com/bellissima_lounge
HOURS: Wed.-Sun. 6 P.M.-late
`Map 2`

A relative newcomer on the scene, cozy Bellissima Lounge has quickly filled a much-needed niche for lesbian nightlife in Midtown. The sexy martini lounge draws a trendy crowd of female patrons;

the name is Italian for "beautiful woman." The smoke-free venue hosts theme nights throughout the week, including Salsa Sundays, wine tastings, and occasional movie screenings. A pool table in the back is a reminder of the venue's former life as a much-loved queer pool hall. On weekend nights, sassy lady DJs play house music.

🌈 BLAKE'S ON THE PARK

227 10th St., 404/892-5786,
www.blakesontheparkatlanta.com
HOURS: Mon.-Sat. 11 A.M.-2:30 A.M.,
Sun. 12:30 P.M.-midnight
`Map 2`

For well over two decades, Blake's on the Park has defied the odds to become one of Atlanta's most resilient gay bars, weathering the city's strict nightlife laws and picking up steam even as the surrounding gayborhood has grown markedly more gentrified. The bar attracts a mostly male clientele to Midtown's quintessential stand-and-model scene; traffic downstairs can be downright brutal, while the breezy patio upstairs usually offers a bit more breathing room for those who don't want to be front row for the drag shows. But for one of the cutest crowds in town, maybe it's worth the hassle.

MARY'S

1287 Glenwood Ave., 404/624-4411,
www.marysatlanta.com
HOURS: Tues.-Sat. 5 P.M.-late
`Map 5`

The Prada boys of Midtown tend to keep their distance from the casual, campy ambience of Mary's in East Atlanta. Known for its wacky karaoke nights, offbeat theme parties, and smarter-than-you DJs, this closet-sized kitsch wonderland is a magnet for eccentric bon vivants and misfit glitterati. The main bar can get crowded to the point of aggravation, but escape the madness by venturing to the upstairs balcony, also a prime spot for cruising new arrivals. Selected as the best gay bar in America by Logo (MTV's gay and lesbian channel) in 2007.

MY SISTER'S ROOM

1271 Glenwood Ave., 404/635-0557,
www.mysistersroom.com
HOURS: Tues.-Thurs. 6 P.M.-late, Fri. 6 P.M.-4 A.M.,
Sat. 7 P.M.-3 A.M.
`Map 5`

Atlanta has a spotty track record for keeping lesbian establishments afloat, though the most defiant exception to the rule may be My Sister's Room. The venerable Sapphic nightspot has enjoyed a long and colorful history in a handful of incarnations around town, most recently popping up in East Atlanta Village. The new home makes sense given the proximity of another hard-to-classify queer bar, Mary's, and fits the watering hole's outsider vibe just fine. Weekend nights find the intimate space packed with butch gals and lipstick ladies bouncing to Top 40 house music. There are also weekly karaoke nights and drag king shows.

NIGHTLIFE

ARTS AND LEISURE

When it comes to the arts, Atlanta sometimes shows symptoms of having an inferiority complex. The city seems to be figuratively always looking over its shoulder, nervous that the finest local artists and arts leaders are planning escapes to towns more hospitable to cultural careers, or eyeing with envy the creative vitality of places like New York or Seattle. Such fears stem from many mitigating circumstances, including the reality that a handful of the city's most successful artists and authors *have* fled Atlanta in the last two decades, coupled with a very Southern fear of being dismissed as a cultural backwater.

The irony is that the city has a bounty of artistic merits to be proud of, with a thriving theater scene, scores of art galleries, exceptional concert halls, and a wealth of performance groups dedicated to everything from opera to improv. Visitors here will find a vast variety of museums filled with classic and modern art, natural history, local culture, and literary matters. The city's many art galleries serve an assortment of tastes, from the bleeding edge to ethnic and outsider art. And the Woodruff Arts Center, which includes the Alliance Theatre, the Atlanta Symphony, and the High Museum, remains a pervasive force in the city's cultural life. It's also the largest arts center in the Southeast.

HIGHLIGHTS

LOOK FOR (TO FIND RECOMMENDED ARTS AND ACTIVITIES.

(**Best Ancient Artwork:** Hidden in plain sight on Emory's campus, the **Michael C. Carlos Museum of Emory University** features one of the most impressive collections of Egyptian funerary artifacts in the nation (page 92).

(**Best Underground Arts Venue:** Expect the unexpected at **Eyedrum Art and Music Gallery,** an off-the-beaten-path setting for envelope-pushing art shows and performances (page 94).

(**Best Small Theater:** With a reputation for excellence, **Actor's Express** has been producing daring stagecraft for two decades (page 95).

(**Best Regional Theater:** After more than 40 seasons, the **Alliance Theatre** is one of Atlanta's most acclaimed cultural institutions. The season typically includes recent Broadway favorites, classics, and world premieres (page 96).

(**Best Music Venue:** The intimate Little Five Points landmark **Variety Playhouse** lives up to its name, featuring a killer line-up of indie rock, folk, pop, and alternative acts (page 100).

(**Best Neighborhood Festival:** In a neighborhood that appears so refined from the outside, the **Inman Park Festival** gives residents a chance to let their freak flags fly, with a colorful costumed parade that's always a highlight of spring (page 102).

(**Biggest Arts Festival:** The **National Black Arts Festival,** held in July but with events year-round, has grown into one of the city's most heavily programmed events, with a mind-blowing schedule of performances, art shows, lectures, and film screenings happening all over town (page 104).

(**Best Recreation Trail:** The **Silver Comet Trail** is a paved multiuse path suitable for walking, biking, and inline skating. The heavily forested corridor runs along a former railroad track and ends in Alabama (page 107).

(**Best Get-to-Know Atlanta Tours:** For a first-rate lesson on local history, the **Atlanta Preservation Center Walking Tours of Historic Atlanta** offer thought-provoking explorations of area sights and neighborhoods (page 110).

(**Best Ball Game:** A day watching the **Atlanta Braves** can be an exhilarating – and also exhausting – affair, thanks to the many distractions at Turner Field (page 111).

© TRAY BUTLER

Michael C. Carlos Museum of Emory University

ARTS AND LEISURE

Atlanta's love of the arts is celebrated most obviously through its many festivals, including the much-hyped Dogwood Festival in April and the world-famous National Black Arts Festival in July. The Atlanta Film Festival has been a regional hit since it began in 1977, and recent years have seen the arrival of an important annual photography festival, Atlanta Celebrates Photography.

The options for outdoor recreation are just as varied and venerated as the arts scene, from hundreds of acres of lush park land inside the city to miles of walking paths that reach from Atlanta to Alabama. Locals are famous for their love of tennis, with one of the largest leagues in the nation, and golf, thanks to dozens of courses around the metro area. The state's sunny and temperate climate makes outdoor fun feasible almost all year round.

Sports fans are also spoiled with an embarrassment of riches here, with major franchises in baseball, basketball, football, and hockey. The Atlanta Braves play in one of the best baseball stadiums in the nation, Turner Field, which was built as Centennial Olympic Stadium in 1996. The Hawks and Thrashers hold court at Philips Arena, an iconic $213 million sports and concert venue. Sure, diehard fans may grumble that too many years have passed since any of the hometown teams landed a championship, but grumbling apparently comes with the territory. Inferiority complex or not, Atlanta isn't a city that likes to settle for second best.

The Arts

MUSEUMS
THE APEX MUSEUM
135 Auburn Ave., 404/521-2739, www.apexmuseum.org
HOURS: Tues.-Sat. 10 A.M.-5 P.M., Sun. 1-5 P.M.
COST: $4 adult, $3 child and senior
Map 1

A downtown fixture since 1978, the African-American Panoramic Experience Museum aims to preserve the culture, traditions, and history of people of African descent. Worth noting is its collection of African art and a detailed replica of the Yates & Milton Drug Store, one of Atlanta's earliest black-owned businesses. The museum deserves high marks for ambition—the small Auburn Avenue space is crammed full of artifacts, photographs, and colorful exhibitions—but could seriously use a more discerning curatorial eye to make the "experience" feel less jumbled.

CENTER FOR PUPPETRY ARTS
1404 Spring St., 404/873-3391, www.puppet.org
HOURS: Tues.-Sat. 9 A.M.-5 P.M., Sun. 11 A.M.-5 P.M.
COST: $8 adult, $6 child, $7 senior
Map 2

The largest American organization dedicated to puppetry theater is more than just a performance space; it also features a must-see museum of puppet history. The permanent collection includes a delightful menagerie of familiar foam faces, from many of Jim Henson's Muppets to prototypes for Disney's Broadway hit *The Lion King*. There's plenty here to keep the ankle-biters busy, from a workshop where kids build their own puppets to an ongoing calendar of family-friendly shows, though adults should hire a sitter and check out the provocative Xperimental Puppetry Theater performances—definitely not for the squeamish.

Fernbank Museum of Natural History is one of the city's favorite family attractions.

FERNBANK MUSEUM OF NATURAL HISTORY

767 Clifton Rd., 404/929-6300,
www.fernbankmuseum.org
HOURS: Mon.-Sat. 10 A.M.-5 P.M., Sun. noon-5 P.M.
COST: $15 adult, $13 child, $14 senior
Map 4

Kids turn out in droves to gasp at the giant *Argentinosaurus* skeleton on permanent display in the Great Hall of Fernbank Museum of Natural History—it's just one of many attractions that has made the museum a much-loved institution. The elegant 160,000-square-foot museum sits on the edge of an urban forest in a corner of the upwardly mobile Druid Hills neighborhood. Permanent exhibits include "A Walk Through Time in Georgia," a series of dioramas that detail the region's geological record, and "Giants of the Mesozoic," which uses fossil casts to explore the diversity of prehistoric life. The Children's Discovery Rooms

take grade-schoolers on a hands-on nature expedition. But not everything here is kids' stuff. Adults can savor the museum's IMAX theater in a cocktail-party atmosphere on Friday nights with Martinis & IMAX.

IMAGINE IT! THE CHILDREN'S MUSEUM OF ATLANTA

275 Centennial Olympic Park Dr., 404/659-5437,
www.imagineit-cma.org
HOURS: Mon.-Fri. 10 A.M.-4 P.M., Sat.-Sun. 10 A.M.-5 P.M.
COST: $11, free under 2
Map 1

Ideal for kids ages eight and under, Imagine It! The Children's Museum of Atlanta is a colorful fantasy land of interactive educational exhibits. The bright, family-friendly space is filled with clever diversions for the Bob the Builder set, specializing in hands-on activities that let kids pull levers, paint on walls, load wagons, and crawl through tunnels. The exhibits are designed

ARTS AND LEISURE

to inspire creative thinking while also teaching concepts such as recycling, environmental awareness, and the importance of teamwork. All kids must be accompanied by an adult, and no adults are admitted without children.

◖ MICHAEL C. CARLOS MUSEUM OF EMORY UNIVERSITY

571 S. Kilgo Circle, 404/727-4282,
www.carlos.emory.edu
HOURS: Tues.-Sat. 10 A.M.-5 P.M., Sun. noon-5 P.M.
COST: $7
Map 4

Although Emory University's impressive collection of artifacts dates back to 1876, the school's Michael C. Carlos Museum has greatly boosted its national reputation in the past 20 years via several high-profile acquisitions and an elegant interior renovation from architect Michael Graves. The 45,000-square-foot museum has become famous especially for a vast and dazzling display of Egyptian mummies and breathtaking relics, though the scope of exhibitions runs the gamut from ancient Greek and Roman ceramics to modern art. Perhaps because of its somewhat remote location in the heart of the Emory campus, the Carlos can be blissfully free of the foot traffic that clogs other Atlanta museums on weekends.

MUSEUM OF CONTEMPORARY ART OF GEORGIA

75 Bennett St., 404/367-4542, www.mocaga.org
HOURS: Tues.-Sat. 10 A.M.-5 P.M.
COST: $3 adult, $1 student
Map 3

A relative newcomer to Atlanta's arts community, the Museum of Contemporary Art of Georgia relocated in 2008 to a grand new home in TULA Art Center, tripling its exhibition space. The new MOCA can host up to five exhibitions in

galleries on two levels, and it also incorporates a classroom facility and storage room for the permanent collection of 550 works by almost 200 Georgia artists. The collection includes pieces in a wide variety of media: paintings, prints, photography, sculpture, and installations. It's off the beaten path but well worth a visit.

RHODES HALL

1516 Peachtree St., 404/885-7800,
www.georgiatrust.org
HOURS: Tues.-Fri. 11 A.M.-4 P.M., Sat. 10 A.M.-2 P.M., Sun. noon-3 P.M.
COST: $5 adult, $4 child and senior
Map 2

True reminders of local history are virtually nonexistent in built-yesterday Atlanta, but stately Rhodes Hall is a lovely exception to the rule. Built in 1904 by furniture magnate Amos Rhodes, the "Rhineland castle on Peachtree" was appointed with high-Victorian flourishes and was one of the first homes in the city to use electricity. Visitors today can marvel at the luminous stained-glass windows depicting the rise and fall of the Confederacy and learn about the evolution of Peachtree Street, where mansions like Rhodes Hall were gradually replaced by today's glass-and-steel office buildings.

WILLIAM BREMAN JEWISH HERITAGE MUSEUM

1440 Spring St., 678/222-3700, www.thebreman.org
HOURS: Mon.-Thurs. 10 A.M.-5 P.M., Fri. 10 A.M.-3 P.M., Sun. 1-5 P.M.
COST: $10 adult, $4 child, $6 senior
Map 2

From the notorious Leo Frank murder trial to the bombing of the Atlanta synagogue in 1958, the local Jewish community has often found itself entangled in issues of justice and equality, even in "the city too busy to hate."

CASTLEBERRY HILL'S ARTS DISTRICT

Art galleries are sprinkled all over Atlanta, with the traditional center of the scene in Buckhead and significant players found in several intown neighborhoods. But the past few years have seen the growth of a new arts district in Castleberry Hill, just south of the Georgia Dome.

The downtown neighborhood was once notorious as a seedy intersection of urban decay and crime, but became a federally recognized historic district in 1985 due to its many traditional brick warehouses dating from the turn of the 20th century. A new, well-heeled generation of residents soon arrived, driving property values up and leading to a renovation boom of decrepit old buildings converted into luxurious lofts. Starting in 2003, a handful of prominent art-gallery owners followed the residential migration, with pioneers like Marcia Wood Gallery, Garage Projects, Wertz Contemporary, and others paving the way for future investment. Though not all of the first transplants survived, the Castleberry Hill Neighborhood Association today lists at least 15 art galleries located in a tight radius around Peters and Walker Streets.

To get a taste for Castleberry Hill's gallery life, hit the **4th Friday ArtStroll** (404/399-7320, www.castleberryhill.org/artstroll.html), held from 7 to 11 P.M. on the fourth Friday of each month. Dozens of galleries, restaurants, shops, and bars take part in the popular free event, and participants vary from month to month. Street parking is available around the neighborhood or in the lot at the corner of Trinity and Spring Streets.

Founded in 1992, the William Breman Jewish Heritage Museum takes visitors on a rich and comprehensive tour of Atlanta's colorful Jewish history. The largest museum of its kind in the Southeast, the Breman hosts permanent exhibitions exploring the roots of the city's Jewish population and its reaction to the Holocaust, with an emphasis on exhibits that highlight the value of tolerance.

WREN'S NEST HOUSE MUSEUM

1050 Ralph David Abernathy Blvd. SW, 404/753-7735, www.wrensnestonline.com

HOURS: Tues.-Sat. 10 A.M.-2:30 P.M.

COST: $8 adult, $5 child, $7 senior

Map 1

Atlanta author Joel Chandler Harris became a household name in the late 1800s thanks to his clever retelling of African-American folktales featuring such now-familiar characters as Br'er Rabbit and Uncle Remus. By the time of his death in 1908, he'd earned a popularity to rival that of his friend Mark Twain. Harris's home, the Wren's Nest, has been a museum and memorial to the writer since 1913. The attractive Queen Anne Victorian farmhouse stands preserved as the Harris family left it, with many original furnishings and interesting heirlooms, including a stuffed owl given to the author by president Teddy Roosevelt. Staff storytellers appear Saturdays at 1 P.M. to bring new life to Harris's Uncle Remus tales; the Wren's Nest also hosts summer and holiday concerts.

GALLERIES

THE ATLANTA CONTEMPORARY ART CENTER

535 Means St., 404/688-1970, www.thecontemporary.org

HOURS: Tues.-Wed. and Fri.-Sat. 11 A.M.-5 P.M., Thurs. 11 A.M.-8 P.M., Sun. noon-5 P.M.

COST: $5 adult, $3 child and senior

Map 2

Founded in 1973 as a cooperative gallery by a

faction of photographers, the Contemporary has since evolved into a cornerstone of the local cutting-edge arts scene. Formerly known as the Nexus Contemporary Art Center, the multidisciplinary center features an expansive exhibition space and a dozen artist studios in an eye-catching 35,000-square-foot warehouse complex. In addition to its popular lecture series, the Contemporary also hosts film screenings and workshops.

THE BILL LOWE GALLERY

1555 Peachtree St., 404/352-8114,
www.lowegallery.com
HOURS: Tues.-Fri. 10 A.M.-5:30 P.M., Sat. 11 A.M.-5:30 P.M.
Map 2

In 2008, Bill Lowe made the bold move of relocating his 20-year-old gallery away from the TULA Art Center in Buckhead to a newly finished office tower in Midtown. The new 12,000-square-foot showroom provides a fitting architectural complement to the artwork Lowe has become known for, specializing in modern, narrative-driven figurative works and rich minimalist creations. The gamble seems to have worked: The gallery's opening parties remain some of the most well-attended art events in town, and the owner refers to his new space as "part temple, part museum, part MTV."

(EYEDRUM ART AND MUSIC GALLERY

290 Martin Luther King Jr. Blvd., 404/522-0655,
www.eyedrum.org
HOURS: Fri. 3-8 P.M., Sat.-Sun. 1-6 P.M.
Map 1

For more than a decade, Eyedrum has been the home for Atlanta's off-the-radar and underground arts scene. This versatile nonprofit blends gallery space with performance venue to create a homey, grungy atmosphere that complements the avant-garde talents featured within. Located in an unlikely warehouse row that you'll swear looks abandoned, Eyedrum delivers an always titillating calendar of cutting-edge art exhibits, improvised music nights, and off-the-wall lectures and workshops. As a rule, the quality of shows varies wildly from divine to dreadful, but such is the nature of experimental art. Atlanta would be a far less interesting place without Eyedrum.

MARCIA WOOD GALLERY

263 Walker St., 404/827-0030,
www.marciawoodgallery.com
HOURS: Tues.-Sat. 11 A.M.-6 P.M.
Map 1

In 2003 longtime Atlanta art guru Marcia Wood decamped from South Buckhead and relocated her popular contemporary gallery to Castleberry Hill, joining a crop of other galleries and studios popping up in the up-and-coming downtown historic district. Castleberry has since become a bona fide gallery destination, with more than a dozen arts-related businesses bringing foot traffic to the still-transitioning neighborhood. Wood's intimate but well-respected gallery specializes in contemporary painting and sculpture, with a taste for provocateurs.

TULA ART CENTER

75 Bennett St., 404/351-3551,
www.tulaartcenter.com
HOURS: Vary
Map 3

At the end of a sleepy industrial street in South Buckhead, the TULA Art Center holds a remarkable enclave of creative activity. The 48,000-square-foot former manufacturing plant houses a handful of commercial galleries, with emphasis ranging from traditional portraiture

© TRAY BUTLER

Young Blood Gallery is a funky blend of indie art gallery, bookstore, and boutique.

to bleeding-edge photography. The Museum of Contemporary Art of Georgia relocated to TULA in 2008, adding new cultural gravitas to an already important arts district. The place can be a ghost town on weekends; it's probably best enjoyed during an evening art opening at one of the galleries or on a weekday afternoon.

YOUNG BLOOD GALLERY AND BOUTIQUE

636 N. Highland Ave., 404/254-4127, www.youngbloodgallery.com

HOURS: Sun.-Thurs. noon-8 P.M., Fri.-Sat. noon-9 P.M.

Map 5

The name says plenty: Young Blood Gallery goes for a youthful, in-your-face vibe with its quirky, urban-inspired exhibitions and wares. The Poncey-Highland gallery and boutique mixes a Little Five Points hipster attitude with a dash of Virginia-Highland refinement to produce an arts emporium that's both

groundbreaking and accessible. Check out the Kraftwerk artist market the first Thursday of each month, featuring a wide range of artwork, jewelry, and crafts created by local artists.

THEATER

ACTOR'S EXPRESS

887 W. Marietta St., Ste. J 107, 404/875-1606, www.actorsexpress.com

Map 2

Since 1988, Actor's Express has put forth some of the most provocative, eyebrow-raising theater in town. Famous for its penchant for male nudity on stage and for championing challenging works by local playwrights, the Express knows how to brew up a season that's both topical and tantalizing. The 200-seat black-box theater is located in the charming King Plow Arts Center, a 19th-century factory whose renovation helped presuppose West Midtown's current building boom.

ARTS AND LEISURE

DISCOUNT TICKETS

Looking to catch a show in Atlanta? **AtlanTIX** is a smart option for finding same-day half-price tickets to theater, dance, and musical performances. Though the ticket selection varies widely, the service lists a plethora of shows daily and almost never disappoints. AtlanTIX operates ticket booths at Underground Atlanta (at the corner of Upper Alabama and Pryor Sts.) and at Lenox Square Mall (3393 Peachtree Rd., in the Simon Guest Services Booth on the main level). Both counters are open Tuesday–Saturday 11 A.M.–6 P.M. and Sunday noon–4 P.M. Go early for the best selection.

Many, but not all, of the discount tickets available at the AtlanTIX booths can also be purchased online at the **Atlanta Performs** website (Tues.–Sat. 8 A.M.–5 P.M., Sun. 8 A.M.–4 P.M., www.atlantaperforms.com), which is also an outstanding resource for locating happenings around town. The official site of the 400-member Atlanta Coalition of Performing Arts, Atlanta Performs serves up a comprehensive list of entertainment choices going on throughout the metro area, with an easy-to-use search engine and an engaging podcast.

◖ ALLIANCE THEATRE

1280 Peachtree St., 404/733-5000,
www.alliancetheatre.org
Map 2

On the crowded stage of Atlanta theater, the Alliance plays the role of the admired prima donna who refuses to give up the spotlight. For more than 40 years, the theater has been a standard-bearer of stagecraft in the Southeast, launching three Tony Award winners to Broadway: *The Color Purple, Aida,* and *The Last Night of Ballyhoo.* The Alliance also took home the 2007 Regional Theatre Tony Award. The 770-seat main auditorium—one of the most comfortable venues in the city—tends to show crowd-pleasers and classics, while more cutting-edge fare is relegated to the smaller Hertz Stage downstairs. Part of the Woodruff Arts Center, the theater shares a grand, eye-popping lobby with Atlanta Symphony Hall and a gorgeous courtyard leading to the High Museum of Art.

DAD'S GARAGE THEATRE

280 Elizabeth St., Ste. C-101, 404/523-3141,
www.dadsgarage.com
Map 5

What was once a fly-by-night improv troupe has evolved into one of the city's preeminent comedy houses. Though it can hardly be called "fringe" anymore, Dad's Garage hasn't lost much of the subversive, sophomoric energy that first put its improv marathons on the map. The cozy black-box theater splits its schedule between a regular season, usually featuring off-the-wall musicals and pop-culture parodies, and weekly improv shows that start at 10:30 P.M. More eclectic fare, including a series for kids, runs in the smaller Top Shelf stage. Drinking and audience participation are expected and encouraged, especially at the late-night improv shows that have the decorum of a college house party.

GEORGIA SHAKESPEARE FESTIVAL

4484 Peachtree Rd., 404/264-0020,
www.gashakespeare.org
Map 7

To be clear, this isn't as much an actual festival as it is a professional repertory theater that happens to produce most—but not all—of its shows in the summer. And even then not all of the plays are by Shakespeare. So maybe the name doesn't fit, but Georgia Shakespeare has been one of the most consistently entertaining and thought-provoking companies in town, with a rich 20-year history in Atlanta. The main season is staged in the well-designed Conant Performing Arts Center on the campus of Oglethorpe University, just north of Buckhead. The troupe also puts on Shake at the Lake, a free outdoor production at Piedmont Park each spring.

HORIZON THEATRE COMPANY

1083 Austin Ave., 404/584-7450,
www.horizontheatre.com

Map 5

Since 1983, cofounders Lisa and Jeff Adler have kept Atlanta audiences hooked on Horizon Theatre. The reliably crowded Little Five Points stage, located in a funky former elementary school, often hosts the Atlanta premieres of off-Broadway plays and works by lesser-known contemporary playwrights. Productions in the intimate 180-seat theater have a certain do-it-yourself charm, though the talent seen on stage tends to be anything but unprofessional. Horizon also hosts the annual New South Play Festival, which develops new plays about the South and works by homegrown playwrights.

THEATRICAL OUTFIT

84 Luckie St., 404/577-5257, www.theatricaloutfit.org

Map 1

Downtown's historic Fairlie-Poplar business district, buzzing by day but deserted by night, has been teetering on the verge of a cultural renaissance at least since the Clinton years. Theatrical Outfit's latest incarnation shows that the long-promised turnaround may happen after all. In 2004, the professional theater company relocated to the lovely 200-seat Balzer Theater at Herren's—a space previously home to one of Downtown's most popular restaurants. Under the leadership of Tom Key, a lion of local theater, Theatrical Outfit stages classic and modern works, with a taste for spiritual themes and stories tied to the South.

PERFORMING ARTS

ATLANTA BALLET

1400 W. Peachtree St., 404/892-3303,
www.atlantaballet.com

Map 2

It may be one of the oldest professional dance companies in America, but the Atlanta Ballet is definitely not acting its age. In recent years the ballet has enjoyed high-profile collaborations with artists such as hip-hop superstar Big Boi and local folk rockers the Indigo Girls—not the kind of fare typically associated with the *Swan Lake* set. Its annual *Nutcracker* production has become an Atlanta holiday tradition; the show usually fills the Fox Theatre to capacity, while the ballet's other performances have moved north to the Cobb Energy Performing Arts Centre.

ATLANTA OPERA

Cobb Energy Performing Arts Centre,
2800 Cobb Galleria Pkwy., 404/881-8801,
www.atlantaopera.org

Map 7

Often dismissed as a genre too stuffy for modern listeners, opera enjoys a surprisingly passionate following here thanks to the efforts of the Atlanta Opera. Founded in 1979, the company has taken steps in recent years to update traditional opera for modern audiences, including providing digital subtitles and staging productions that often turn conventions on their ear. The Atlanta Opera's five annual productions at the Cobb Energy Performing Arts Centre attract a mature, well-heeled crowd mixed with savvy young fans out for a high-culture fix. The performances are almost always thrilling experiences.

© 2009 KEVIN C. ROSE/ATLANTAPHOTOS.COM

Atlanta Symphony Orchestra

ATLANTA SYMPHONY ORCHESTRA

1280 Peachtree St., 404/733-5000,
www.atlantasymphony.org

Map 2

Atlantans have a love-hate relationship—mostly hate—with the acoustically challenged **Symphony Hall,** but their derision doesn't extend to its resident arts company, the Atlanta Symphony Orchestra. Under the musical direction of Robert Spano and Donald Runnicles since 2004, the Grammy-winning orchestra has bolstered its international credentials and cultivated a new reputation for commissioning works by living composers. Its annual events honoring Martin Luther King Jr. and outdoor performances are just a few highlights of the season, along with always-popular holiday shows and concerts featuring the 200-voice Atlanta Symphony Orchestra Chorus.

CONCERT VENUES
CHASTAIN PARK AMPHITHEATER

4469 Stella Dr., 404/233-2227,
www.classicchastain.com

Map 7

The upside: Because many of the seats at Chastain Park Amphitheater have built-in tables or room for picnic baskets, concertgoers usually bring snacks and beverages to enjoy before the show. The downside: At some shows, the dinner conversation and noise of wineglasses clinking can drown out the performance itself. Still, Chastain Park Amphitheater remains one of Atlanta's most popular concert venues, and a $2.3 million renovation has only boosted its credentials. The summer Classic Chastain series features familiar faces your parents would love, along with a handful of younger talents and appearances by the Atlanta Symphony Orchestra. The best parking lots are reserved for season ticket holders, leaving other visitors to search for spots in the residential streets surrounding the venue. Check signs carefully to avoid being towed.

COBB ENERGY PERFORMING ARTS CENTRE

2800 Cobb Galleria Pkwy., 770/916-2800,
www.cobbenergycentre.com

Map 7

Atlanta's affluent northern suburbanites finally got the concert hall they've long howled for with the arrival of the Cobb Energy Performing Arts Centre. The resplendent 2,750-seat venue opened in 2007 at a cost of $145 million and quickly became the default stage for two of the city's most respected cultural institutions, the Atlanta Ballet and the Atlanta Opera. Though designed with touring Broadway shows in mind, the acoustically sound concert hall has been more likely to host big-name pop stars

ARTS AND LEISURE

and country acts. Its 10,000-square-foot ball-room has also been a big attraction for private events. The Cobb Energy Centre is about a 15-minute drive from Downtown, potentially much longer with traffic.

LAKEWOOD AMPHITHEATRE

2002 Lakewood Ave., 404/443-5000

Map 7

It may not be the most comfortable concert venue in town, nor the best maintained, but Lakewood Amphitheatre has a certain scruffy charm. The open-air arena offers 4,000 covered seats, 3,000 "starlight" seats, and room on the sloped lawn for an additional 12,000 fans. (Tip: Spring for the reserved seats, because the lawn has a tendency to turn into a mudslide.) Summers find Lakewood's concert schedule packed with high-profile pop and country stars and music festivals, and the season usually runs late due to Atlanta's temperate autumns. Parking and traffic around the amphitheater can be an utter nightmare, so plan to arrive—and exit—early.

SPIVEY HALL

2000 Clayton State Blvd., 678/466 4200, www.spiveyhall.org

Map 7

Spivey Hall at Clayton State University is one of the region's most respected concert halls. Its reputation hinges on the space's superior acoustics; Spivey Hall is regularly ranked as one of the best small performing-arts venues in the nation. The warm 400-seat theater features a busy series of jazz and classical music performances, which are often heard on American Public Media's *Performance Today* on NPR. The venue also boasts an impressive 4,413-pipe Albert Schweitzer Memorial Organ, installed in 1992. Located 25 minutes from Downtown, Spivey is well worth the hike.

© TRAY BUTLER

Tabernacle

TABERNACLE

152 Luckie St., 404/659-9022, www.tabernacleatl.com

Map 1

From 1910 until the 1980s, this historic downtown venue was an active Baptist church with a congregation of over 4,000. It sat vacant until the 1996 Olympics, when it was converted to a House of Blues club. These days the Tabernacle has become one of the city's favorite midsize music venues, with a total capacity for 2,600 fans spread out over four stories of the historic building. Few flourishes from the church era remain other than the sheer size of the sanctuary (now the main stage) and the striking chandelier. Most interior walls are decorated with funky folk-art designs left over from the New Orleans–inspired House of Blues days.

ARTS AND LEISURE

𝗖 VARIETY PLAYHOUSE

1099 Euclid Ave., 404/524-7354,
www.variety-playhouse.com
Map 5

Little Five Points just wouldn't be the same without the Variety Playhouse. The no-frills music club features a calendar of acts that's about as eclectic as they come: indie rock one night, bluegrass the next. The sloped space, a former movie theater, provides clear sightlines to the bands on stage; the standing-room-only pit up front is almost always jam-packed, but more relaxed fans can see and hear just as well in the upper balcony. The staff is low-key and always friendly, serving microbrews and cocktails at reasonable prices. It's great for a casual night out and close to the restaurants and bars around Little Five Points.

CINEMAS

FERNBANK MUSEUM'S IMAX THEATRE

767 Clifton Rd., 404/929-6300,
www.fernbankmuseum.org
Map 4

Atlanta suffers from a strange dearth of IMAX options: There are only two large-scale film projectors in the entire state of Georgia. Regardless, don't expect Fernbank to start showing Hollywood blockbusters on its five-story screen anytime soon. The science museum reserves the theater for educational films only. (Sorry, Batman.) Every Friday night the museum hosts Martinis & IMAX, a festive cocktail party featuring pre-show drinks and tasty hors d'oeuvres in the Great Hall before screenings of movies such as *Wild Ocean* and *Dinosaurs Alive!* Shows do sell out, so call ahead for reservations.

MIDTOWN ART CINEMA

931 Monroe Dr., 678/495-1424, www.landmarktheatres.com
Map 2

In 2003, national cinema chain Landmark

Theatres bought and dramatically refurbished a shabby eight-screen cinema in a shady corner of Midtown, creating one of the city's most sought-after movie houses. The renovated lobby and concession area, decked in kitschy-cool foreign-language film posters, serves pastries, espresso drinks, and beer. The theater plays Hollywood blockbusters and off-the-radar art-house fare, and also hosts the annual Atlanta Film Festival and Out on Film: the Atlanta Gay and Lesbian Film Festival.

PLAZA THEATRE

1029 Ponce de Leon Ave., 404/873-1939,
www.plazaatlanta.com
Map 4

It may not have the amenities of today's stadium-seating megaplexes, but the quaint Plaza Theatre remains a cheeky and adored flashback to the golden age of small neighborhood cinemas. The oldest movie house in Atlanta makes its presence on Ponce de Leon known via a huge and nostalgic neon sign out front. The theater shows art-house and indie flicks on two screens, mixed with big Hollywood productions and cult classics. A live cast of costumed actors do the "Time Warp" at midnight screenings of *The Rocky Horror Picture Show* every Friday—truly a must-see phenomenon.

STARLIGHT SIX DRIVE-IN

2000 Moreland Ave., 404/627-5786,
www.starlightdrivein.com
Map 7

During the 1950s, Georgia could brag of having almost 130 drive-in movie theaters. Today that number is down to just four, with the venerable Starlight Six Drive-In the only one left in Atlanta. Open since 1949, this local institution remains an attraction by showing current Hollywood releases—usually double features—at the bargain price of $7 per person ($1 for kids under 9). The drive-in also hosts the immensely popular **Drive Invasion** film and music festival every Labor Day weekend, featuring kitschy classic flicks, a hot-rod show, wild tailgating, and bikini-clad car washes.

Festivals and Events

SPRING
ATLANTA DOGWOOD FESTIVAL
Piedmont Park, www.dogwood.org
Map 2

An Atlanta springtime tradition since 1936, the Dogwood Festival draws upwards of 300,000 people to Piedmont Park. Though the event is timed to coincide with April's dogwood blossoms, spectators are more likely to be caught up watching the *actual* dogs competing in the U.S. Disc Dog Southern Nationals, which stars the top Frisbee-catching canines in the country. A vibrant artist's market features more than 200 vendors selling paintings, pottery, jewelry, and tchotchkes. Food and family-friendly fun abounds, though the crowds can be oppressive midday Saturday.

ATLANTA FILM FESTIVAL
Various locations, 404/352-4225,
www.atlantafilmfestival.com

The 10-day Atlanta Film Festival brings up-and-coming cinema to 130,000 moviegoers every April. Festival staffers sort through more than 1,600 entries to select around 160 titles to screen; of those, 20 films compete for the

© TRAY BUTLER

ARTS AND LEISURE

The Dogwood Festival brings the nation's top Frisbee-catching canines to Piedmont Park.

festival's coveted jury prize. The event also features an absorbing roster of panels, screenplay readings, movie discussions, and plenty of parties. Recent years have seen festival screenings centralized into one or two Midtown locations. Atlanta Film Festival 365, the nonprofit group that produces the festival, hosts workshops and screenings year-round.

DECATUR ARTS FESTIVAL

Decatur Square, 404/371-9583,
www.decaturartsfestival.com
Map 6

The best thing about the Decatur Arts Festival may be the city of Decatur itself. With vendors galore in and around Decatur Square, located six miles from downtown Atlanta, the festival has the charm and scale of a small-town street fair, but with the benefits of big-city sophistication. The annual Memorial Day weekend event features more than 140 artists selected through a competitive jury process. An expansive art walk takes visitors on stops all around the city, from art galleries to coffee shops. Kids get their own mini-festival, with events all day Saturday and even their own parade.

◖ INMAN PARK FESTIVAL

Euclid Ave. at Elizabeth St., 770/242-4895,
www.inmanparkfestival.org
Map 5

Spring and summer finds no shortage of neighborhood street festivals here, but the annual Inman Park Festival may well be the city's most vibrant. The stately Victorian homes of the area provide a stunning, if somewhat unexpected, backdrop for the hippie vibe of the two-day festival, which includes an extensive artist market, live dance and musical performances, and a raucous street parade that is usually the highlight of

the weekend. The festival is rounded out by a tour of Inman Park homes. Street parking on festival weekend can be almost impossible to find, so be prepared to walk or take MARTA to the Inman Park Station.

MARTIN LUTHER KING JR. WEEK

Various locations, 404/526-8900,
www.thekingcenter.org

Kicking off with the January 15 birthday of Martin Luther King Jr., this celebration usually spills over to become more of a month-long observance. King Week incorporates a wide range of events all over the city, from an annual concert by the Atlanta Symphony Orchestra to lectures and workshops on many local college campuses. The King Center is the hub for most King Week activities, hosting its largest fundraiser of the year as well as a memorial service for the late civil rights leader. Some happenings are tied with programming for Black History Month in February and the Season for Nonviolence.

SWEET AUBURN SPRINGFEST

Auburn Ave. and Courtland St., 770/912-7221,
www.sweetauburn.com
Map 1

Usually held around the first week in May, this multicultural street festival has expanded its scope to include more than just the vendor tents that fill Auburn Avenue. The event dates back to 1984, but recent years have seen the Sweet Auburn Springfest tackle issues ranging from raising environmental awareness to hosting one of the largest outdoor health and fitness fairs in the country. The festival's primary draw remains the weekend artist market and its many international food options, along with activities aimed at kids and even a beauty pageant.

SUMMER

ATLANTA PRIDE FESTIVAL

Piedmont Park, 770/491-8633, www.atlantapride.org

Map 2

The largest gay and lesbian pride celebration in the South is truly a regional affair. The three-day festival includes a parade, marketplace, full performance schedule, and mass commitment ceremony, among dozens of other unofficial events. Typically held the last weekend in June to commemorate New York's Stonewall Riots of 1969, the Atlanta festival started as a march by local gay activists in 1970. National acts such as the B-52s and the Indigo Girls have headlined Pride over the years; the highlight of the weekend is the sprawling Sunday-afternoon parade that winds its way from Downtown to Piedmont Park. Expect the biggest crowds to gather outside Outwrite Bookstore on Piedmont Avenue.

In 2009 the festival moved to October; check the website for future dates.

DRAGON*CON PARADE

Downtown, 770/909-0115, www.dragoncon.org

Map 1

No longer just Dungeons & Dragons–playing fanboys rolling 20-sided dice in someone's basement all weekend, Atlanta's annual Dragon*Con has grown into one of the largest pop-culture conventions in the country. Held Labor Day weekend, the 30,000-plus member convention delivers some of the city's most outlandish people-watching of the year, best experienced at the annual street parade. Picture an army of Storm Troopers invading Downtown, followed by a fleet of Hobbits or a legion of superheroes. Around 1,000

MOVIES UNDER THE STARS

As if summers in Atlanta weren't packed enough with neighborhood festivals, concerts, and events every night of the week, city dwellers have also come to love outdoor movie screenings. The biggest and best open-air film series is **Screen on the Green** (www.peachtreetv.com), presented by Peachtree TV. Launched in 2000 in Piedmont Park, the festival relocated to Centennial Olympic Park in 2008 due to Georgia's drought. Typically starting in late May and running for five or six weeks, the free Thursday-night series shows Hollywood favorites on a super-sized portable screen. Moviegoers can bring picnic baskets into the park, but glass containers, alcoholic beverages, pets, and umbrellas are prohibited.

The annual **Flicks on Fifth** film series (www.flickson5th.gatech.edu), presented by Georgia Tech, takes place at Technology Square in Midtown, on 5th Street between Spring and Williams Streets. The free Wednesday-night screenings tend toward recent releases and draw a chatty college-age crowd. The series runs for six weeks in June and July. Guests can bring blankets and chairs, but coolers, pets, and umbrellas aren't allowed.

The always entertaining **Coca-Cola Film Festival** at the Fox Theatre (www.foxtheatre.org) also happens under the stars – albeit fake ones. (The historic movie palace's enormous ceiling is painted to mimic a romantic night sky, complete with twinkling stars.) A beloved Atlanta summer tradition, the series features a pre-show sing-along with the Mighty Mo pipe organ and vintage cartoons. The movies shown on the Fox's gigantic screen vary from summer blockbusters to classics. The festival typically kicks off in July or August. Doors open at 6:45 P.M. and tickets are $7. It's perfect for folks who prefer their summer movies in the comfort of air conditioning.

costumed characters take part in the parade, held the Saturday morning of the four-day convention.

◖ NATIONAL BLACK ARTS FESTIVAL
Various locations, 404/730-7315, www.nbaf.org
`Map 1`

What was once a biannual arts festival has expanded into a year-round cultural institution. The summer festival takes place in July, with dozens of events all over the city and a huge, colorful vendor market filling Centennial Olympic Park. Previous festivals have featured appearances by Alice Walker, Wynton Marsalis, and Gladys Knight—to name only a few—as well as performances of Broadway's *The Color Purple* and *Dream Girls*. The festival also offers dance concerts, a lecture series, literary events, and film screenings. No one person can take in all the NBAF has to offer, and tickets to many events do sell out, so advance planning is definitely recommended.

PEACHTREE ROAD RACE
Lenox Square to Piedmont Park, 404/231-9064, www.atlantatrackclub.org

Every July 4, some 55,000 runners brave the blistering Georgia heat to run 6.2 miles along Peachtree Street, huffing past Lenox Square Mall, the glass towers of Buckhead, and the Woodruff Arts Center to finally reach the waiting oasis of Piedmont Park in Midtown. The annual race, first run in 1970, is one of Atlanta's most talked-about local traditions, its coveted T-shirts worn by locals long after the logos have faded. The course's most challenging stretch, dubbed "Heart Attack Hill," happily coincides with Piedmont Hospital—just in case. It's fun for spectators and runners alike, but everyone should avoid driving in Midtown or Buckhead on July 4.

FALL

ATLANTA CELEBRATES PHOTOGRAPHY
Various locations, 404/634-8664, www.acpinfo.org

Since 1999, early fall has signaled an onslaught of photography shows in the city, thanks to the efforts of Atlanta Celebrates Photography. The wide-reaching "festival" feels more like a movement, with more than 100 exhibitions mounted in spaces all over town, as well as parties, film screenings, and a lecture series honoring photographers. An annual gala fundraiser and photography auction helps to keep the nonprofit entity behind Atlanta Celebrates Photography afloat. You could easily visit a couple of ACP shows per day in October and still not take in the full scope of the festival.

EAST ATLANTA STRUT
Flat Shoals and Glenwood Aves., www.eastatlantastrut.com

More than 12,000 people descend upon East Atlanta Village each September for the East Atlanta Strut, a rambunctious street festival with three stages of live entertainment. The community-organized one-day event lasts from 10 A.M. to 10 P.M. and kicks off with a 5K run. The parade features wildly decorated art cars and floats. Younger strutters will enjoy the Kids Village, which gives a funky East Atlanta twist to face painting and wacky removable tattoos. The festival is a fundraiser for local charities.

GRANT PARK MOTHBALL AND TOUR OF HOMES
Various locations, 404/586-9999, www.themothball.org
`Map 5`

Grant Park's tongue-in-cheek Mothball began

in the '70s as a potluck during the annual Tour of Homes; its name is a parody of neighboring Inman Park's formal Butterfly Ball. Now almost 40 years later, the annual costume party and fundraiser for the neighborhood association has spread its wings to become an autumn tradition not just for Grant Park residents. The event features a silent auction, live music, and a spirited "Miss Mothball" competition. The party traditionally takes place on the Saturday evening of the Grant Park Tour of Homes (in September or October), which gives a peek inside some of the prestigious residences of Atlanta's largest historic neighborhood. The date of the event varies.

LITTLE FIVE POINTS HALLOWEEN FESTIVAL

Euclid and Moreland Aves.,

www.l5phalloween.com

Map 5

Most any Saturday night finds all sorts of freaks and funky characters roaming the streets of Little Five Points, so just try and imagine the place around Halloween. The alternative-minded neighborhood's annual Halloween festival embraces the spooky spirit of the season with rare enthusiasm, though its daytime events make this horror show a (mostly) family-friendly function. Kids and adults can enter the festival's costume contest or just sit back and enjoy the afternoon parade, featuring some of the most imaginative get-ups found this side of Dragon*Con. The festival usually takes place a couple of weekends before October 31, thereby stretching Halloween into a much longer celebration.

WINTER

LIGHTING OF MACY'S GREAT TREE

Lenox Square Mall, 770/913-5639

Map 3

Since its start in 1947, this homegrown holiday tradition has changed with the times. It was first held at the now-defunct Rich's department store Downtown, but has since moved to Macy's at Lenox Square Mall. More than 100,000 spectators turn out for the Thanksgiving-evening event, which includes a lot more than just throwing the switch on the store's towering 70-foot Christmas tree. Previous years have seen performances by pop and country stars and the Macy's holiday choir. Even better, the annual tree lighting signals the arrival of the **Pink Pig,** a beloved children's ride that returns each year to the mall's upper parking deck. (It's one of those things you just have to see to understand.)

NEW YEAR'S EVE PEACH DROP AT UNDERGROUND

50 Upper Alabama St., 404/523-2311,

www.peachdrop.com

Map 1

Times Square drops a magnificent Waterford Crystal ball every New Year's Eve at midnight; Atlanta drops an 800-pound fiberglass peach. The city's 16-hour New Year's celebration features a full day of live performances, family games, and fireworks leading up to the closing of the calendar. At midnight, the eight-foot-tall fruit takes less than a minute to crawl down its metal light tower as thousands of onlookers below ring in the new year. It's one of the most well-attended outdoor New Year's Eve events in the nation, but not recommended for anyone averse to rowdy crowds.

ARTS AND LEISURE

Sports and Recreation

PARKS

Atlanta's two most famous parks, Piedmont Park and Centennial Olympic Park (both profiled in the *Sights* chapter), are prime destinations for tourists and locals alike. The city boasts 338 parks in all, which cover a total of 3,570 acres—which is actually one of the smallest park systems for any major American city. If lacking in acreage, Atlanta's parks certainly don't hurt for usage or loyalty. Neighborhood groups here are known to be fierce defenders of their nearby parks, and heavy investors in the green spaces' maintenance and future.

CHASTAIN PARK

Powers Ferry and W. Wieuca Rds., 404/817-6744, www.chastainpark.org

Map 7

Chastain Park, Atlanta's largest, often gets overshadowed by the more centrally located Piedmont Park, but this splendid 250-acre green space has plenty to offer. Once the site of a Creek Indian village, the land was first developed as North Fulton Park in the late 1930s and renamed Troy G. Chastain Memorial Park in 1945 to honor the civic leader who'd been the biggest booster of the project. The park today incorporates a diverse slate of options: Chastain Park Amphitheatre, an arts center, jogging trails, a horse park, ball fields, aquatic center, tennis courts, and a golf course.

FREEDOM PARK

North Ave. and Freedom Pkwy., 404/875-7284, www.freedompark.org

Map 5

More than six miles long, the spider-shaped Freedom Park marks a large green *X* in the center of Poncey-Highland. The park offers 210 acres of open terrain that draws a symbolic line from the Martin Luther King Jr. National Historic Site Downtown to the Jimmy Carter Presidential Library, with ample jogging paths and rolling hills for communing with nature. The city has dubbed it an Atlanta Art Park, designating the area for seven permanent installations of public art.

LULLWATER PARK

1463 Clifton Rd., 404/875-7284, www.emory.edu/admissions/about/lullwater.htm

HOURS: Daily dawn-dusk

Map 4

Hidden—almost literally—on the edge of Emory University's campus, Lullwater Park has a noticeably more natural ambience than some of the city's other parks. The 185-acre wooded green space is used most often by Emory students, but is open to the public. The park features jogging trails, a pond, manicured gardens, and several colonies of ducks and swans. The English Tudor mansion of Emory's president also sits on Lullwater's grounds. Enter near the intersection of Clifton Road and Haygood Drive.

HIKING, BIKING, AND JOGGING TRAILS

CHASTAIN PARK TRAIL

West Wieuca and Lake Forest Rds., 404/875-7284, www.chastainpark.org

Map 7

It's a handsome three-mile loop around one of the city's most graceful public parks—but don't expect to have the Chastain Park Trail to yourself. An average of 250 walkers, joggers, cyclists, and inline skaters use this immensely popular trail each *hour*. The nonprofit PATH Foundation, local advocates for trail-building, have announced plans for a second loop of the Chastain Park Trail on the northern end of the park. Still, it's a lovely getaway just minutes from the bustle of Buckhead.

◀ SILVER COMET TRAIL

Starts at S. Cobb Dr. and East-West Connector in Cobb County, 404/875-7284, www.silvercometga.com

Map 7

Built over abandoned railroad lines, the massive Silver Comet Trail stretches 95 miles from suburban Atlanta to Anniston, Alabama. The fully paved two-lane path winds through three counties and provides an up-close encounter with the raw Georgia countryside, from the 25,000-acre Paulding Forest to the remote and charming Chief Ladiga Trail outside Cedartown. Named for the Silver Comet passenger train that once occupied its rail line, the trail's first section opened in 1998, and further expansions have occurred incrementally. It's a great and unique option for walking, biking, inline skating, and even horseback riding.

Bike Rentals
SKATE ESCAPE

1086 Piedmont Ave., 404/892-1292, www.skateescape.com

HOURS: Mon.-Fri. 11 A.M.-6:30 P.M., Sat.-Sun. 11 A.M.-6 P.M.

Map 2

You can't beat the location of this family-owned bike shop, which sits just across the street from one of Piedmont Park's busiest entrances. Come springtime, the place is always full. The funky, friendly little store rents inline skates, bikes, recumbents, and even tandems by the hour or for the day at reasonable prices. The shop also sells a wide line of skateboarding

goods and safety equipment, and offers repair services for bikes and rollerblades.

BOWLING
TEN PIN ALLEY

261 19th St., 404/872-3364, www.dolcegroup.com/tenpinalley

HOURS: Mon.-Thurs. 7 P.M.-1 A.M., Fri.-Sat. 6 P.M.-2 A.M., Sun. 6 P.M.-midnight

COST: Lanes around $80 an hour

Map 2

It's a funky concept: a plush, high-end bowling alley remixed to include a 1950s-style lounge and upscale snack bar. But with big-name backers and a killer location in Atlantic Station, this unusually themed bar appears to work. The alley doesn't get busy until late, when buzzed diners from parent restaurant Dolce downstairs start stumbling in. Upstairs, don't miss the plush pool tables. It's not for the budget-conscious, but definitely a change of pace from tired old cosmic bowling. Note that the lounge has an exclusive vibe and, oddly enough, a dress code: No sweats, athletic wear, or sleeveless shirts for men.

GOLF COURSES
BOBBY JONES GOLF COURSE

384 Woodward Way, 404/355-1009, www.bobbyjones.americangolf.com

COST: Tee times $20-40

Map 3

In 1930 legendary Atlanta athlete Bobby Jones won the golf Grand Slam: the British Amateur, U.S. Open, British Open, and U.S. Amateur. His namesake golf course, an 18-hole 71-par course situated on an old Civil War battlefield, has been a Buckhead favorite since 1931. Though sometimes derided for shoddy maintenance, the course has undergone renovation and installed new Champion Bermuda greens. It's not considered to be a particularly

ARTS AND LEISURE

challenging course, but the location alone makes this a worthwhile local destination.

CANDLER PARK GOLF COURSE

585 Candler Park Dr., 404/371-1260, www.candlerpark.americangolf.com

COST: Tee times $7-13

Map 5

In terms of value, Candler Park Golf Course can't be beat. Sure, the 9-hole course may be noticeably light on amenities, but it's heavy on a casual live-and-let-live outlook that fits the vibe of the surrounding Candler Park neighborhood. Devoid of the pretension found at some of the city's more exclusive golf clubs, Candler Park is a good option for beginners or those who love the game but hate its uppity trappings. The attractive course sits adjacent to Freedom Park and is located a stone's throw outside of Little Five Points.

GYMS AND HEALTH CLUBS

ATHLETIC CLUB NORTHEAST

1515 Sheridan Rd., 404/325-2700, www.athleticclubnortheast.com

HOURS: Mon.-Fri. 5:15 A.M.-10 P.M., Sat.-Sun. 8 A.M.-8 P.M.

COST: $15 daily guest pass; yearly membership varies

Map 7

Fitness club or shopping mall? The cavernous Athletic Club Northeast could single-handedly swallow up most other gyms in Atlanta and still have a locker room to spare. It incorporates six racquetball courts, a full-sized basketball gymnasium, two pools, a pilates studio, two weight rooms, and eight outdoor tennis courts—just to name a few of the high points. The clientele tilts toward old-timers who've belonged to the club long enough to see their grandkids become members, but don't hold that against this noteworthy sports megaplex.

JAI SHANTI YOGA

1630-D Dekalb Ave., 404/370-0579, www.jaishantiyoga.com

COST: $8-25 per class

Map 5

Although Jai Shanti Yoga offers a full range of instruction for advanced devotees, it's also known for being especially friendly and welcoming to newcomers. The informal Candler Park studio has a soothing, understated atmosphere. The studio offers more than 30 weekly classes devoted to the yoga practices of Kripalu and Integral Yoga, plus classes in Vinyasa, Yin and Restorative Yoga, breathwork and meditation and even a nude yoga class for men. Check out one of the occasional workshops on philosophy and asana practice.

URBAN BODY FITNESS

742 Ponce de Leon Place, 404/885-1499, www.urbanbodyfitness.com

HOURS: Mon.-Fri. 5 A.M.-10 P.M., Sat. 8 A.M.-8 P.M., Sun. 8 A.M.-7 P.M.

COST: $15 daily guest pass, which includes classes; membership around $55/month

Map 4

In a city dominated by chain athletic clubs, Urban Body Fitness brings some much-needed local flavor and an upscale, metropolitan vibe to the gym scene. The well-appointed loft-like club features state-of-the-art equipment, comfortable locker rooms, and complimentary towel service. The slate of classes can't be beat: In addition to the spin, boot camp, and kickboxing classes offered at UBF, check out the affiliated **Urban Body Studios** (730 Ponce de Leon Pl., 404/201-7994, www.urbanstudios.com, Mon.–Thurs. 6 A.M.–9 P.M., Fri. 6 A.M.–8 P.M., Sat.–Sun. 8:30 A.M.–6 P.M.) next door for a full line-up of yoga and pilates instruction.

CANOEING, KAYAKING, AND RAFTING

CHATTAHOOCHEE RIVER NATIONAL RECREATION AREA

Island Ford Visitor Contact Station, 1978 Island Ford Pkwy., www.nps.gov/chat

Map 7

The mind boggles that such an enormous national park can exist so close to the sprawling metropolis, but the Chattahoochee River National Recreation Area makes for a natural treasure tucked just out of plain sight. Covering a 48-mile section of the Chattahoochee River, the recreation area consists of 16 different segments that stretch from Peachtree Creek near Atlanta to Lake Lanier. In additional to the ample hiking/jogging trails along the river, the recreation area offers 11 separate areas appropriate for canoeing, kayaking, or rafting. Some are more easily accessed than others: Spend time on the National Park Service website to decide which area best suits your needs.

HIGH COUNTRY OUTFITTERS

3906 Roswell Rd., 404/814-0999, www.highcountryoutfitters.com

Map 7

For generations, "shooting the 'Hooch"—rafting down the Chattahoochee—has been a homegrown summertime tradition, one that's been overshadowed in recent years by reports of pollution in the river and concerns over the ongoing drought that has shook that region. Still, High Country Outfitters is one of a small handful of local companies offering rafting trips down the river. Rafters can choose from two starting points within the Chattahoochee River National Recreation Area—one that takes four hours, another that takes only two—and pay $125 per day for a six-person raft. Canoes and kayaks are also offered.

TENNIS

ATLANTA LAWN TENNIS ASSOCIATION

6849 Peachtree Dunwoody Rd., tournaments in various locations, 770/399-5788, www.altatennis.org

COST: $20 per year adult, $10 per year age 8-18

One of the most popular sports organizations in Atlanta, this nonprofit started league play in 1971 with less than 1,000 members. Today ALTA has more than 80,000 members, assigned to leagues based on skill level, gender, and geography. Separate tiers exist for women, men, youth, and wheelchair-bound competitors. The tournaments, though cordial, can push the envelope on friendly competition to become heated battles with longstanding rivalries.

BITSY GRANT TENNIS CENTER

2125 Northside Dr., 404/609-7193,

COST: $1.50-2.25 per hour

Map 3

Atlanta tennis legend Bryan M. Grant Jr.—nicknamed "Bitsy" because of his diminutive frame—enjoyed a long and illustrious career on the world stage. For years, he was also a fixture at the Buckhead tennis center that bears his name. The center today offers 13 clay courts and 10 hard courts at reasonable prices. Courts are available on a first-come, first-served basis with no reservations. The center also offers lessons for players of all skill levels.

TOURS

ATLANTA GHOSTS AND LEGENDS TOUR

50 Upper Alabama St., Ste. 256, 877/734-8687, www.citysegwaytours.com/atlanta

COST: $60 adult

Map 1

As if learning to drive a Segway weren't scary enough, this unique tour takes visitors on a rolling itinerary of some of Downtown's spookiest spots. The two-hour trip starts at Underground

ARTS AND LEISURE

Atlanta (again, not for the faint-hearted even on a sunny afternoon) and continues through supernaturally charged sites in the Fairlie-Poplar district and on to Georgia State University. Segway novices get a 30-minute driving lesson before the tour begins. Recommended for guests 12 and older; reservations required.

(ATLANTA PRESERVATION CENTER WALKING TOURS OF HISTORIC ATLANTA

327 St. Paul Ave., 404/688-3350,
www.preserveatlanta.com
COST: $10 adult, $5 child and senior
`Map 1`

Since 1980, the Atlanta Preservation Center has been an advocate for protecting local historic landmarks. It's credited with saving more than 175 threatened sites. The agency also offers some of the most insightful guided walking tours in town, serving up educational explorations of the Fox Theatre, Sweet Auburn, and intown neighborhoods including Ansley Park, Druid Hills, Inman Park, and Midtown. Each tour lasts around an hour and a half and is led by knowledgeable, professionally trained volunteers passionate about local history.

AMUSEMENT PARKS
SIX FLAGS OVER GEORGIA

7561 Six Flags Pkwy., Austell, 770/948-9290,
www.sixflags.com/overgeorgia
COST: $40 adult, $30 child
`Map 7`

Six Flags Over Georgia has been the state's premier amusement park for more than four decades. Situated 10 miles from Downtown, the 230-acre theme park retains some of the Southern-fried flair from its early days, with location names that include the Cotton States Exposition and a Confederate section. The

Six Flags Over Georgia features nine roller coasters.

ARTS AND LEISURE

overall branding these days has given way to DC Comics superheroes and Warner Brothers cartoon characters. The park features nine roller coasters, including the gigantic new Goliath, billed as one of the tallest in the world. The dearly loved Monster Plantation, an animatronic kids' ride, went through a major renovation in 2008 and was renamed the Monster Mansion. The longstanding Great American Scream Machine from 1973 also remains a perennial favorite. Parking and crowds can be oppressive in summer; consider parking in one of the unofficial lots on the other side of the interstate to save a few bucks.

favorite that features almost two dozen water rides for kids and adults. The daunting Cliffhanger, billed as one of the tallest freefall water slides in the world, hurls guests nine stories down into the drink below. Younger visitors might be better off exploring the colorful Georgia Treehouse Island, which features three stories of water fun, or Captain Kid's Cove. If you want to relax, float over to the 700,000-gallon Atlanta Ocean, where the waves rarely climb above four feet. Tykes under 12 might also want to check out **American Adventures** (www.americanadventures funpark.com), a kiddie park next door filled with low-impact rides and a mini-golf course.

SIX FLAGS WHITE WATER

250 Cobb Pkwy. N., Marietta, 770/948-9290, www.sixflags.com/whitewater
COST: $37 adult, $27 child
Map 7

Get wet at Six Flags White Water, a summertime

SPECTATOR SPORTS
⟨ ATLANTA BRAVES

Turner Field, 755 Hank Aaron Dr., 404/522-7630, http://atlanta.braves.mlb.com
Map 1

The only thing an Atlanta Braves fan loves

Turner Field, "Home of the Braves"

ARTS AND LEISURE

more than cheering for the home team is griping about them. The much-loved—but also much-maligned—baseball franchise came to Atlanta in 1966. The Braves rose from last place to win the World Series in 1995 and have earned 10 division titles in the years since. They play in **Turner Field,** built as the Centennial Olympic Stadium in 1996—it's where Muhammad Ali lit the torch to launch the summer games. The stadium has the feeling of a small amusement park, with bars, restaurants, costumed characters, and interactive fan contests always going on in the periphery. The **Ivan Allen Jr. Baseball Museum** inside the stadium contains many fascinating artifacts of the game, including the ball and bat Hank Aaron used to set his home-run record.

ATLANTA FALCONS

Georgia Dome, 1 Georgia Dome Dr., 404/249-6400, www.atlantafalcons.com

`Map 1`

Atlanta's National Football League franchise since 1965, the Falcons enjoyed a brief stint as the city's most admired sports team when they made it to the Super Bowl in 1999. Sadly, the years since have not been as kind to the "dirty birds," due mainly to the controversy surrounding former quarterback Michael Vick and his very public dog-fighting trial in 2007. The Falcons, owned by Home Depot co-founder Arthur Blank, have since retooled both the team and the coaching staff and worked to rebuild the fan base. Since 1992 the Falcons have played in the gargantuan **Georgia Dome,** which seats more than 71,000 fans and is part of the greater entertainment campus that includes Philips Arena, the Georgia World Congress Center, and CNN Center.

ATLANTA HAWKS

Philips Arena, 1 Philips Dr., 404/827-3800, www.nba.com/hawks

`Map 1`

Experiencing an Atlanta Hawks basketball game at Philips Arena may well be one of the most adrenaline-inducing sports events in the city, not just because of the constant hustle on the court but also thanks to the energized Hawks Dance Team cheering on the sidelines. The franchise dates back to 1946 as the Tri-Cities Blackhawks (in the Quad Cities area straddling Iowa and Illinois), and later moved to Milwaukee and St. Louis before migrating to Atlanta in 1968. Since 1999 the team has played in **Philips Arena,** a state-of-the-art sports complex that doubles as a concert venue and the home of the Atlanta Thrashers.

ATLANTA THRASHERS

Philips Arena, 1 Philips Dr., 404/875-3800, http://thrashers.nhl.com

`Map 1`

Hockey? In Atlanta? As incredible as it may seem, the Atlanta Thrashers have built up a dedicated fan following even here in the heat of the sunny South. The National Hockey League franchise launched in 1999 as the city's second foray into professional hockey (the Atlanta Flames left for Calgary in 1980). The years since have seen the team qualify for the Stanley Cup playoffs and compete in division championships. The team plays at Philips Arena, which seats more than 18,000 fans for hockey games.

SHOPS

Any sentence that involves the words "shopping" and "Atlanta" most often ends with "Buckhead"—which makes sense given that two of the city's largest upscale malls are located there, including some of the region's most chic designer boutiques. But it would be a crying shame for anyone to devote their entire time here to Lenox Square Mall and Phipps Plaza, because the city has countless other options for a discerning shopaholic. Unlike Chicago's Magnificent Mile, Atlanta's retail treasures tend to require a little more digging and footwork. Though a few shopping districts feature tempting clusters of must-see stores, finding the best shops in Atlanta will entail patience and perseverance.

For years, Virginia-Highland has been dotted with interesting boutiques, home stores, and gift shops, making it a destination for sharp customers seeking an alternative to Buckhead. Midtown has more recently seen a major crop of stylish businesses popping up in the street-level spaces of the newly risen condo towers that increasingly define the neighborhood. Just across the Downtown Connector, brand-new Atlantic Station has brought a density of hot new shops to an instant neighborhood whipped up from scratch.

Customers in search of more independent-minded options and shops that are anything but mainstream should make a beeline for the

HIGHLIGHTS

LOOK FOR **(** TO FIND RECOMMENDED SHOPS.

(**Best Independent Bookstore:**
Outwrite Bookstore and Coffeehouse is
not only the default gathering spot for gay
Atlantans, it's also a surprisingly well-stocked
indie bookseller appealing to customers of all
persuasions (page 117).

(**Best Fashion-Forward Clothes:**
Local fashion guru Bill Hallman has built his
own small empire of cutting-edge boutiques,
including **Bill Hallman Men** and Bill Hallman
Flaunt (page 118).

(**Best Consignment Shop:** From vintage lovers and picky hipsters to Halloween
shoppers and aspiring drag queens, everyone
loves the always-provocative goods at **Psycho
Sisters Consignment** (page 121).

(**Best Gourmet Goodies:** A sister shop
to be-seen restaurant Bacchanalia, **Star
Provisions** is Atlanta's best high-end gourmet market (page 123).

(**Best Castle of Kitsch:** Oddball gift and
clothing shop **Junkman's Daughter** could be
called a pop-culture blender, garish knickknack
store, and trippy sideshow all at once. No place
sums up the spirit of Little Five Points better
(page 123).

(**Best Mall:** It was Georgia's first mall and
one of the first enclosed shopping centers in
the region. Today, **Lenox Square Mall** remains

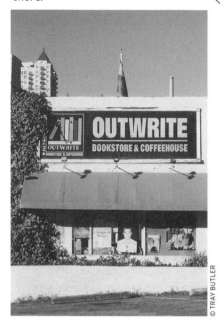

© TRAY BUTLER

an in-demand retail palace, home to 250 shops
(page 128).

(**Best Spa:** Blue MedSpa is the city's premier go-to destination for a luxurious day of
pampering (page 129).

eccentric emporiums of Little Five Points, still
a mecca for thrift stores, record shops, and tattoo parlors. The neighborhoods of Decatur and
East Atlanta Village offer a similar mix of offbeat urban goodies.

As a city with a relatively low cost of living and a vast array of businesses, Atlanta gets
props as the Southeast's premier destination
for racking up credit-card debt. The blend of
sprawling department stores, funky flea markets, reliable chains, and elegant boutiques

means there's something here for everyone—
even window shoppers.

SHOPPING DISTRICTS
Atlantic Station

No single development in modern history has
impacted intown Atlanta as thoroughly as
Atlantic Station, which transformed an ugly
and polluted steel-mill site into a dense 138
acres of retail, commercial, and residential
space. Hailed as a model for the New Urbanist

movement, the new "city within a city" opened in 2005. Its central shopping district, which has the feeling of a small town square perched atop an enormous parking deck, includes many brand-name clothing stores most often found in malls (such as Banana Republic, Express, H&M, and Dillards), a multiplex movie theater with stadium seating, an athletic club, a wide range of restaurants, and a handful of small boutiques.

East Atlanta Village

Concentrated around the intersection of Glenwood and Flat Shoals Avenues, the heart of East Atlanta Village has enjoyed a dramatic renaissance since the middle 1990s. Many businesses in the area maintain a hipster-ish, post punk attitude, influenced no doubt by the proximity of the Earl, one of the city's favorite indie music venues, and an off-the-radar gay bar, Mary's. The annual East Atlanta Strut, a popular street festival held every September, brings big crowds to the neighborhood for its artist market and parade.

Little Five Points

Atlanta's longtime capital of all things alternative, Little Five Points is a must-see shopping destination for those with eclectic, envelope-pushing tastes. The commercial district branches out from the intersection of Moreland and Euclid Avenues, with a diverse blend of new and vintage boutiques, novelty shops, independent bookstores and record stores, tattoo parlors, bars, and restaurants. A few blocks south, a new commercial development has added big-box shopping to the mix. Many locals cried foul when the mixed-use

Edgewood strip mall went in, but its proximity hasn't stifled the anti-corporate Little Five Points vibe so far.

Midtown Mile

Billed as Atlanta's answer to Chicago's Magnificent Mile, the still-developing Midtown Mile runs along Peachtree Street from North Avenue to 15th Street. Spurred by the outburst of new condo and office towers rising in this part of town, the shops of the new Midtown Mile will eventually fill an estimated one million square feet of street-level retail space—most of which is brand new. The stores popping up here tend to be cosmopolitan and on the expensive side, a mix of designer furniture galleries, ritzy boutiques, and specialty shops. It also offers a nice blend of food options, from casual noodle houses to four-star restaurants.

North Highland Avenue

Think of it as Atlanta's answer to New York's West Village—spread out in a single-file line over almost two miles. North Highland Avenue isn't home to just one commercial district but, depending on how you slice it, three or four strips of noteworthy shops. The biggest cluster rests at the intersection of North Highland and Virginia Avenue, home to several frilly boutiques, two gift shops, and a hardware store. A few blocks south, another collection of storefronts (mostly bars and restaurants) includes a couple of must-see shops and salons. Even more options pop up here and there as the avenue heads north into Morningside, including a couple of art galleries and a really great video store.

Books and Music

A CAPPELLA BOOKS

484 Moreland Ave., 404/681-5128,
www.acappellabooks.com
HOURS: Mon.-Thurs. 11 A.M.-9 P.M.,
Fri.-Sat. 11 A.M.-10 P.M., Sun. noon-8 P.M.
`Map 5`

In the war between big-box stores and independent booksellers, the chains are winning in Atlanta. But A Cappella Books remains a proud hold-out from an earlier age. The small shop is crammed pleasantly full of new and used titles, with a sales floor that's quirky and curiously organized. Owner Frank Reiss seems to pay particular emphasis to Southern and local authors, though he confesses that his own interests in ancient history, baseball, and country music also inform the inventory. The store carries rare and out-of-print titles and a wide selection of books that reflect the counterculture tastes of surrounding Little Five Points.

CHARIS BOOKS AND MORE

1189 Euclid Ave., 404/524-0304,
www.charisbooksandmore.com
HOURS: Mon.-Tues. 10:30 A.M.-6:30 P.M.,
Wed. 10:30 A.M.-8 P.M., Thurs. 10:30 A.M.-7:30 P.M.,
Fri.-Sat. 10:30 A.M.-8 P.M., Sun. noon-6 P.M.
`Map 5`

Billed as the South's oldest and largest feminist bookstore, Charis Books has operated in Little Five Points since 1974. The homey and accommodating shop offers a full line of fiction and nonfiction books of interest to women, including a comprehensive catalog of progressive and lesbian literature and countless cultural studies titles. It also carries a full line of children's books and an intriguing collection of music by independent artists. **Charis Circle** (www.chariscircle .org), the programming arm of the bookstore, is a separate nonprofit entity that hosts frequent evening events, including writing groups, social

the Criminal Records sign, as interpreted by Atlanta artist R. Land

© TRAY BUTLER

justice seminars, poetry readings, and author appearances.

CRIMINAL RECORDS

1154-A Euclid Ave., 404/215-9511,
www.criminal.com
HOURS: Mon.-Thurs. 10 A.M.-9 P.M.,
Fri.-Sat. 10 A.M.-11 P.M., Sun. noon-7 P.M.
Map 5

More than just another CD store, Criminal Records also sells comic books, toys, and DVDs to a hip and discerning clientele. It's one of Atlanta's only independently owned record shops that has not only survived but thrived despite earth-shaking changes in the music market. The business defiantly relocated to a larger space on Euclid Avenue in 2008. It's the kind of place where you'll find obscure indie gold, vinyl accessories, slacker T-shirts, and oddball graphic novels. Criminal also features an unrivaled series of in-store events, ranging from concerts to book signings.

OUTWRITE BOOKSTORE AND COFFEEHOUSE

991 Piedmont Ave., 404/607-0082,
www.outwritebooks.com
HOURS: Daily 10 A.M.-11 P.M.
Map 2

The corner of 10th Street and Piedmont Avenue used to be Atlanta's intersection of Gay and Gayer. Now, the neighborhood is growing noticeably more mixed, but Outwrite Bookstore remains ground zero for the city's queer population, an always-busy crossroads where the books aren't the only thing being browsed. The store carries a wide catalog of contemporary fiction and nonfiction, as well as a full line of campy coffee-table titles, cheeky gifts, and irreverent greeting cards. Weekly events bring in authors of all stripes, making Outwrite an

important Southern literary landmark that transcends its niche market.

OXFORD COMICS & GAMES

2855 Piedmont Rd., 404/233-8682,
www.oxfordcomics.com
HOURS: Mon.-Sat. 10 A.M.-10 P.M., Sun. 11 A.M.-7 P.M.
Map 3

A true fanboy (or fangirl) paradise, Oxford Comics is Atlanta's most popular comic-book shop. With a colossal display of current and past titles and a supersized selection of graphic novels, the 20-year-old store is the only surviving member of a once-cherished local chain of independent booksellers. That hometown vibe lives on in the friendly staff and laid-back atmosphere. But comics are only half the story: The entire front of the store features action figures, trading cards, games, anime and cult film DVDs, manga, and even an adults-only section. Even better, most every day is Free Comic Book Day at Oxford, with three or four freebies available per visit.

WAX 'N FACTS

432 Moreland Ave., 404/525-2275
HOURS: Mon.-Sat. 11 A.M.-8 P.M., Sun. noon-6 P.M.
Map 5

Fact: Wax 'N Facts is one of Atlanta's oldest record stores and also one of the city's best. OK, so maybe that last part is opinion, but this dusty Little Five Points vinyl shop must be doing something right to have stayed in business since 1976. The store specializes in used and hard-to-find vinyl, organized in a system that might make you snap were it not for the staff's encyclopedic knowledge of music. A big bin of used CDs also gets plenty of traffic, but much of the clientele consists of hardcore vinyl junkies obliviously digging through the stacks.

SHOPS

Clothing, Accessories, and Shoes

CHILDREN'S CLOTHING

SPROUT
1198 Howell Mill Rd., 404/352-0864,
www.sproutatlanta.com
HOURS: Mon.-Sat. 10 A.M.-6 P.M.
`Map 2`

If you're grooming your progeny to be a pint-sized fashionista, search no further than Sprout, a playground for Atlanta's most pampered tots and its most particular parents. The meticulously well-groomed children's boutique sells clothing, toys, and furniture for the Nick Jr. set, though it shies away from blatantly corporate products. The aesthetic feels both modern and timeless, offering accessories for childhood that are playful and understated

WIGGLE
305 E. College Ave., 404/373-2522,
www.wiggleatlanta.com
HOURS: Tues.-Fri. 9 A.M.-5 P.M.,
Sat. 10 A.M.-5:30 P.M., Sun. noon-5 P.M.
`Map 6`

As a mom-to-be, Kolby Sanders-Lewis was dismayed to find a dearth of quality kids' clothing stores in Atlanta, so she opened Wiggle, which specializes in upscale and unique clothes for children. The shop carries sizes for newborns through size 8, with clothes for girls and more for boys than some other boutiques. An in-house monogramming service will let you customize the goods with your little ones' initials. The shop works with a handful of local artists to feature bibs, onesies, and storybooks that can't be found elsewhere.

MEN'S CLOTHING AND ACCESSORIES

◖ BILL HALLMAN MEN
792 N. Highland Ave., 404/876-6055,
www.billhallman.com
HOURS: Mon.-Wed. noon-8 P.M., Thurs. 11 A.M.-9 P.M.,
Fri.-Sat. 11 A.M.-10 P.M., Sun. noon-7 P.M.
`Map 4`

Once in the not-so-distant past, Bill Hallman ran one of the only boutiques in town known for introducing a certain flavor of fashion-forward looks to Atlanta. These days the number of similar shops has exploded, but Hallman's mini-empire of boutiques remains a popular favorite. The men's store features up-to-date collections of designer labels, shoes, and accessories (including some really killer sunglasses) in a sleek Virginia-Highland space. The emphasis here is definitely on a younger and rambunctious market, though the prices can be anything but budget friendly. A separate **women's store** (784 N. Highland Ave., 404/607-1171) sits across the courtyard, and

Look for this sign outside Bill Hallman's Virginia-Highland shop.

© TRAY BUTLER

Bill Hallman Flaunt (424 Moreland Ave., 404/522-1010) offers mostly women's clothes with a few choice items for guys in a smaller Little Five Points location.

BOY NEXT DOOR

1447 Piedmont Ave., 404/873-2664
HOURS: Mon.-Sat. 10 A.M.-8 P.M., Sun. noon-6 P.M.
`Map 2`

A Midtown staple since 1980, Boy Next Door features casual and club-ready menswear in a small boutique that's always throbbing with a heavy house beat. Intimate without feeling cramped, it's also a great destination for designer undies, jeans, and swimsuits. The prices can lead to occasional sticker shock, but the store's large clearance area is usually ripe for bargains. The adorable sales staff are some of the most helpful (and hands-on) in town, though be forewarned: The transparent curtains of the "changing rooms" leave little to the imagination.

SID MASHBURN

1198 Howell Mill Rd., 404/350-7135,
www.sidmashburn.com
HOURS: Mon.-Sat. 10:30 A.M.-6:30 P.M.
`Map 2`

Think of it as a sort of modern style concierge—equal parts gracious tailor's shop, off-the-rack boutique, and remixed gentlemen's club from a more refined era. Sid Mashburn, a former design director for Ralph Lauren and J. Crew, sells both trendy labels and his own classically inspired creations, clothes with a whiff of New England privilege but tempered by a friendly, down-to-earth sales floor. The offbeat accessories and Sid's gasp-worthy attention to detail have made the shop yet another West Midtown success story.

WOMEN'S CLOTHING AND ACCESSORIES

DRESSCODES

201 W. Ponce de Leon Ave. #117, 404/343-2894,
www.dresscodesatl.com
HOURS: Mon.-Tues. 11 A.M.-8 P.M.,
Wed.-Sat. 11 A.M.-9 P.M., Sun. 11 A.M.-6 P.M.
`Map 6`

A sleek and easy emporium for big-city fashions, without the big-city attitude, DressCodes has quickly attracted a devoted following in Decatur. Owners Karen and Brett Mascavage are transplanted New Yorkers who bring plenty of SoHo sophistication to this small boutique, which sells both women's and men's casual wear. Check out the lust-worthy denim wall and unexpected accessories from Europe and Southeast Asia, and don't forget to say hello to the store's mascots, two welcoming terriers. The DressCodes blog (www.dresscodesatl.com/blog) can be an interesting read in its own right.

FAB'RIK

1114 W. Peachtree St., 404/881-8223,
www.fabrikatlanta.com
HOURS: Mon.-Sat. 11 A.M.-7 P.M., Sun. noon-5 P.M.
`Map 2`

Shopping and drinking mix splendidly at stylish fab'rik, combination boutique and upscale water bar. The chic, minimalist showroom specializes in high-fashion concepts sans the Paris prices; most pieces in the store are less than $100 (with the exception of the denim selection, one of the best in the city). The trendy water bar sells flavored, carbonated, and even caffeinated water drinks—as well as alcoholic beverages. The space doubles as a commercial art gallery focused on local talent; monthly events include wine tastings and martini nights.

THE FICKLE MANOR

1402-4 N. Highland Ave., 404/541-0960,
www.theficklemanor.com
HOURS: Mon.-Fri. 11:30 A.M.-7:30 P.M.,
Sat. 10 A.M.-6 P.M., Sun. 1-5 P.M.
Map 4

The word "fickle" might inspire images of up-pity salesgirls rolling their eyes at spoiled house-wives, but the vibe at Fickle Manor couldn't be more relaxed. The store is actually named after owner JJ Tomlinson's capricious dog, Manor. This popular Morningside boutique launched in 2002 with a mission to sell hip and comfort-able fashions in a no-pressure setting. Familiar designer labels are mixed in with more obscure up-and-coming brands, and the store also fea-tures a cool assortment of greeting cards, mag-nets, and picture frames.

JEFFREY ATLANTA

Phipps Plaza, 3500 Peachtree Rd., 404/237-9000,
www.jeffreyatlanta.com
HOURS: Mon.-Wed. and Fri. 10 A.M.-8 P.M.,
Thurs. 10 A.M.-9 P.M., Sat. 10 A.M.-7 P.M.,
Sun. 12:30-6 P.M.
Map 3

Jeffrey Kalinsky, a former buyer for Barneys, built his fashion fiefdom with boutiques in Atlanta and New York's Meatpacking District. His Phipps Plaza location, formerly devoted exclusively to high-end footwear from the likes of Manolo Blahnik or Jil Sander, has ex-panded in recent years to include a full line of women's clothing from names such as Prada and Michael Kors. The strikingly minimal storefront is heavy on attitude and light on merchandise; the staff can be standoffish to customers who aren't dressed to impress. But Kalinksy, a South Carolina native, always ex-udes hospitality and he certainly knows his way around a showroom.

LUXE ATLANTA

1000 Marietta St., Ste. 102, 404/541-0960,
www.luxeatlanta.com
HOURS: Tues.-Sat. 11 A.M.-7 P.M.
Map 2

West Midtown has been a magnet for buzzed-about restaurants and contemporary furniture galleries but slower to attract much of a boutique scene. Luxe Atlanta is one obvious exception, a too-good-to-be-true fashion depot that features women's designer clothing, shoes, and accessories at deep discounts from the original retail prices. In this case "discount" doesn't mean "down mar-ket." Luxe represents more than 40 high-end and hard-to-find designers, and most looks are not more than two seasons old. The staff is gracious to a fault and new items arrive often.

MITZI & ROMANO

1038 N. Highland Ave., 404/876-7228
HOURS: Mon.-Thurs. 10 A.M.-9 P.M.,
Fri.-Sat. 10 A.M.-10 P.M., Sun. 11 A.M.-7 P.M.
Map 4

Though it sits in the heart of Virginia-Highland, this longstanding women's bou-tique feels decidedly more like a Buckhead transplant—which is to say, more upscale, more exclusive, and a bit more expensive. From evening dresses to casual wear, jewelry to de-signer accessories, owner Mitzi Ugolini has an eye for refined elegance with a contemporary twist. There are discoveries to be found on the sales racks, but this is one shop best enjoyed if money isn't an object. Nearby, **Mitzi's Shoe Box** (1004 Virginia Ave., 404/873-4718) sells designer footwear and handbags.

SHOES

ABBADABBA'S

421-B Moreland Ave., 770/491-6775,
www.coolshoes.com

HOURS: Mon.-Sat. 10 A.M.-7:30 P.M., Sun. noon-6 P.M.

Map 5

Abbadabba's has grown into a locally based chain of casual footwear warehouses with five Atlanta locations. The original Little Five Points store has been a treasure trove of offbeat fashions since 1981. Though brands such as Puma, Crocs, Vans, and Reef are represented heavily, Abbadabba's has long been known as a great source for sandals. The **Buckhead location** (4389 Roswell Rd., 404/262-3356) became Georgia's first Birkenstock Specialty Store in 1998, with the other locations quickly following suit, a designation that allows the chain a greater selection than other Birkenstock dealers.

VINTAGE
THE CLOTHING WAREHOUSE

420 Moreland Ave., 404/524-5070,
www.theclothingwarehouse.com

HOURS: Mon.-Sat. 11:30 A.M.-8:30 P.M., Sun. noon-7 P.M.

Map 5

This homegrown dealer of vintage threads started in Atlanta in 1992 and has since spread throughout the country. Since 2000, the always-busy Moreland Avenue location has lured hipsters with a huge inventory of gently used T-shirts, dresses, and denim. The clothes tend to be grouped by color, making for a playful sales floor that can require a bit of patience to find just the right piece. The shop probably won't ever win customers based on bargain prices— you'll find similar stuff much cheaper at most any large thrift store in town—but the Clothing Warehouse culls out the fashion don'ts for a selection that's suitably ironic and trendy.

PSYCHO SISTERS CONSIGNMENT

428 Moreland Ave., 404/523-0100,
www.psychosistersshops.com

HOURS: Daily 10 A.M.-10 P.M.

The Clothing Warehouse

© TRAY BUTLER

Map 5

The name says it all: Psycho Sisters carries clothes on the crazy side. The tiny Little Five Points consignment shop buys and sells sizzling clubwear and casual attire, from vintage polyester disco pants to '80s miniskirts and practically hubcap-sized belt buckles. The store gets especially wild around Halloween, when seemingly every would-be hippie, pimp, and go-go kitten in town crams inside searching for the perfect pink boa. But there's more to the store than retro costumes: Check out the rock T-shirts and the always eye-catching display of sunglasses.

STEFAN'S VINTAGE CLOTHING

1160 Euclid Ave., 404/688-4929,
www.stefansvintage.com

HOURS: Mon.-Sat. 11 A.M.-7 P.M., Sun. noon-6 P.M.

Map 5

While some other vintage shops in town go for frills and thrills, Stefan's aims for more subtle delights. The oldest store of its kind in Atlanta, this is the place to find an authentic evening gown from the Jazz Age or a pillbox hat from the Kennedy years. Though the store does include some men's items, such as antique tuxedos, evening jackets, and bowling shirts, most of the inventory centers around high-end women's fashions from before 1970. The only thing not retro is the price, which can be jarring on some of the rarer items.

Gifts and Specialty

ANTIQUES
PROVIDENCE

1409 N. Highland Ave., 404/872-7551,
www.providenceantiques.com

HOURS: Mon. 11 A.M.–6 P.M., Tues.–Thurs. 11 A.M.–9 P.M., Fri.–Sat. 11 A.M.–10 P.M., Sun. noon–6 P.M.

Map 4

A mainstay in Morningside for almost 20 years, Providence is an antiques store masquerading as a nifty gift shop—or maybe it's the other way around. The comfortable exposed-brick showroom does offer some vintage merchandise—mainly assorted pieces of traditional furniture—but much of the inventory is best described as new gift items, from groovy stationery and innovative office supplies to distinctive children's toys and home accessories. The store also trades in unpredictable "found items" and a line of fashions for pet lovers.

FLOWERS
TWELVE BOUTIQUE AND FLOWERS

1000 Piedmont Ave., Ste. D, 404/541-2357,
www.twelveatlanta.net

HOURS: Mon.–Wed. 11:30 A.M.–10 P.M., Thurs.–Sat. 11:30 A.M.–11 P.M., Sun. noon–9 P.M.

Map 2

Perhaps the "twelve" refers to the number of incarnations the perennial gift shop has gone through. Owner John McDonald has toyed with various locations and concepts over the years, at one point

ANTIQUES HEAVEN

The sprawling Lakewood Antiques Market was an Atlanta tradition for more than 20 years, drawing upwards of 12,000 customers to its monthly wonderland of vintage treasures. Held in the Spanish colonial livestock exhibition halls at the historic Lakewood Fairgrounds near the airport, the acclaimed event shut down in 2006 when the City of Atlanta bought back the property lease from the market's owners with vague plans to redevelop the site.

The good news for antiques addicts is that the show continues, only now north of the city near the tiny town of Cumming. The new **Lakewood 400 Antiques Market** (1321 Atlanta Hwy., 770/889-3400, www.lakewoodantiques.com, Fri. 9 A.M.–5 P.M., Sat. 9 A.M.–6 P.M., Sun. 10 A.M.–5 P.M., $3) takes place the third weekend of each month in a shiny new 75,000-square-foot showroom with more than 500 dealer spaces and an on-site restaurant. The featured merchandise tends to be a captivating hodgepodge of high-end furniture, classic jewelry, pop-culture artifacts, and bizarre bric-a-brac. Reaching the Lakewood 400 Antiques Market requires at least a 40-minute drive from the city center up Georgia 400, but it's well worth the effort – and the $0.50 toll.

splitting his boutique and floral businesses into two separate locations. Now the Twelve family is united again on Piedmont Avenue, and the resulting store is a hodgepodge of home accessories, fresh-cut flowers, and other oddities such as jewelry, purses, and greeting cards. The floral selection can be limited when compared to other neighborhood florists, but the helpful design staff knows how to make a few petals go a long way.

GOURMET TREATS

ALON'S

1394 N. Highland Ave., 404/872-6000, www.alons.com
HOURS: Mon.-Fri. 7 A.M.-8 P.M., Sat. 8 A.M.-8 P.M., Sun. 9 A.M.-4 P.M.
Map 4

Part café, part gourmet market, Alon's was inspired by European specialty markets that carried more than just pastries. Alon Balshan's original Virginia-Highland bakery opened in 1992 and quickly expanded to include gourmet prepared foods, wine, flowers, and an artisan cheese selection with more than 120 varieties from local and international producers. The mouth-watering sandwiches and soups bring in a full lunch business, but Alon's is probably still best known as a bakery, with fresh breads made daily and some of the most delicious birthday cakes and cookies in the city.

◖ STAR PROVISIONS

1198 Howell Mill Rd., 404/365-0410, www.starprovisions.com
HOURS: Mon.-Sat. 10 A.M.-8 P.M.
Map 2

Foodies go ga-ga over the delectable selection of meats, cheeses, wines, and pastries at Star Provisions, a market owned by five-star restaurant Bacchanalia next door. There's more to the shop than its edible offerings; the store also carries charming tableware and a colorful range of food-related gifts. Hit the take-out counter for ready-made meals, or enjoy a heaping deli sandwich at one of the few tables there in the

store. Not for the budget-conscious shopper, but it's a sweet extravagance for a gourmand with dough to spare.

KNITTING

KNITCH

1052 St. Charles Ave., 404/745-9276, www.knitchknitting.com
HOURS: Mon.-Fri. 11 A.M.-6:30 P.M., Sat.-Sun. 11 A.M.-5 P.M.
Map 4

A visit to Knitch feels like stumbling upon a top-secret clubhouse for crafty women—that is, women who like to knit. Nearly hidden on the backside of a Virginia-Highland strip of stores, this warm, two-story loft is equal parts yarn shop, hobby warehouse, and workshop, with a wide central workspace where eager knitters gather for classes and conversation. The inventory includes a huge selection of luxury yarn, books on knitwear designs, and some truly gorgeous knitting needles. The weekly schedule ranges from ongoing classes to free evening knitting sessions—with no secret password needed to participate.

NOVELTY SHOPS

◖ JUNKMAN'S DAUGHTER

464 Moreland Ave., 404/577-3188
HOURS: Mon.-Thurs. 11 A.M.-7 P.M., Fri. 11 A.M.-8 P.M., Sat. 11 A.M.-9 P.M.
Map 5

Atlanta's high temple of all things kitschy, Junkman's Daughter has been peddling oddball knickknacks, kooky collectibles, and pop-culture detritus for more than 25 years. It's possible to lose hours of your life browsing through the 10,000-square-foot store, which includes rack after rack of hipster gear for guys and girls, crass and cutting-edge gifts and housewares, offbeat picture books, and more *A Nightmare*

© TRAY BUTLER

Junkman's Daughter

Before Christmas goodies than you ever knew existed. Climb the 20-foot high-heeled staircase and check out the shoe department upstairs, or browse the fully stocked tobacco shop in back, but be careful not to piss off the sales staff, who are notoriously surly.

POSTER HUT
2175 Cheshire Bridge Rd., 404/633-7491
HOURS: Sun.-Thurs. 10 A.M.-9 P.M.,
Fri.-Sat. 10 A.M.-10:30 P.M.
Map 3

It's not technically a hut, nor does it specialize in posters. Instead, this longstanding novelty shop carries a full line of adult-themed gag gifts, fetish-ready outfits, smoke accessories, and greeting cards you probably wouldn't want to give to Grandma. Not that everything here earns an NC-17 rating; the store also offers plenty of offbeat tchotchkes, glass

doodads, and bachelorette-party goods, but the kids should probably wait in the car in any case.

RICHARD'S VARIETY STORE
2347 Peachtree Rd, 404/237-1412
HOURS: Mon.-Fri. 9 A.M.-7 P.M., Sat. 9 A.M.-6 P.M.,
Sun. 12:30-5:30 P.M.
Map 3

Although the first couple of aisles feature the kind of stuff found in most any pharmacy, like light bulbs and reading glasses, Richard's Variety quickly shows its true colors as an unpredictable menagerie of nostalgic toys, provocative gifts, and party supplies. Open since 1951, the family-owned store has a unique affinity for all things retro, from Baby Boomer lunch boxes and classic hobby horses to Halloween costumes you might remember from childhood. It's a fun throwback to the five-and-dime era, and with prices still competitive to much larger stores.

PETS
HIGHLAND PET SUPPLY
1186 N. Highland Ave., 404/892-5900,
www.highlandpet.com
HOURS: Mon.-Fri. 9 A.M.-8 P.M., Sat. 9 A.M.-7 P.M.,
Sun. noon-6 P.M.
Map 4

Dog and cat lovers adore this locally owned pet supply store for its huge selection of high-end accessories and toys. It also features a crafty do-it-yourself dog-wash area, with elevated tubs, shampoos, towels, and blow dryers. Highland Pet Supply's selection of organic pet foods and treats is also hard to match, as is the friendly customer service. The store offers a five-week off-site canine training program that'll take your problem pup and teach him some decent doggy manners.

PIEDMONT BARK

501 Amsterdam Ave., 404/873-5400,
www.piedmontbark.com
HOURS: Mon.-Fri. 7 A.M.-7:30 P.M., Sat. 8 A.M.-5 P.M.,
Sun. noon-6 P.M.
Map 2

Atlanta's most pampered pooches get to spend weekdays at doggy daycare at Piedmont Bark, which features 8,000 square feet of exercise space in a simulated outdoor setting, complete with trees and park benches. Designated run areas separate out the small, medium, and large dogs, with a similar categorical approach to the kennels. Piedmont Bark's walk-in dog wash is also a popular draw. You can even throw your puppy a private birthday party here, with a birthday cake, handmade doggie treats for all four-legged guests, and the run of the facility for two hours. Bow wow!

Home Furnishings and Accents

BELVEDERE

996-B Huff Rd., 404/352-1942,
www.belvedereinc.com
HOURS: Tues.-Sat. 11 A.M.-5 P.M.
Map 2

You could say that Julia-Carr Bayler is stuck in the past—in a very good way. Since 1999, she's been hyping her love for stylish mid-20th-century designs at Belvedere, her West Midtown furniture gallery that sells both vintage and new goods. The store specializes in hard-to-find pieces from the 1930s through the 1960s, though its sense of style mixes modern accents in seamlessly with the vintage items. Also on the menu: accessories, jewelry, and artwork.

INTAGLIA HOME COLLECTION

1544 Piedmont Ave., Ste. 105, 404/607-9750,
www.intagliahome.com

HOURS: Mon.-Sat. 10:30 A.M.-7 P.M.,
Sun. noon-6 P.M.

Map 2

After years in Amsterdam Walk, this perpetu-
ally tasteful furniture store relocated to Ansley
Mall in 2008, more than doubling its showroom
space and re-creating the same earth-toned interior color palette that made the former location such a refreshing shopping experience. It's
the kind of place where the furniture whispers
and never screams, a purveyor of stylishly comfortable sofas and elegant dining room tables
aimed at a polished Martha Stewart market.
Don't miss the fun display of greeting cards.

TRADERS NEIGHBORHOOD STORE

485-B Flat Shoals Ave., 404/522-3006,
www.tradersatlanta.com

HOURS: Mon. 11 A.M.-9 P.M., Tues.-Sat. 11 A.M.-8 P.M.,
Sun. noon-6 P.M.

Map 5

East Atlanta Village has clearly benefited from
the presence of Traders, a combination furniture
gallery and gift shop that brings an upwardly
mobile set of tastemakers to the neighborhood's
retail scene. The furniture here feels both urban
and refined, edgy enough to be interesting
without being outlandish. The shop does just
as much business for its accessories and gifts,
from candles and picture frames to whimsical
magnets and stand-alone Hula girls.

YES HOME

921-B Peachtree St., 404/733-5909,
www.yes4me.com

HOURS: Mon.-Fri. 10 A.M.-7 P.M., Sat. 10 A.M.-6 P.M.,
Sun. noon-6 P.M.

Map 2

Tasteful, contemporary home goods? Yes.

HOMING IN ON HOME GOODS

As a rule, Atlanta isn't overflowing with shopping areas dedicated to one category of goods,
like New York's Diamond District or L.A.'s Fashion District. But for every rule, there are always
exceptions: The city has no shortage of high-
end home stores selling everything from fashionable furniture and accessories to upmarket
antiques and art. Some of the best shops are
tucked in out-of-the-way pockets of the city.
The best example may be **Miami Circle,** an
easily overlooked commercial cul-de-sac that
branches off Piedmont Road a block north of
the Lindbergh Plaza shopping center. Businesses on the meandering street specialize in
tasteful, traditional home decor aimed at the
luxury market, with a concentration of exclusive
European and Asian antiques, classic furniture,
fine fabrics, and rugs. It's a fun drive for window
shopping no matter what your budget is.

A couple of miles west, **Bennett Street** is
also a great destination for discerning home
goods. Unlike Miami Circle, this former warehouse has a quirky post-industrial vibe; it
saw a stint as a nightlife district in the 1970s
before morphing into its current mix of art galleries and antiques shops. The 48,000-square-
foot TULA Art Center is by far the biggest
draw, featuring the Museum of Contemporary
Art of Georgia. Bennett Street sits in South
Buckhead and intersects with the 2100 block
of Peachtree Road.

Meanwhile, **West Midtown** has lately
emerged as Atlanta's newest hot spot for chic
home accessories. The tastes you'll find here
tend to be more modern, with contemporary
furniture stores and cutting-edge art galleries. Though the businesses are spread out,
there's an obvious critical mass on Huff Road,
Ellsworth Industrial Boulevard, and Howell Mill
Road near Marietta Street.

Dazzling light fixtures? Yes. High-end floor coverings? Yes! For such an unassuming space on the ground floor of the Metropolis condo tower, Yes Home packs a lot of bang for the buck. The selection of furniture and accessories gets all the fanfare, but this crowded Midtown showroom also deserves a look for its titillating collection of eccentric, off-the-wall paintings and photography, including many works by local artists.

Markets

GREEN MARKET FOR PIEDMONT PARK

14th St. and Piedmont Ave., 404/876-4024, www.piedmontpark.org
HOURS: May-Dec. Sat. 9 A.M.-1 P.M.
`Map 2`

The movement toward buying organic, locally grown fruits and vegetables has given Piedmont Park's nascent farmer's market a fresh sense of relevance. Started in 2004 with only a few sleepy-eyed neighbors browsing the produce booths, the market has evolved into one of Midtown's Saturday-morning traditions—still with plenty of room to grow. Beyond the veggies, vendors also sell a range of "natural products," though the term apparently applies to everything from pet supplies to greeting cards.

MORNINGSIDE FARMERS MARKET

1393 N. Highland Ave., 404/313-5784, www.morningsidemarket.com
HOURS: Sat. 8-11:30 A.M.
`Map 4`

With roots reaching back to the late 1980s,

© JEFFREY L. REED/FLICKR.COM

some of the produce available at the Green Market in Piedmont Park

this year-round produce market has become a perennial favorite in Morningside. Held every Saturday of the year rain or shine, the Morningside Farmers Market features only local vendors (who live no more than two hours outside the city) selling certified organically grown fruits and vegetables, along with freshly baked breads, handmade soaps, and floral arrangements. The small market sets up in a parking lot and can be very crowded with customers some Saturdays; arrive early to catch the cooking demonstrations by local chefs held at 9:30 A.M.

SWEET AUBURN CURB MARKET

209 Edgewood Ave., 404/659-1665,
www.sweetauburncurbmarket.com
HOURS: Mon.-Sat. 8 A.M.-6 P.M.
Map 1

Though it was founded in 1918, the Sweet Auburn Curb Market has the feel of a modern food court mixed with a big-city deli counter—with a dash of flea market thrown in for extra flavor. A friendly assortment of stands offer fresh produce, cheeses, baked goods, and seafood. Its 10 cafés feature a wide range of ethnic foods, from Indian to Jamaican, but the less courageous can stick with Pizza Hut. The market also includes a bath shop, pharmacy, and gift store. Parking is free for the first 90 minutes in the nearby lot.

YOUR DEKALB FARMERS MARKET

3000 E. Ponce de Leon Ave., 404/377-6400,
www.dekalbfarmersmarket.com
HOURS: Daily 9 A.M.-9 P.M.
Map 6

The term "market," which often implies an outdoor space and haggling with actual farmers, barely suits this 140,000-square-foot food complex, which functions more like a massive suburban grocery store. The difference comes in freshness and variety, with Your DeKalb Farmers Market offering hard-to-find gourmet items and produce that hasn't been in transit for a month. The market also includes a popular cafeteria that charges for meals by the pound.

Shopping Malls

◖ LENOX SQUARE MALL

3393 Peachtree Rd., 404/233-6767,
www.lenoxsquare.com
HOURS: Mon.-Sat. 10 A.M.-9 P.M., Sun. noon-6 P.M.
Map 3

Since it opened in Buckhead in 1959, Lenox Square Mall has been one of the city's premier gathering places—not just for shopping, but also for annual traditions such as an enormous Independence Day fireworks display and the Lighting of the Great Tree at Macy's. What was originally an open-air shopping center was enclosed in the early 1970s and has gone through many sweeping renovations since then. The result today is a sprawling and upscale urban mall, with 250 shops spread out over four levels. Anchor stores include Macy's, Bloomingdales, and Neiman Marcus; you'll also find Anthropologie, Burberry, Calvin Klein, Cartier, David Yurman, Louis Vuitton, Kate Spade, Ralph Lauren, and Zara.

PHIPPS PLAZA

3500 Peachtree Rd., 404/262-0992,

www.phippsplaza.com
HOURS: Mon.-Sat. 10 A.M.-9 P.M., Sun. noon-5:30 P.M.
Map 3
Diagonally across Peachtree Road from Lenox Square sits its sibling property, Phipps Plaza. The playing field between these two shopping malls has become arguably more level in recent years, though Phipps retains a more upmarket atmosphere and clientele. Specialty shops include Armani Exchange, Barney's Co-Op, Gucci, and Giorgio Armani. Saks Fifth Avenue, Nordstrom, and Belk are the largest tenants. The mall also includes a 14-screen AMC cineplex, though the arrival of more stadium-seating theaters in the city in recent years has diminished the cache of this once favorite theater.

Spas and Salons

BLUE MEDSPA
190 10th St., 404/815-8880, www.bluemedspa.com
HOURS: Mon. 10 A.M.-6 P.M., Tues.-Fri. 10 A.M.-8 P.M., Sat. 9 A.M.-8 P.M., Sun. 1-6 P.M.
Map 2
Wedged in an unlikely 10th Street building with funky geometric windows, Blue MedSpa is a swanky retreat from the bustle of Midtown. Visitors pass a gushing outdoor water wall before entering the hushed, all-white world of the spa's well-appointed interior. The suite of services ranges from massage and manicures to facials and Botox. The locker rooms may be on the small side, but the interior vibe is appropriately posh and tranquil, and the treatments never disappoint. Call early for reservations; it's often booked solid.

HELMET
970 Piedmont Ave., 404/815-1629, www.helmethairworx.com
HOURS: Mon. noon-8 P.M., Tues.-Fri. 9 A.M.-9 P.M., Sat. 9 A.M.-5 P.M., Sun. noon-5 P.M.
Map 2
Too many stylish hair salons ooze a subtle attitude of derision, but not Helmet. Located on two floors of a renovated Midtown home, the salon retains a gracious Southern charm mixed with big-city sophistication. The stylists are both hip and approachable, and even though the place always seems to be full, it's usually easy to get an appointment. Men's haircuts range from around $35 to $50, women's cuts closer to $60, and the salon also offers full color services, manicures, pedicures, and eyebrow waxing.

KEY LIME PIE SALON AND WELLNESS SPA
806 N. Highland Ave., 404/873-6512, www.keylimepie.net
HOURS: Tues. 10 A.M.-6 P.M., Wed.-Thurs. 11 A.M.-8 P.M., Fri. 10 A.M.-6 P.M., Sat. 9 A.M.-5 P.M.
Map 4
If you just want a haircut, Key Lime Pie is probably not for you. If you want a one-of-a-kind color consultation, an aquatherapy tub and body massage, an underarm waxing, or a relaxing afternoon in one of the city's most sought-after day spas, this might be the place. Owner DJ Freed has created a quirky Virginia-Highland refuge that's both an Aveda Concept Salon and also a full-service spa known for its celebrity clientele. The comprehensive suite of spa services includes French manicures, custom facials, and body treatments. Sweet!

SALON RED & SPA

1642 DeKalb Ave., 404/373-2868, www.salonred.com

HOURS: Tues.-Thurs. 10 A.M.-8 P.M.,

Fri.-Sun. 9 A.M.-6 P.M.

Map 5

Casual Candler Park, one of the more laid-back intown 'hoods, may seem an unlikely setting for a high-end hair salon, but Salon Red defies easy pigeonholing. The local chain of salons strives to offer a "creative, compassionate environment" (according to its mission statement) to bring out the best in clients, which means a full selection of professional beauty services in a clean, modern environment. The DeKalb Avenue location includes a day spa, offering massage and reflexology, while the Decatur branch includes **Salon Red Kids** (123 East Ponce de Leon Ave., 404/377-6230)—a rare haircuttery aimed only at the squirming set.

SUGARCOAT

256 Pharr Rd., 404/814-2121,

www.sugarcoatbeauty.com

HOURS: Tues.-Sat. 10 A.M.-7 P.M.

Map 3

If Barbie had a nail salon, it would probably look a lot like Sugarcoat. An explosion of girly pink and white furnishings accented by a crystal chandelier, the small Buckhead salon pampers its clients with manicure and pedicure services that feel lifted straight out of a chick flick. First-time clients are given their own personal pouch of nail tools—files, toe separators, pumice stones—that they bring back on subsequent visits, a testament to the shop's obsession with sanitation. The store also sells scents, bath goods, and small gift items. Book a private mani-pedi party for up to 12 of your best girlfriends.

HOTELS

Thanks to Atlanta's busy convention schedule, the city doesn't hurt for hotels. According to the Atlanta Convention and Visitors Bureau, there are more than 90,000 rooms in the metro area—10,000 of them in an eight-block area of Downtown. But visitors shouldn't limit their search for lodging to the gargantuan mega-properties that fill the skyline of the central business district.

Buckhead abounds with luxurious high-rises representing some of the most sophisticated accommodations in the South—and also some of the most expensive. Even if your budget won't allow a stay in one of these lavish towers, the hotels can be worth a visit for their swanky bars and restaurants. The same is true for the high-end properties found in Midtown, a neighborhood that offers a mixed range of options, including Atlanta's primary youth hostel.

The past few years have seen a burst of new boutique hotels—designer properties that tend to be smaller and dripping with a heady sense of style. The boutique craze has caused even some international hotel brands to attempt to get in on the action, offering their own answers to the concept. Atlanta has also experienced an influx of properties that are mixed-use: posh condo towers with a designated number of hotel rooms included. It's a harder task to locate a well-regarded bed-and-breakfast in the

HOTELS

HIGHLIGHTS

LOOK FOR (TO FIND RECOMMENDED HOTELS.

(Most Dramatic Lobby: After undergoing an extensive renovation, the dramatic 47-story atrium at the **Atlanta Marriott Marquis** has never looked better (page 133).

(Best Hotel for Kids: With plenty of room for the family to spread out, **Embassy Suites Atlanta at Centennial Olympic Park** is convenient to some of the city's main kid-friendly attractions, including the Georgia Aquarium and Imagine It! The Children's Museum of Atlanta (page 134).

(Best Boutique Hotel: The plush **Glenn Hotel** in a historic former office building Downtown is one of the city's most buzzed-about properties (page 134).

(Best Spot for Sports Fans: The **Omni Hotel at CNN Center** connects to Philips Arena (home of the Hawks and the Thrashers) and is an easy walk to the Georgia Dome (home of the Falcons) and a short MARTA ride to Turner Field (home of the Braves) (page 134).

(Best Pool: Twelve Hotel Centennial Park wows guests with a large and comfortable pool deck that offers striking views of the Atlanta skyline (page 134).

(Best Place to Film a Music Video: It's hard not to feel like a rock star while staying at the fresh and sexy **W Atlanta Midtown** (page 138).

(Best 24-Hour Fine Dining: The flashy **InterContinental Buckhead** features an ex-

© TRAY BUTLER

W Atlanta Midtown hotel

cellent French brasserie, Au Pied de Cochon, which never closes (page 140).

(Most Charming Bargain Hotel: It'll never be known as the most lavish property in town, but the **Highland Inn** is a lovely intersection of genuine character and reasonable rates (page 142).

city; intown options seem to be limited in the category. With a few notable exceptions, the best bed-and-breakfasts tend to be found farther out from the city center.

CHOOSING A HOTEL

It may seem like a no-brainer, but selecting the best hotel has everything to do with location—or, more specifically, transportation.

If you're planning to visit the city and not rent a car, it's essential that you find a property with effortless access to public transit or within walking distance of the sights you want to experience. Travelers on a mission to take in the city's most obvious tourist attractions—including the Georgia Aquarium, CNN Center, and the Martin Luther King Jr. National Historic Site—will probably want

PRICE KEY

$ Less than $150 per night
$$ $150-250 per night
$$$ More than $250 per night

to stick with a hotel in pedestrian-friendly Downtown. Keep in mind that the availability of rooms Downtown can depend greatly on what conventions are going on around town. Add to that the usual week-day business travelers, and you may find that some properties have limited availability for certain dates. Downtown hotels run the full gamut from budget-busters to bare-bones options.

A hotel in Midtown can be a great choice for folks whose itineraries will take them to several different areas of town, thanks to the neighborhood's central location. Visitors out to get a taste of Atlanta's arts scene should consider staying here. Many locations in Midtown will put you within walking distance of the High Museum of Art, Piedmont Park, and the Atlanta Botanical Garden. The area's three

MARTA stations can connect you to parts of the rest of the city.

Staying in Buckhead can be an unforgettable and extravagant experience, and it will also land you in the lap of Atlanta's ritziest shopping and dining district. At the same time, the neighborhood is removed from the best museums and sights. Though MARTA runs along Peachtree Road, the subway isn't necessarily an ideal choice for getting to other parts of town.

For the cheapest, no-frills hotels, the district around Hartsfield-Jackson Atlanta International Airport is overflowing with familiar chain properties. Tempting as it might be to try to save a few bucks, staying near the airport could easily make getting in and out of the city a major hassle.

Because Atlanta has no lack of ubiquitous chain hotels, this chapter attempts to focus on more distinctive properties, including brand-name hotels that qualify as iconic Atlanta institutions. All rates listed here are based on double occupancy in the high season (June–August). Many hotels here include parking services, with prices around $15 per day.

HOTELS

Downtown   Map 1

◖ ATLANTA MARRIOTT MARQUIS $$$

265 Peachtree Center Ave., 404/521-0000, www.marriott.com

It's been a downtown landmark since 1985, and the graceful Marriott Marquis celebrated its 20th anniversary with a much-needed interior makeover. The $138 million facelift, finished in 2007, has drop-kicked the 50-story convention hotel into the new millennium, updating all of the 1,663 guest rooms with

amenities like granite countertops in the bathrooms and down comforters on the beds, and also injected a newly modern attitude into its common areas. The revamped main bar, **Pulse** (404/586-6081, www.pulsebaratlanta .com), is particularly metropolitan and sexy. Cosmetic upgrades aside, the John Portman-designed building remains one of Atlanta's architectural gems, with a jaw-dropping atrium that spans the height of the building and is often cited as one of the largest in the world.

ELLIS HOTEL $$

176 Peachtree St., 404/523-5155, www.ellishotel.com

Opened in late 2007, the Ellis Hotel is part of the new generation of boutique properties braving Downtown's convention-centered market. Located on a busy stretch of Peachtree Street and within walking distance of the neighborhood's attractions, the intimate Ellis features 127 rooms and suites, each appointed with 32-inch LCD televisions and beds with ritzy ostrich-leather headboards. Women can request a room on the hotel's female-only floor, with keyed entry access and—believe it or not—straightening irons in each room. The Ellis has a thoroughly contemporary style overall, but it also gives a nod to its Southern setting with homegrown recording artists playing in the lobby and peach-flavored refreshments at check-in. As with most downtown hotels, parking can be a challenge.

(EMBASSY SUITES ATLANTA AT CENTENNIAL OLYMPIC PARK $$

267 Marietta St., 404/223-2300, www.atlantacentennialpark.embassysuites.com

This eight-story all-suite property gets high marks for its location next to Centennial Olympic Park; popular tourist spots like the Georgia Aquarium, the World of Coca-Cola, and CNN Center are practically in the hotel's front yard. The suites are big and clean, if a little sterile. All suites come with a separate living room with sleeper sofa, refrigerator, microwave, coffeemaker, and two televisions. It's a great option for parents traveling with kids: Guests can request cribs, and the hotel often offers special family packages. Don't miss the view of the downtown skyline from the rooftop pool.

(GLENN HOTEL $$

110 Marietta St., 404/521-2250, www.glennhotel.com

Hear that noise? It's the inescapable buzz surrounding the Glenn Hotel, billed as "downtown Atlanta's first boutique hotel" and raved about as if it were the best thing to hit the city since Asa Candler started bottling sugar water. Luckily, the Glenn turns out to be worth (most of) the hype, with 10 floors of sophistication tucked in the heart of Downtown. The 110 rooms can be on the cramped side, but make up for their lack of space with a slate of unique details, such as Herman Miller Aeron chairs, soothing rain showerheads, and LCD televisions among a host of other pricey creature comforts. Though the hotel pays lip service to business travelers, its recurring motif of "meeting desires" makes it feel more like an ideal option for romance-seekers.

(OMNI HOTEL AT CNN CENTER $$

100 CNN Center, 404/659-0000, www.omnihotels.com

This 28-story four-star property located within CNN Center is the closest Atlanta comes to Las Vegas–style lodging, with a massive food court, upscale restaurants, convention center, and sports arena all seconds outside your door. The Omni Hotel's two towers house 1,067 guest rooms with appropriately modern amenities (Chinese granite countertops, Italian marble floors, boutique toiletries, and flat-screen televisions), though rooms in the newer tower, completed in 2003, tend to be better than those in the original building. Centennial Olympic Park, the Georgia Aquarium, the World of Coca-Cola, and Philips Arena are all less than a five-minute walk away.

(TWELVE HOTEL CENTENNIAL PARK $$

400 W. Peachtree St., 404/418-1212, www.twelvehotels.com

The recent building boom that has reshaped

©2000 STARWOOD HOTELS

Westin Peachtree Plaza

Downtown's northern edge has brought a glossy new crop of luxury condos to the neighborhood, including the handsome Twelve Centennial Park. Opened in 2007, the 39-story glass tower features 102 hotel suites (along with more than 500 residential units) each appointed with full-sized kitchens, 10-foot ceilings, VoIP phone service, complimentary Wi-Fi, and multiple flat-screen televisions in each unit. But the biggest perk—other than

the spectacular views from most balconies—may well be the large size of each room, especially noteworthy given the prices. Twelve's elevated pool deck is also larger than those at most other hotels and well worth checking out. Don't let the name fool you: The hotel is actually located several blocks from Centennial Olympic Park.

WESTIN PEACHTREE PLAZA $$$

210 Peachtree St., 404/881-9898,
www.westin.com/peachtree

The downtown Atlanta skyline wouldn't be the same without the Westin Peachtree Plaza, a shining black-glass cylinder that towers 73 stories above the city. The building opened as the tallest hotel in the world back in 1976 and was Atlanta's tallest skyscraper for the next decade. Although the hotel comes with many of the signature features of the Westin brand, including better-than-average bedding and bathroom supplies, the decor of the common areas hasn't exactly kept up with the level of lavishness found in many nearby hotels. The hotel sustained some exterior damage when a tornado hit Atlanta in 2008, and repair efforts have been slow going. Still, the revolving **Sun Dial Restaurant** (404/935-5279, www.sundialrestaurant.com) on the hotel's top three floors boasts some of the most jaw-dropping views of the city to be found anywhere.

HOTELS

Midtown Map 2

ATLANTA INTERNATIONAL HOSTEL $

223 Ponce de Leon Ave., 404/872-1042, www.atlantahostel.com

Atlanta's first full hostel opened in 1992 and features 100 beds in a dormitory setting. It's a real steal at only $22 per night for students and holders of foreign passports, and is located in an interesting old Victorian house in residential Midtown. The Fox Theatre, Piedmont Park, and The Varsity are close by; it's a 10-minute walk to MARTA. You can expect to share a room with as many as six other guests at a time, but really, who expects privacy in a hostel? The hostel features lockers, a pool table, and a laundry room. Ponce de Leon Avenue can attract shady characters so use extra caution if returning late at night.

FOUR SEASONS HOTEL $$$

75 14th St., 404/881-9898, www.fourseasons.com/atlanta

For luxury in a prime location, you can't beat the Four Seasons. Located within easy walking distance of the Woodruff Arts Center, Crescent Avenue's restaurant row, and MARTA, the hotel almost dispels Atlanta's reputation for being anti-pedestrian. Though the Four Seasons received a five-diamond designation from AAA, its atmosphere and attitude are less stuffy and more casual than you might expect. The service is impeccable. Its celebrated restaurant, **Park 75** (404/253-3840), does a brisk business independent of hotel guests, with an especially popular afternoon tea. Also check out the small but well-appointed day spa.

GEORGIAN TERRACE HOTEL $$

659 Peachtree St., 404/897-1991, www.thegeorgianterrace.com

Atlanta International Hostel

The Georgian Terrace qualifies as a bona fide Atlanta landmark, for good reason. Built in 1911, the Beaux Arts building was for decades one of the city's grandest hotels, host to Vivian Leigh and Clark Gable for the 1939 *Gone With the Wind* premiere. These days the hotel has worked to regain some of its Old Hollywood glamour (after going through a sad stint as an apartment building), with a handsome lobby and an opulent ballroom. The rooms, however, can be unpredictable in terms of size and cleanliness. Don't miss the stunning view from the rooftop pool.

HOTEL INDIGO $$

683 Peachtree St., 800/948-0424, www.hotelindigo.com

Part of the InterContinental Hotels Group's

STAY IN THE LAP OF LUXURY

Despite the national real estate slowdown, Atlanta has experienced a rash of new luxury hotels rising around town. **The Mansion on Peachtree** (3376 Peachtree Rd., 404/995-7500, www.rwmansiononpeachtree .com) opened in 2008 and immediately set a new standard for over-the-top opulence – even in pampered Buckhead. The 42-story boutique hotel has the appearance of a fashion model: impossibly thin and ridiculously stylish. With 127 ultra-high-end rooms and 45 residences (which sell for up to $12 million), the hotel also offers one of the neighborhood's most gorgeous spas, which is open to the public. Rooms in the plush property run around $360 per night.

Not to be outdone, Midtown has fired back with exclusive accommodations of its own. The 304-room **Hotel Palomar Atlanta** (866 W. Peachtree St., 800/546-7866, www. hotelpalomar-atlantamidtown.com), the first foray into the Atlanta market by upscale giant Kimpton Hotels, opened in 2009 in a rapidly changing pocket of new high-rises and development. The attractive 21-story tower offers Kimpton's signature in-room spa services and a unique design aesthetic tailored toward lovers of the arts.

A few blocks northeast, the **Mandarin Oriental** (1138 Peachtree St., www.mandarin-oriental.com) is due to open in 2011 along Peachtree

© TRAY BUTLER

The Mansion on Peachtree

Street's up-and-coming Midtown Mile. The $250 million project will further transform Midtown's skyline with a new 53-story glass skyscraper. The hotel will feature 200 guest rooms, 70 residences, and a three-story spa.

new line of "branded boutique hotels," the Hotel Indigo gets high marks for its playful interior design and commitment to using environmentally friendly materials. Previously an easily missed Days Inn property, the hotel underwent a sweeping renovation and opened in 2004. Its bar attracts a busy pre-show crowd heading to the nearby Fox Theatre. The Indigo is also known as one of the city's most pet-friendly hotels, with a weekly Canine Cocktail Hour for four-legged visitors (and their owners).

SHELLMONT INN ⬤⬤
821 Piedmont Ave., 404/872-9290, www.shellmont.com

For a city its size, Atlanta suffers a shortage of quality bed-and-breakfasts—at least in the center of town. One notable exception is the Shellmont Inn, a lovingly restored 1891 Victorian home on the National Register of Historic Places that looks like a photo spread from *Southern Living* brought to life. The six-room inn drips with antiques and authentic Southern charm. Shared meals are served twice daily, and the property features multiple porches

HOTELS

© TRAY BUTLER

Shellmont Inn

sophistication in an emerging new neighborhood. The 26-story building is split between residential units and hotel rooms, giving each of the 101 deluxe suites a homey, condominium feel, with large kitchens, luxurious bathrooms, and flat-screen televisions in every room. Wide balconies offer splendid views of the downtown skyline, though recent construction has obscured the sightlines of some units. Best of all, the hotel's prime location puts the restaurants, shops, and nightlife of Atlantic Station within a four-block radius, including a grocery store and dry cleaner.

❰ W ATLANTA MIDTOWN ❸❸

188 14th St., 404/892-6000,
www.whotels.com/atlantamidtown

Who could have guessed that the dingy Sheraton Colony Square would be reborn as one of Atlanta's sexiest hotels? With a vibe lifted straight from South Beach, the W Atlanta Midtown features flourishes aimed at a fun-loving younger clientele, from 37-inch flat-screen TVs with laptop plug-ins to iPod-ready clock radios. The lobby bar, **Living Room,** attracts a be-seen glitterati crowd; Saturdays can be a mob scene. Though the standard rooms are cozy and cool, the pricey Wow Suite is truly a spectacle, with a bar, two-person bathtub, and a den ready for *The Real World.*

for relaxing, as well as a Victorian fishpond out back. The innkeepers, Debbie and Ed McCord, are gracious without being overbearing and treat guests more like friends than strangers.

TWELVE HOTEL
ATLANTIC STATION ❸❸

361 17th St., 404/961-1212, www.twelvehotels.com

One of the first high-rises at Atlantic Station, Twelve Hotel raised the bar on urban

Buckhead

Map 3

BEVERLY HILLS INN ❺

65 Sheridan Dr., 404/233-8520,
www.beverlyhillsinn.com

Housed in a 1929 neoclassical apartment building built for elderly single women, the stately Beverly Hills Inn bills itself as Atlanta's first bed-and-breakfast. Opened in 1982, the inn itself hasn't aged as gracefully as some other nearby properties in Buckhead, but it does offer a nice and comfortable option close to the neighborhood's busy commercial district and a nice change of pace from the glass towers farther north. The inn's 18 suites feature small kitchenettes, large closets, and sitting areas decorated with traditional European flourishes.

COUNTRY INN AND SUITES BUCKHEAD ❺

80 Sidney Marcus Blvd., 404/949-4000,
www.countryinns.com/hotels/gabuckhd

Budget travelers who need to stay in Buckhead but can't stomach the luxury prices will find a more reasonable alternative at this basic hotel, part of the Carlson chain. The suburban-style six-story complex offers 147 rooms that are clean and serviceable, if on the small side. The hotel sits across the street from the large Lindbergh Plaza shopping complex, which includes big-box shops such as Target and Best Buy, several restaurants, and a hair salon. The Lindbergh MARTA station appears close on the map but is probably too far to hike with luggage.

HOTELS

© TRAY BUTLER

Beverly Hills Inn

Grand Hyatt Atlanta

GRAND HYATT ATLANTA ⑤⑤
3300 Peachtree Rd., 404/237-1234,
www.grandatlanta.hyatt.com

Not to be confused with the Hyatt Regency Downtown, Buckhead's Grand Hyatt Atlanta features 438 rooms in two 25-story towers on one of the busiest stretches of Peachtree Road. Formerly the Hotel Nikko, the Grand Hyatt knows from comfort: The rooms offer luxurious linens, down comforters, and plush pillow-top mattresses; some rooms overlook a soothing Japanese Zen garden. The new Terminus office tower nearby adds a great wealth of fine dining options to the equation; a complimentary shuttle service will take you to any destination within two miles of the hotel.

◖ INTERCONTINENTAL BUCKHEAD ⑤⑤⑤
3315 Peachtree Rd., 404/946-9000,
www.ichotelsgroup.com

Beyond being one of the neighborhood's most opulent hotels, the InterContinental Buckhead is also known as the host for the annual Peachtree Road Race 10K and its pre-race sports expo. The 22-story property has a refined, big-city vibe, with a ritzy pool deck that feels more like South Beach than Buckhead. The high-end French restaurant, **Au Pied de Cochon** (404/946-9070, www.aupiedde cochonatlanta.com), is open 24 hours. The 422 spacious guest rooms feature whirlpool tubs, Wi-Fi, CD players, and, for business travelers, work desks with speakerphones. Lenox Square Mall and the Buckhead MARTA station are within walking distance.

RITZ-CARLTON BUCKHEAD ⑤⑤⑤
3434 Peachtree Rd., 404/237-2700,
www.ritzcarlton.com/en/properties/buckhead/default.htm

It's a real shame that such a luxurious hotel has to make do with such an unattractive building, a sulking brown box that represents the worst of early '80s architecture. But the Ritz-Carlton Buckhead overcompensates for the drab exterior by sparing no expense on its elegant, fussy decor inspired by classic European lavishness. The hotel celebrated its 25th anniversary in 2008 with a stunning $38 million renovation that mainly affected the guest rooms; the total number of rooms was reduced from 553 to 517, with the number of suites doubling. All rooms are appointed with custom-designed furnishings, including marble-topped cabinets and roomy walk-in showers. The hotel's five-star restaurant, the **Dining Room,** is often cited as one of the best in Atlanta.

WESTIN BUCKHEAD ATLANTA ⑤
3391 Peachtree Rd., 404/365-0065,
www.westin.com/buckhead

Compared with neighboring high-end hotels the Ritz-Carlton and InterContinental

© TRAY BUTLER

Ritz-Carlton Buckhead

Buckhead, the Westin Buckhead Atlanta deserves a prize for giving guests the most bang for their buck. Built as a Swissôtel, the shining white 22-story building has a lobby and common areas that still whisper of sleek European design and a jet-set sophistication. The 376 rooms feature Biedermeier-style furnishings, with freshly cut flowers, floor-to-ceiling windows, and marble bathrooms. The popular **Palm restaurant** (404/814-1955, www.thepalm.com) attracts a busy scene of locals and hotel guests alike. Sitting adjacent to Lenox Square Mall, the Westin Buckhead is an ideal choice for travelers who'd rather spend their savings at Neiman Marcus than on accommodations.

HOTELS

Virginia-Highland

Map 4

EMORY CONFERENCE CENTER HOTEL ⑤⑤

1641 Clifton Rd., 404/712-6000,
www.emoryconferencecenter.com

In the rush to go green, no local hotel can match the Emory Conference Center Hotel's efforts toward environmental responsibility. The only Green Seal–certified hotel in Georgia has gone above and beyond in its commitment to recycling and using sustainable resources; an on-site recycler processes approximately 40 tons of waste each year, while the housekeeping staff uses only natural, non-toxic cleaning supplies. The building itself, with an architectural style inspired by Frank Lloyd Wright, features 198 guest rooms that are decorated in a classic style. The hotel underwent a major (and environmentally friendly) expansion in 2008 and

is surrounded by 28 acres of forest preserve on the Emory University campus.

GASLIGHT INN BED & BREAKFAST ⑤

1001 Saint Charles Ave., 404/875-1001,
www.gaslightinn.com

As the name would imply, many of the common areas in this quainter-than-quaint bed-and-breakfast are indeed lit by flickering gaslight lanterns, which gives the 1913 Craftsman-style home a genuinely old-fashioned ambience. The property offers four guest rooms and four suites (some of which are located across the street from the main house), which include standard amenities and off-street parking— a real perk in busy Virginia-Highland. Most rooms are decorated in a traditional Southern or Victorian style; some include fireplaces but not all have in-room bathrooms. It's located within walking distance of the busiest bars and restaurants of Virginia-Highland.

UNIVERSITY INN AT EMORY 🄢🄢

1767 N. Decatur Rd., 800/654-8591, www.univinn.com

The best thing about this small family-owned hotel is its proximity to the Emory University campus and medical facilities, which are just across the street. The property offers a total of 60 rooms split among three buildings; the main building itself is probably your best bet, with rooms that offer kitchenettes and Wi-Fi access. The Guest House and Oxford Hall are aimed at guests who plan longer visits; some suites require a seven-night stay. The size of rooms seems to vary greatly, as does the quality of services. Don't be afraid to ask for an upgrade to a larger room.

VIRGINIA HIGHLAND BED AND BREAKFAST 🄢🄢

630 Orme Circle, 877/870-4485, www.virginiahighlandbandb.com

Staying in this tiny bed-and-breakfast feels something like a visit to a distant cousin's house for the holidays—cozy, casual, but with the potential for awkward familiarity in close quarters. The restored 1920s Craftsman bungalow hasn't been modified much from its days as a private home and features three guest rooms, one of which is a suite with its own entrance. Innkeeper Adele Northrup pays particular attention to the property's gardens, which are in bloom year-round. A lovely screened porch with a Pawley's Island hammock makes for a sweet respite from the rush of the city. The Virginia-Highland commercial district is a 15-minute walk through a residential area.

Little Five Points and East Atlanta   Map 5

1890 KING-KEITH HOUSE BED AND BREAKFAST 🄢🄢

889 Edgewood Ave., 404/688-7330, www.kingkeith.com

From the street, the King-Keith House looks good enough to eat—a playful peach and purple Queen Anne mansion that has been tenderly restored to its Victorian grandeur. No wonder it's one of the most photographed buildings in the city. Inside, the six guest rooms and common areas are appointed with period-style antiques and handsome stained-glass windows. It's located on a quiet street in Inman Park, near the historic Trolley Barn and within walking distance from MARTA, though the owners will also pick up you up from the station.

☾ HIGHLAND INN 🄢

644 N. Highland Ave., 404/874-5756, www.thehighlandinn.com

The Highland Inn is, if nothing else, true to the bohemian character of its neighborhood: quirky, charming, and capricious. The hotel's biggest perk—its prime location in a busy part of Poncey-Highland's shops and restaurants—may also be its biggest weakness, due to the potential noise factor. The upside is its value, with rooms starting under $90 per night. The inn is housed in a historic two-story 1927 building that was refurbished for the 1996 Olympic Games. The popular **Cafe di Sol** (640 N. Highland Ave., 404/724-0711, http://cafedisol.com) nearby does a packed dinner and bar business.

HOTELS

© TRAY BUTLER

The Highland Inn sits within easy walking distance of Virginia-Highland.

INMAN PARK BED & BREAKFAST $

100 Waverly Way, 404/688-9498,
www.inmanparkbandb.com

Travelers thirsty for Atlanta history will marvel at the story behind this gracious Inman Park property; the 1912 home was built as a honeymoon residence for Coca-Cola king Robert Woodruff. It features heart-of-pine floors, 12-foot ceilings, and enough antiques to fill a small museum. A Charleston-style private garden in back feels like a private park in the city. The three guest rooms are furnished with either queen or twin beds; all offer private restrooms, which is not always a given at other area bed-and-breakfasts. Guests also receive a complimentary pass to one of the city's finest health clubs.

SUGAR MAGNOLIA BED & BREAKFAST $

804 Edgewood Ave., 404/222-0226,
www.sugarmagnoliabb.com

With a name that sounds like an Anne Rivers Siddons novel, Sugar Magnolia Bed & Breakfast is the kind of place perfect for nostalgic dreamers and hopeless romantics. The attractive three-story Victorian manor shines like a yellow beacon among the historic homes along Edgewood Avenue. The interior features four guest rooms, the best being the enormous Royal Suite with two balconies, a whirlpool tub, and a king-size bed in a recessed alcove. Other highlights of the 1892 home include its grand three-story turret and staircase, oval beveled windows, decorative plasterwork, and amazing crystal chandelier.

Decatur   Map 6

LAUREL HILL BED & BREAKFAST $

1992 McLendon Ave., 404/377-3217,
www.laurelhillbandb.com

There's a Confederate Suite and a Union Suite—but who says the South can't stop fighting the Civil War? Despite the historical nomenclature, Laurel Hill Bed & Breakfast is decorated with a modern, tasteful sensibility, a change of pace from many of the other bed-and-breakfasts in town that could double as antiques showrooms. The property consists of twin English Tudor homes located in a quiet neighborhood near Lake Claire Park. The two houses offer a total of five suites each with unique characteristics ranging from whirlpool tubs to private balconies.

MILEYBRIGHT FARMHOUSE BED & BREAKFAST $$

3244 Covington Highway, 404/508-6060,
www.mileybright.com

Close enough to the city to still be convenient and yet far enough to feel like it's in the countryside, this 1900 residence was built as a dairy farm—400 acres of which later became part of the city of Avondale Estates. Restored to a classic 1930s Southern character, the pleasant bed-and-breakfast is split into one guest room and a one-, two-, or three-bedroom apartment. Modern amenities include Wi-Fi, a gas log fireplace, satellite TV, 11-foot ceilings, hardwood floors, a hand-painted sink, large private porch, and an outdoor spa tub.

EXCURSIONS FROM ATLANTA

A journey outside Atlanta's Perimeter can feel like visiting a different state altogether, so striking is the difference between the metropolitan area and the Georgia countryside. Though suburban sprawl stretches in all directions around the city, visitors might be surprised by how quickly a more relaxed rural ambience sets in. But it's not all peanut fields and pine forests. Scenic Stone Mountain, about 30 minutes east of the city, is a dramatic geological curiosity, a chunk of solid granite surrounded by a busy theme park and recreation area. To the northeast, Atlantans escape the summer heat with dips in Lake Lanier and trips to the foothills of the Blue Ridge Mountains, which come into view after about an hour's drive. The area has no shortage of lake houses and mountain cabins to rent, as well as picturesque bed-and-breakfasts and genuine down-home dining. Northwest of the city, history buffs flock to Kennesaw Mountain, site of a famous Civil War battle, and nearby Marietta, full of genteel charm.

A different energy lives in the streets of Athens, a bohemian college town known for the alternative rock bands that have risen from its manic music scene over the past 25 years. Located 70 miles from Atlanta, Athens promises a diverse mix of fun day-trip possibilities, including primo dining, historic sightseeing,

HIGHLIGHTS

LOOK FOR ◖ TO FIND RECOMMENDED SIGHTS, ACTIVITIES, DINING, AND LODGING.

◖ **Best Destination for Scarlett O'Hara Groupies:** The **Marietta Gone With the Wind Museum: Scarlett on the Square** is one of three museums in the metro area devoted to Margaret Mitchell's classic novel, but this noteworthy collection pays particular attention to rare volumes of the book – including foreign-language texts and a first edition signed by the author (page 150).

◖ **Best View:** The trip to the top of **Kennesaw Mountain National Battlefield Park** is worth the effort even if Civil War history isn't your cup of tea (page 150).

◖ **Best Way to Climb a Mountain:** Stone Mountain Park has dozens of attractions aimed at the whole family, but none can beat the simple thrill of the **Summit Skyride,** a slow-moving cable car that lifts visitors to the peak of the granite monadnock (page 155).

◖ **Best Place to Beat the Heat:** The sandy beach at **Lake Lanier Islands Resort** is a favorite getaway for landlocked, water-starved Atlantans (page 157).

◖ **Most Romantic Getaway:** Modeled after a 16th-century French château, the resplendent **Château Élan Winery and Resort** features a vast vineyard and lots of chances to sample Georgia wines with the one you love (page 157).

◖ **Most Colorful Downtown:** More than just a college town, **Downtown Athens** is a hip and artsy destination for offbeat shopping, eclectic restaurants, and tipsy nightlife (page 160).

◖ **Best Place to Reconnect with Nature:** With five miles of nature trails and 300 acres of forest, **The State Botanical Garden of Georgia** offers manicured plant collections, a great conservatory, and lots of raw woodlands to explore (page 160).

© MARCUS WILLIAMS

The Grill's retro-styled restaurant and welcoming neon glow has been a mainstay of Downtown Athens for decades.

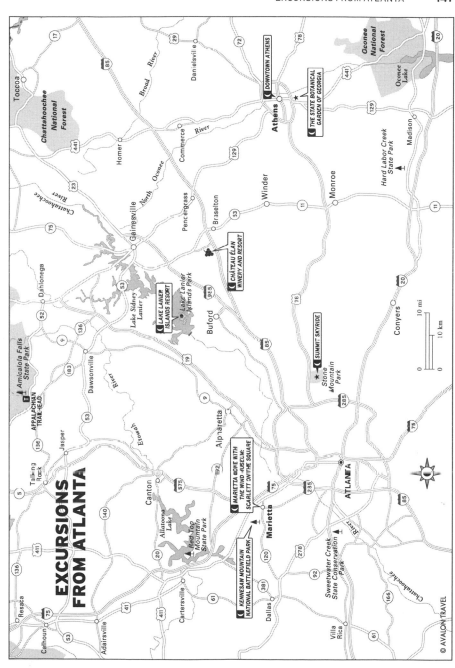

EXCURSIONS

EXCURSIONS FROM ATLANTA

Chattahoochee National Forest

Oconee National Forest

◀ DOWNTOWN ATHENS

◀ THE STATE BOTANICAL GARDEN OF GEORGIA

◀ CHÂTEAU ÉLAN WINERY AND RESORT

◀ LAKE LANIER ISLANDS RESORT

◀ SUMMIT SKYRIDE

◀ MARIETTA GONE WITH THE WIND MUSEUM: SCARLETT ON THE SQUARE

◀ KENNESAW MOUNTAIN NATIONAL BATTLEFIELD PARK

Amicalola Falls State Park

APPALACHIAN TRAILHEAD

Hard Labor Creek State Park

Red Top Mountain State Park

Stone Mountain Park

Sweetwater Creek State Conservation Park

Lake Sidney Lanier

Lake Lanier Islands Park

Allatoona Lake

Toccoa

Homer

Danielsville

Commerce

Athens

Madison

Winder

Monroe

Conyers

Gainesville

Pencergrass

Braselton

Buford

Dahlonega

Dawsonville

Jasper

Talking Rock

Canton

Alpharetta

Marietta

ATLANTA

Dallas

Villa Rica

Cartersville

Calhoun

Adairsville

Resaca

Broad River

North Oconee River

Chattahoochee River

Etowah River

Chattahoochee River

10 mi

10 km

an amazing botanical garden, and a raucous bar scene.

Although the destinations profiled in this chapter are some of the best and most popular, they're by no means the only options. A traveler with time to spend exploring—and who doesn't mind lazy drives through lush farmland and forgotten country crossroads—can discover many hidden treasures in the state's varied landscape.

PLANNING YOUR TIME

Most of the excursions detailed in this chapter can be completed in a day or less, though traffic on Atlanta-area interstates is notoriously unpredictable—especially on holiday weekends. For a real taste of Georgia, venture off the expressway and experience the small towns on their own terms, choosing perhaps Athens or Marietta as your home base for an overnight or weekend visit. Attractions in Cobb County (including Kennesaw Mountain) are closest to the city, not quite 30 minutes away, though the area can be a mixed bag of noteworthy sites alongside unattractive big-box strip malls. Stone Mountain and its theme park are also

about a half hour outside the city and have dozens of family-friendly activities. It's a great option for a full afternoon and easy drive back inside the Perimeter. Destinations near Lake Lanier and Athens are farther away, between 60 and 90 minutes respectively.

The best way to travel to these areas is by car, though a couple of companies do provide shuttle services between Hartsfield-Jackson Atlanta International Airport and Athens. Marietta is accessible via public transportation from downtown Atlanta, but it's a long trek requiring lots of patience. As with Athens, you'd need a car once you arrived there. Biking is probably not a good idea anywhere other than central Athens or on the trails around Stone Mountain Park.

Georgia's temperate climate makes most any destination a year-round draw, with crowds at the lowest during the winter months and heaviest in July or August—despite the pervasive humidity. Spring arrives early, and autumn brings in a huge explosion of colorful foliage—the backroads north of Lake Lanier can be crammed with "leaf-lookers." Lake Lanier Islands puts on a magnificent display of holiday lights, which attracts throngs of visitors.

Marietta and Vicinity

At first glance Marietta isn't so different from many other suburban county seats, a bedroom community of 58,000 that's stubbornly proud of its small-town heritage. But the town, and especially its quaint downtown square, has an interesting history dating back to the 1830s, which includes some of Atlanta's most famous—and infamous—moments. The Civil War Battle of Kennesaw Mountain raged here in 1864, and the town was set afire as the

first strike during General William Sherman's March to the Sea. Marietta achieved national notoriety in 1915 with the lynching of Leo Frank, a Jewish factory owner wrongfully accused of murder. The city gained a reputation during the 1990s as one of the most conservative pockets of the country, the home base of Republican congressman Newt Gingrich and a center of controversy during the 1996 Olympic Games.

These days the town has grown increasingly diverse and tolerant, with plenty of local culture and no lack of antiques shopping, sightseeing, and dining. The area can be explored in one leisurely afternoon, starting at the square and working your way out to the museums and Civil War sites.

SIGHTS
Marietta Square

This charming antebellum square has the spirit of a Frank Capra film, brimming with hospitality from a bygone era. Start at the **Marietta Welcome Center** (4 Depot St., 770/429-1115, www.themariettasquare.com), located in a renovated train depot one block off the square, where you can pick up brochures leading you through the area's five National Historic Districts and a guide to the plethora of historic buildings and homes. Next door, the **Marietta Museum of History** (1 Depot

St., 770/794-5710, Mon.–Sat. 10 A.M.–4 P.M., www.mariettahistory.org, $5 adult, $3 student and senior) offers four galleries of Native-American artifacts, Georgia Gold Rush relics, and of course, Civil War weapons. It's located on the 2nd floor of the Kennesaw House, built in 1845 as a cotton warehouse. The square is located at the intersection of Roswell and Atlanta Streets, and has several fine lunch and dinner options.

Marietta-Cobb Museum of Art

The best thing about the museum (30 Atlanta St., 770/528-1444, www.mariettacobbart museum.org, Tues.–Fri. 11 A.M.–5 P.M., Sat. 11 A.M.–4 P.M., $5 adult, $3 student and senior) may be the building itself, a grand Greek Revival monolith that opened as a post office in 1910. The artwork, dedicated to American masters from Wyeth to Warhol, often pales in comparison. Don't miss the unusual gift

EXCURSIONS

© TRAY BUTLER

An antique boxcar sits next to the Marietta Welcome Center.

shop, a marketplace for artists who live in metro Atlanta.

◖ Marietta Gone With the Wind Museum: Scarlett on the Square

Not to be confused with the Midtown museum at the Margaret Mitchell House, this attraction near the Marietta Square houses a privately owned collection of movie and book memorabilia. Highlights of the museum (18 Whitlock Ave., 770/794-5576, www.marietta ga.gov/gwtw, Mon.–Sat. 10 A.M.–5 P.M., $7 adult, $6 student and senior) include the original Bengaline honeymoon gown Vivien Leigh wore in the film and several rare volumes of the novel, including a first edition signed by the author. It's an extensive collection replete with trivia, but a stroll through the museum shouldn't take more than 45 minutes.

◖ Kennesaw Mountain National Battlefield Park

Located about three miles from Marietta Square, this national park (900 Kennesaw Mountain Dr., 770/427-4686, www.nps .gov/kemo, daily dawn–dusk) preserves the battlefield that saw some of the heaviest fighting of the Atlanta Campaign, where more than 5,300 soldiers were killed in the summer of 1864. Today the 2,923-acre park features 18 miles of trails for hiking and a visitors center that brings historical context to the area. The trek to the top of the mountain is a steep climb more than a mile long. But it's worth the hike, with a stunning view of Atlanta, Stone Mountain, and Marietta. A shuttle bus runs to the mountaintop every 30 minutes on weekends; driving is permitted on weekdays. Note that food options inside the park are limited, so you might want to pack a lunch.

© TRAY BUTLER

EXCURSIONS

© TRAY BUTLER

Kennesaw Mountain National Battlefield Park

Southern Museum of Civil War and Locomotive History

Just in case you haven't gotten your fill of Civil War trivia elsewhere, the Southern Museum of Civil War and Locomotive History (2829 Cherokee St., 770/427-2117, www.southern museum.org, Mon.–Sat. 9:30 A.M.–5 P.M., Sun. noon–5 P.M., $7.50 adult, $5.50 child, $6.50 senior) explores yet another aspect of the "War of Northern Aggression," the 1862 hijacking of a Confederate locomotive by Union spies. The train, the General, is on display here along with a narrative of the episode and its context in the greater war, as well as other artifacts from the era. Probably best for hard-core history buffs and train enthusiasts only.

More Marietta Sights

The **Root House Museum** (145 Denmead St., 770/426-4982, www.cobblandmarks.com/root-house.html, Tues.–Sat. 11 A.M.–4 P.M., $4

adult, $3 child and senior) was built in 1854 by one of Marietta's early merchants and gives a glimpse at everyday life before the Civil War. The Greek Revival home is furnished with period furniture.

The **Marietta Fire Museum** (112 Haynes St., 770/794-5491, www.marietta ga.gov, Mon.–Fri. 8 A.M.–5 P.M., free) features fire-fighting clothing, equipment, and antique gadgets used by the Marietta Fire Department dating back to the 1800s.

Near the square, **National Cemetery** (500 Washington Ave.) was founded in 1866 and features the graves of more than 10,000 Union soldiers, 3,000 of them unknown. Farther south, the 1863 **Confederate Cemetery** (381 Powder Springs St.) houses the remains of 3,000 Confederate dead. It's thought to be the oldest Confederate cemetery and the largest one south of Virginia.

Finally, no trip to Cobb County would be complete without a sighting of the **Big**

Chicken. It's actually an otherwise nondescript KFC (1970 N. Cobb Pkwy., 770/422-9716) with a bizarre sign, a 53-foot bird whose eyes gyrate and beak opens. The landmark is used often for local directions and as a reference point by pilots heading to Dobbins Air Reserve Base.

RESTAURANTS
Marietta Square is teeming with cozy options for lunch or dinner, as well as a handful of small bars. **Marietta Pizza Company** (3 Whitlock Ave., 770/419-0900, www.marietta pizza.com, Mon.–Thurs. 11 A.M.–10 P.M., Fri.–Sat. 11 A.M.–11 P.M., Sun. 4–9 P.M., $6–25) serves tasty pies and slices in a fun, funky environment. The mom-and-pop pizza shop also sells sandwiches and subs.

You can eat breakfast all day at **Three Bears Café** (105 N. Park Sq., 678/290-0017, www.threebearscafe.com, Mon.–Thurs.

© TRAY BUTLER

Marietta's famous Big Chicken

7 A.M.–midnight, Sat.–Sun. 8 A.M.–midnight, $15). The diner becomes more of a bar after dark, with live music on weekends. The dinner menu is reliable American and pub grub.

Two miles from the square, ◖ **Williamson Bros. Barbecue** (1425 Roswell Rd., 770/971-3201, www.realpagessites.com/williamsonbros, $7–18) is a much-adored local spot for Alabama-style barbecue. The menu includes hot dogs, hamburgers, and even catfish for non-barbecue lovers.

SHOPS
Of the three or four dozen tiny shops and boutiques around Marietta, the vast majority sell antiques. The concentration creates not just competition but also the chance to discover some truly unique heirlooms. **DuPre's Antiques and Interiors** (17 Whitlock Ave., 770/428-2667, www.dupresai.com, Mon.–Sat. 10 A.M.–5:30 P.M., Sun. 1–5:30 P.M.) is one of the largest and best antiques markets in the area, a 17,000-square-foot showroom that houses 90 dealers. It's the kind of cavernous flea market where you can lose two hours without even realizing it.

Around the corner, the **Brumby Chair Company** (37 W. Park Square, 770/425-1875, www.brumbyrocker.com, Mon.–Sat. 10 A.M.–5 P.M.) has been selling its unique handcrafted rocking chairs since 1875. Made from fine Appalachian Red Oak, the furniture is quintessentially Southern and homespun.

HOTELS
Located a block off Marietta Square, the **Whitlock Inn** (57 Whitlock Ave., 770/428-1495, www.whitlockinn.com, $150 d) is a charming Victorian bed-and-breakfast that doubles as an event space for high-end receptions and dinner parties. The 1900 inn's

five guest rooms all have private baths, old-fashioned ceiling fans, and central heat and air. The front porch is a comfortable place for afternoon naps in a rocking chair; the gardens in back are also worth seeing.

The **Stanley House** (236 Church St., 770/426-1881, www.thestanleyhouse.com, $125 d) just oozes with romance, which is probably the main reason this handsome bed-and-breakfast is so popular for weddings. The 1897 mansion is fabulously appointed, with antiques in every nook and cranny. Most of the seven rooms are named for Georgia locales ("Buckhead," "Dahlonega") and each has its own distinctive personality.

GETTING THERE AND AROUND

Marietta sits about a half hour northwest of Atlanta, best accessed via I-75. The county bus system, **Cobb County Transit** (770/427-4444, www.cobbdot.org/cct.htm), connects with MARTA at the Five Points and Arts Center stations and includes a few stops in the city proper, but taking the bus is probably not ideal for anyone wishing to visit more than just Marietta Square. Attractions are spread out,

so having a car is usually your best bet. Luckily, parking tends not to be a major issue.

The **Historic Marietta Trolley Company** (131 Church St., 770/425-1006, www.marietta trolley.com, $20 adult, $12 child, $18 senior) offers one-hour tours of the town, with stops at the Western & Atlantic Depot, National Cemetery, and Kennesaw Mountain. It's a great, easy, and relatively cheap way to take in Marietta's top attractions in a short amount of time.

INFORMATION

The **Marietta Welcome Center** (4 Depot St., 770/429-1115, www.themariettasquare.com) has a thorough website with loads of information on local attractions, hotels, shopping, and events. The center also sells a **Heritage Passport** ($10), which includes admission to Marietta Museum of History, Root House Museum, and the Marietta Gone With the Wind Museum.

The **Cobb County Convention & Visitors Bureau** (1 Galleria Pkwy., Ste. 1A2A, 800/451-3480, www.cobbcvb.com) offers similar information, geared more toward convention visitors.

Stone Mountain

It's not only the state's most-visited tourist spot, but also one of the most-attended attractions in the nation. Stone Mountain is actually a giant monadnock that towers 825 feet at its highest point—the single largest piece of exposed granite on earth. The northern face of the mountain features its famous **Confederate Memorial,** a three-acre carving of three mounted generals from the Civil War. Stone Mountain Park, the 3,200-acre recreation area that surrounds the mountain, is home to a huge range of family-friendly entertainment, including a theme park, resort, antebellum plantation, museums, campsites, and hiking trails. This is not to be confused with Stone Mountain Village, the sleepy railroad town nearby. The village's quaint tourist district is listed on the National Register of Historic Places and has a handful of souvenir shops and restaurants, but your time is better spent inside Stone Mountain Park itself. All of the sights discussed here are within park property and have various admission fees and open times, which change seasonally.

SIGHTS

Stone Mountain Park (1000 Robert E. Lee Blvd., 770/498-5690, www.stonemountainpark .com, daily 6 A.M.–midnight, $8 per car, cash only) has numerous museums and attractions. Admission prices and hours vary among attractions, and not all sights are open year-round. A one-day **Adventure Pass** ($25 adult, $20 child) grants access to all the major attractions.

© 2009 KEVIN C. ROSE/ATLANTAPHOTOS.COM

The Confederate Memorial carving depicts three Southern heroes of the Civil War: Confederate President Jefferson Davis, General Robert E. Lee, and General Thomas J. "Stonewall" Jackson.

Discovering Stone Mountain Museum at Memorial Hall

Any visit to Stone Mountain Park should start at the Discovering Stone Mountain Museum at Memorial Hall, which presents a detailed history of the mountain. The main exhibition hall explains not only the mountain's geology and unique natural habitat but also its early settlers, featuring artifacts from ancient Native-American dwellers through the Civil War era. A timeline traces Stone Mountain's fate as disputed piece of land, stone quarry, and eventual site of a major Confederate memorial. A separate exhibition details the colossal endeavor involved with the carving, a task that took almost 50 years to complete and required three subsequent teams of artisans. The finished memorial was finally dedicated in 1970.

Summit Skyride

The Summit Skyride transports visitors to the top of the mountain via a hanging Swiss cable car. Though the vehicle doesn't exceed 30 miles per hour, it can be a dizzying experience on windy days. The breathtaking view from the gently sloped peak reveals the vast forest of the Georgia Piedmont, with the Atlanta skyline and Kennesaw Mountain visible. Catch the Summit Skyride at Skyride Plaza, located next to the Discovering Stone Mountain Museum. Lines can be long in the busiest summer months, but they tend to move quickly. Adventurous types can also choose to hike to the summit along a 1.3-mile trail.

Other Park Attractions

Beyond the majesty of Mother Nature, the park includes plenty of manmade attractions, most of them aimed at children. **Crossroads**

EXCURSIONS

Antebellum Plantation at Stone Mountain

re-creates a lively 1870s Southern town, where demonstrators in period costume show off craftmaking skills. A short hike away, the poorly curated **Antebellum Plantation and Farmyard** preserves an actual homestead built in 1845, appointed with period furnishings.

Other park attractions include the **Antique Car and Treasure Museum**—which uses the term "treasure" loosely—and a 19th-century style paddleboat, *Scarlett O'Hara.* The boat takes guests on a 20-minute cruise around the park's 383-acre lake.

FESTIVALS AND EVENTS

Beyond Memorial Hall, the great lawn facing the Confederate monument hosts a variety of festivals, concerts, and events year-round. The most popular is the summertime **Lasershow Spectacular,** a 40-minute light show on the mountain's face set to music. Get there early to claim a spot on the lawn. The **Indian Festival and Pow-Wow** each autumn celebrates Native-American culture through dance, cooking, crafts, and storytelling. December brings a park-wide holiday celebration and **Snow Mountain**—three football fields of fresh (artificial) snow, along with tube racing and a snow lift.

SPORTS AND RECREATION

Many visitors to Stone Mountain each year never set foot in any of the hyped attractions, instead focusing on the plethora of outdoor activity options in the serene 3,200-acre park. The area features 15 miles of hiking trails, including the six-mile **National Recreation Trail,** which traces the base of the mountain. Visitors can rent **pedal boats** (Riverboat Marina Complex off Robert E. Lee Blvd., $9 adult, $7 child) for 30-minute

excursions into the water. Swimming in the lake is not permitted, but fishing is. The lake is stocked with bass, carp, catfish, and brim; a valid Georgia fishing license is required ($9 annual, $3.50 one-day) and sold at the Campground Grocery Store, located at the campground's entrance on Stonewall Jackson Drive.

Golfers can explore the two courses at **Stone Mountain Golf Club** (770/465-3278), which wind through a forest of Georgia pines around the lake. Trained PGA professionals staff the club, which features instruction options and precision club fitting. The club includes a golf shop and full-service restaurant.

HOTELS AND CAMPING

The **❰ Marriott Evergreen Marriott Conference Resort** (4021 Lakeview Dr., 770/879-9900, www.evergreenresort.com, $199 d) is an expansive lodge where many of the 311 rooms offer balconies with serene lakeside views. The modern hotel has beautiful grounds, well-appointed suites, and a spa.

Expect a different sort of experience at the nostalgic **Marriott Stone Mountain Inn** (1058 Robert E. Lee Dr., 770/469-3311, www.marriott.com/hotels/travel/atlsi-stone-mountain-inn, $164 d), a white-columned replica of a 19th-century plantation. The 92-room hotel offers easy access to the mountain, and some rooms feature sleeper sofas.

Stone Mountain Park's extensive (and heavily used) **campground** (770/498-5710, www.stonemountainpark.com, $25–60) includes 441 wooded campsites, 147 full hook-ups and 247 partial hook-ups with water and electricity (for tents, pop-ups, and motor homes), plus another 47 primitive tent sites. Reservations can be made online. There's a two-night minimum stay on some lots.

GETTING THERE AND AROUND

Stone Mountain is located about 17 miles east of Atlanta, best accessed via U.S. 78. Traffic can be cumbersome during morning or evening weekday crunch times, but an afternoon drive shouldn't take more than 20 or 30 minutes. If coming from outside the city via I-285, take exit 39B for U.S. 78 East (Snellville/Athens). Travel 7.7 miles and take exit 8, which leads to the park's East Gate entrance. Road signs in the area will point you toward nearby Stone Mountain Village, if you're so inclined.

There's ample parking inside the park, but expect a day with lots of walking since most attractions are fairly spread out. The **Stone Mountain Railroad** ($9 adult, $7 child, free with Adventure Pass) journeys around the mountain via a 1940s-era locomotive with open-air cars. The five-mile trek takes about half an hour, and the train can be boarded and de-boarded from Memorial Depot in Crossroads or Confederate Hall at the base of the Walk-Up Trail.

Lake Lanier and Vicinity

More than seven million visitors a year flock to Lake Sidney Lanier, the 38,000-acre reservoir that serves as one of Atlanta's primary water sources. Named for the 19th century Georgia poet who wrote "The Song of the Chattahoochee," the lake was created in 1956 when the U.S. Army Corps of Engineers completed work on Buford Dam. Water from the Chattahoochee River slowly filled the valley between Hall and Forsyth Counties. At its normal water level, the lake's shoreline stretches for almost 700 miles and touches five counties, though recent years have seen lake levels occasionally reaching record lows due to Georgia's pervasive drought. Rowing and canoeing competitions were held here during the 1996 Summer Olympics, which led to a rush of new development along the lake's northern fingers.

SIGHTS
(Lake Lanier Islands Resort

One unintended consequence of the filling of the reservoir was the creation of a handful of islands in the lake's southeast corner. Rather than trying to correct the problem, the state of Georgia decided to dedicate the land for recreational use. Today Lake Lanier Islands Resort (7000 Holiday Rd., 800/840-5253, www.lakelanierislands.com) has grown to include a luxury hotel, golf club, conference center, equestrian center, and spa. Its half-mile sandy beach and **water park** (hours vary, roughly 10 A.M.–6 P.M. May–Sept., $28 adult, $18 child) are packed during the summer months; the water park features Georgia's largest wave pool and several waterslides. The resort also hosts a wildly popular display of holiday lights in late November and December. The islands are accessible by car and located about a half mile from I-985. The resort includes three restaurants on-site.

(Château Élan Winery and Resort

Napa Valley it isn't, but Georgia has developed a small and growing wine industry, with almost a dozen vineyards and wineries popping up in the northeast corridor. The most famous is Château Élan Winery and Resort (100 Rue Charlemagne,

GOLD IN THEM HILLS

Located just over an hour north of the city, the tiny town of Dahlonega is worth the drive for a visit to the **Dahlonega Gold Museum Historic Site** (1 Public Sq., 800/864-7275, www.gastateparks.org/info/dahlonega, Mon.-Sat. 9 A.M.-5 P.M., Sun. 10 A.M.-5 P.M., $5). Two decades before the 1849 discovery of gold in California, fortune-seekers flooded Dahlonega during America's first gold rush. The story of the mountain town's meteoric rise – and fall – as a mining mecca is told in the 1836 Lumpkin County Courthouse, the oldest courthouse in the state. Featured exhibits in the museum include U.S. coins minted from Dahlonega gold and equipment used in mining. The surrounding downtown district is a popular tourist destination with folk-art galleries, dining, and stands where kids can pan for "gold" and gemstones. Every October Dahlonega hosts **Gold Rush Days** (www.dahlonega.org), a colorful street festival that commemorates the gold rush and brings in a crowd of over 200,000 for events that include a parade, fashion show, gold-panning contest, wheelbarrow race, hog calling and buck-dancing contests, gospel singing, and other live acts.

800/233-9463, www.chateauelan.com), the largest producer of premium wines in the state. The 42,000-square-foot winery is housed in a surprising 16th-century-style French château surrounded by vineyards, with a golf club, spa, and conference center included. Located in Braselton, about 40 miles outside of the city, the winery is easily one of the area's most romantic day-trip destinations. Die-hard oenophiles can also use the château as the starting point for following the **Georgia Wine Highway** (www.georgiawine.com), a meandering itinerary of 10 wineries spread from Dahlonega to Clayton. Just be sure to pick a designated driver!

SPORTS AND RECREATION
Boating
The area around Friendship Road in Buford includes several places to rent or purchase boats and personal watercraft for use on the lake. **Harbor Landing,** part of Lake Lanier Islands Resort, rents out ski boats, pontoon boats, houseboats, sailboats, and even some yachts.

Golf
For golfers, the resort's two courses ($29–65)

are some of the most scenic in the state, with a total of 21 waterfront holes. **Pineisle Golf Club** is a par-72 18-hole championship course, while **Legacy Golf Club** launched a sweeping renovation and facelift, reopening in summer 2009.

Hiking and Biking
Closer to Gainesville, **Elachee Nature Science Center** (2125 Elachee Dr., 770/535-1976, www.elachee.org, Mon.–Fri. 10 A.M.–2 P.M., $5 adult, $3 child) is a serene environmental conservancy and museum located in the 1,500-acre Chicopee Woods Nature Preserve. It includes more than 12 miles of hiking trails, which are free to visit and are open daily 8 A.M.–dusk. For a somewhat bumpier forest experience, the nearby **Chicopee Woods Mountain Bike Trails** (www.gainesvillesorba.org) offer 13 miles of trails for mountain bikers.

SHOPS
The tiny hamlet of Buford, Georgia, may seem like an unlikely place to plant the region's largest shopping mall, but that's exactly

what happened when the **Mall of Georgia** (3333 Buford Dr., 678/482-8788, www.mall ofgeorgia.com) sprouted in 1999. With more than 225 stores, the sprawling commercial megaplex has the feel of a small municipality, complete with its own town square out front. Anchor tenants include Dillard's, Macy's, Nordstrom, and JCPenney, as well as designer stores like Coach and A|X Armani Exchange. The plush Regal Cinema 20 is the only IMAX theater in the state that shows Hollywood fare on a supersized screen.

GETTING THERE AND AROUND

Lake Lanier is approximately 40 miles northeast of Atlanta, best accessed via I-85. Merge onto I-985 and exit at Friendship Road, exit 8. For Château Élan, take I-85 to exit 126, Farm Market Road.

Athens

Though it's best known as a college town, there's more to Athens than the University of Georgia. True, the nation's oldest public research university takes up a whopping 600 acres of the city's prime real estate, with a student population of 33,000 flooding the downtown streets each academic year. The university's influence reaches beyond the classroom and informs all aspects of life in the Classic City, making this a mecca for intellectuals, bohemians, artists, and misfits of all stripes.

Since the early 1980s, Athens has also been

EXCURSIONS

COURTESY OF ATHENS CONVENTION & VISITORS BUREAU

Downtown Athens

recognized nationally for its ever-churning alternative music scene, thanks to the success of wildly popular bands like the B-52s and R.E.M. A variety of chart-topping acts have since emerged from this important indie incubator, including Widespread Panic, Matthew Sweet, Danger Mouse, and the Elephant Six family of artists—to name just a smattering of dozens.

As home to the University of Georgia Press, Hill Street Press, and the *Georgia Review,* the city has a vibrant literary scene, as well as a hot arts community and a busy clique of local theaters. The luxuriant State Botanical Garden of Georgia is located here, as well as a famous "Tree that Owns Itself" and enormous Stanford Stadium, home of the Georgia Bulldogs.

SIGHTS
◖ Downtown Athens

The University of Georgia campus meets the animated downtown commercial district along Broad Street. The 20-square-block center of town is a picturesque and walkable collection of classic pre-war American buildings filled with restaurants, bars, music clubs, boutiques, bookstores, and gift shops. Any exploration of the area should start at the University's **Arch** (Broad and College Streets), the 1858 wrought-iron gate that serves as the school's symbol and mimics the design of the state seal of Georgia. The Arch once supported heavy swinging gates, but they vanished around 1885. The best of downtown's commercial district radiates outward from here to the north and tapers off around Dougherty Street.

About half a mile to the west, the **Tree that Owns Itself** stands proudly at the intersection of Dearing and Finley Streets. The large white oak is technically the offspring of the original self-owning tree, so deemed because of the final wishes of its landowner in the late 1800s.

◖ The State Botanical Garden of Georgia

Approximately three miles from downtown Athens, the splendid State Botanical Garden of Georgia (2450 S. Milledge Ave., 706/542-1244, www.uga.edu/botgarden, Tues.–Sat. 9 A.M.–4:30 P.M., Sun. 11:30 A.M.–4:30 P.M., free) is a serene sanctuary away from the commotion of campus. The garden's grounds spread over 300 acres, much along the Middle Oconee River, and features more than five miles of nature trails. A gorgeous three-story conservatory hosts a permanent collection of tropical plants with an emphasis on beneficial species. Outdoors, visitors can stroll through six themed gardens, including native flora, ornamentals, and a prize-winning rhododendron collection. The grounds of the garden have longer hours than the visitors center and conservatory: daily 8 A.M.–6 P.M. October–March, and 8 A.M.–8 P.M. April–September. The garden is also popular for bird-watchers. Its nearby Whitehall Forest has been designated an Important Bird Area by the Georgia Audubon Society.

RESTAURANTS

For such a small town, Athens offers a sophisticated selection of restaurants, from much-loved dive spots to high-end eateries. ◖ **Five & Ten** (1653 S. Lumpkin St., 706/546-7300, www.fiveandten.com, Mon.–Thurs. 5:30–10:30 P.M., Fri.–Sat. 5:30–10:30 P.M., Sun. 10:30 A.M.–2:30 P.M. and 5:30–10:30 P.M., $14–32) gets ranked not only as one of the best restaurants in Athens, but as one of the best in the state. Chef-owner Hugh Acheson deserves the hype around his seasonally changing menu of New American fare with French and Southern influences. The cozy and low-key restaurant is located in Five Points southwest of downtown.

The Grill (171 College Ave., 706/543-4770, www.thegrillathensga.com, $6) is a 1950s-style diner open 24 hours, making it a great spot to get a grease fix and enjoy some of the best late-night people-watching downtown. The menu varies from diner standards like hamburgers and hot dogs to breakfast favorites and some of the best fresh-cut french fries you'll find anywhere, served with decadent gobs of feta cheese.

Rabid fans of R.E.M. make a point to find **Weaver D's Delicious Fine Foods** (1016 E. Broad St., 706/353-7797, Mon.–Sat. 7:30 A.M.–6 P.M., $7), the soul-food shack whose iconic sign gave the band the name for its 1992 breakthrough album *Automatic for the People*. Despite its landmark status, the humble cinder-block building just oozes authenticity, serving Southern staples like fried chicken, pork chops, and meatloaf along with sweet-potato casserole and buttermilk cornbread.

Contrary to its name, **Last Resort Grill** (174-184 W. Clayton St., 706/549-0810, www.lastresortgrill.com, Mon.–Thurs. 11 A.M.–3 P.M. and 5–10 P.M., Fri.–Sat. 11 A.M.–3 P.M. and 5–11 P.M., Sun. 11 A.M.–3 P.M. and 5–10 P.M., $15) has been a first choice for fine dining in Athens since 1992. It's a funky little New American bistro with an atmosphere that's both comfortable and upscale. Billed as "nouvelle Southern," the menu is tinged with Southwestern influences; the signature dish is an amazing praline chicken served with a medley of cheeses. The menu also gets points for its many healthy options.

NIGHTLIFE

Bars, bars, and more bars dot the streets of downtown Athens, where noisy packs of students keep up UGA's party-school reputation most nights of the week. White-hot nightspots filled with barely legal undergrads are a dime a dozen, but you can usually find a more relaxed crowd at **The Globe** (199 N. Lumpkin St., 706/353-4721, www.classiccitybrew.com/globe.html), modeled after a classic British pub. It's a favorite gathering spot for professors and grad students, the kind of place where heated debates erupt over Chaucer or Keats. The Globe carries 70 bottled beers and 14 drafts, along with a full wine menu.

Nearby, **Georgia Theatre** (215 N. Lumpkin St., 706/549-9918, www.georgiatheatre.com) is a music venue, watering hole, and sometime dance club, with a full and diverse calendar of acts. Formerly a movie house, the venue has hosted a Who's Who of Athens music royalty over the years, from Pylon to Widespread Panic.

Around the corner, the **40 Watt Club** (285 W. Washington St., 706/549-7871, www.40watt.com) is a must-see temple for indie-rock pilgrims. The legendary nightspot first opened in 1979 and has moved often around town, finally settling in this gritty former furniture showroom in 1990. Countless national acts have passed through the club on their way to stardom.

Flicker Theater and Bar (263 W. Washington St., 706/546-0039, www.myspace.com/flickerbar) is, as the name suggests, both a bar and a cinema of sorts, featuring artsy screenings, live performances, puppet shows, and other eclectic ephemera.

A relative newcomer to the scene, the **Arch Bar** (288 N. Lumpkin St., 706/548-0300) brings in a young crowd for an atmosphere that's a strange blend of sleek urban lounge and whiskey-soaked honky-tonk. It's especially fun if you're into beer pong.

EXCURSIONS

HOTELS

Athens isn't known for a stunning selection of hotels. **Hilton Garden Inn** (390 E. Washington St., 706/353-6800, www.hiltongardeninn.com, $149 d) is a popular choice for visitors heading to the Classic Center, a major downtown event venue. The inviting eight-floor hotel has 185 guestrooms that include large work desks, two phones (each with two lines) and data ports. The fitness center, indoor pool, and hot tub are all better than average, but really the best aspect of this hotel is its location.

A less obvious choice for travelers is the **UGA Center for Continuing Education** (1197 S. Lumpkin St., 706/542-2635, www.georgiacenter.uga.edu, $99 d), an upscale conference center in the heart of the university's campus. Recently renovated, the hotel has 200 well-appointed rooms with a modern aesthetic that isn't necessarily reflected in some of the more traditional common areas. It also features two restaurants on-site. It's convenient to the Stegeman Coliseum and Stanford Stadium, but downtown's commercial district is a good 20-minute uphill walk through North Campus.

Many chain hotels can also be found west of downtown, including but not limited to **Holiday Inn Express** (513 W. Broad St., 706/546-8122, www.hi-athens.com, $90 d), **Best Western Colonial Inn** (170 N. Milledge Ave., 706/546-7311, www.bestwestern.com/colonialinnathens, $70 d), and **Perimeter Inn** (3791 Atlanta Hwy., 706/548-3000, www.perimeterinn.com, $44 d).

GETTING THERE AND AROUND

Athens is located about 70 miles east of Atlanta, roughly 1.5 hours by car. The fastest route is via I-85 north to Hwy. 316. Exit at Lexington Road for destinations downtown. There is no public transportation from Atlanta to Athens.

You won't necessarily need a car to see some the best of the downtown district or the university campus, but parking can be a challenge in the Classic City. The **College Avenue Parking Deck** (265 College Ave., 706/613-1417) is a great and central place to leave your wheels while walking around town. **Athens Transit** (www.athenstransit.com) runs an extensive network of bus routes through the city and is a real bargain at only $1.25 per ride.

INFORMATION

The Athens Welcome Center (280 E. Dougherty St., 706/353-1820, www.athenswelcomecenter.com, Mon.–Sat. 10 A.M.–5 P.M., Sun. noon–5 P.M.) is an indispensable source of information about the city. It's located in the historic Church-Waddel-Brumby House, dating to 1820 and believed to be the oldest residence in town. You can also find plenty of local insights and assistance at the **University of Georgia Visitors Center** (Four Towers building, College Station Rd., 706/542-0842, www.uga.edu/visit, Mon.–Fri. 8 A.M.–5 P.M., Sat. 9 A.M.–5 P.M., Sun. 1–5 P.M.). It's housed in a former dairy barn on East Campus.

BACKGROUND

The Setting

GEOGRAPHY

In his seminal 1903 essay collection *The Souls of Black Folk*, W. E. B. Du Bois wrote of Atlanta:

> South of the North, yet north of the South, lies the City of a Hundred Hills, peering out from the shadows of the past into the promise of the future. I have seen her in the morning, when the first flush of day had half-roused her; she lay gray and still on the crimson soil of Georgia; then the blue smoke began to curl from her chimneys, the tinkle of bell and scream of whistle broke the silence, the rattle and roar of busy life slowly gathered and swelled, until the seething whirl of the city seemed a strange thing in a sleepy land.

More than a century later, the "City of a Hundred Hills" might still be described as "a strange thing in a sleepy land," an audacious Southern metropolis with its eyes fixed on the future. Today the whistles, rattles, and roars have been replaced with sirens, horns, and the pervasive hum of traffic on the Downtown

© 2009 KEVIN C. ROSE/ATLANTAPHOTOS.COM

Connector. To say Atlanta has a hundred hills might be an exaggeration; decades of development have tamed the wild landscape, but the city's topography still features plenty of peaks and valleys, which are especially obvious in Piedmont or Freedom Parks.

Located in the central northern half of the state, Georgia's capital city lies in the foothills of the Appalachian Mountains at an elevation of 1,010 feet above sea level. It's the largest city on the vast Piedmont Plateau, which stretches from Alabama to New Jersey. The greater metropolitan area spans 8,376 square miles, comprising 28 counties and 140 municipalities. Atlanta's city limits encompass 132 square miles, most of which lie in Fulton County, with a smaller slice in DeKalb County. Of that area, less than one square mile consists of water. The city depends upon reservoirs in North Georgia for its water supply, via the Chattahoochee River. The Brevard Fault

Zone runs alongside the river, but geologists consider it extinct. However, Atlantans have occasionally reported minor earthquakes, including one in 2003 measuring 4.9 on the Richter scale.

The Chattahoochee traditionally defined the northwestern border of Atlanta, but the city is otherwise in the unusual position of having no natural boundaries—which has been both a blessing and a curse to its development. Unfettered by mountains or ocean, the metro area has extended rapidly into surrounding counties over the past few decades, leading to legendary traffic congestion and making Atlanta an unfortunate poster child for suburban sprawl.

CLIMATE

Due to its high elevation, Atlanta enjoys four distinct seasons and is known for having a temperate climate. The average low temperature in

Dogwoods bloom in the spring.

© 2009 KEVIN C. ROSE/ATLANTAPHOTOS.COM

January still dips to 33°F (0.5°C). The hottest month of the year is July, with average highs around 89°F (32°C). Summers in the city are notorious for their humidity, and occasional heat waves can cause highs around 98°F (37°C), with heat indexes that reach potentially unhealthy levels.

Classified as having a humid subtropical climate, Atlanta receives an average of 50 inches of rainfall per year. The driest month here is October, which gets an average of 3.11 inches of precipitation. March ranks as the wettest, with 5.38 inches. However, recent years have seen the entire region plagued by an unusually severe drought. The city's total rainfall was 16 inches below normal in 2007, which led to record low levels in nearby lakes Lanier and Allatoona and serious fears of a shortage of drinking water. The U.S. Army Corps of Engineers, controllers of the reservoirs, and city leaders were able to work together to avoid

catastrophe; the city also put in place strict bans on outdoor watering. Though some of the restrictions have since been relaxed, residents remain vigilant and antsy about potential future shortages.

Atlanta sees occasional ice storms during the winter months, but only two inches of snow fall here annually. Most years experience frost on 36 days. Sporadic thunderstorms are known to pass through during the warmer months. Georgia's tornado season runs March–May, with an average of six twisters per year statewide. In March 2008, a tornado swept through Atlanta's Downtown business district, damaging landmarks like CNN Center, the Georgia Dome, and the Westin Peachtree Plaza Hotel. Two fatalities were reported and officials estimated that the tornado cost the city $150 million. Luckily, such extreme weather events are rare inside the city.

History

In the family of major East Coast cities, Atlanta might qualify as the overachieving baby sister. By the time the town was incorporated in 1847, New York City had already been around for 223 years. Charleston, South Carolina, was turning 167, and even nearby Milledgeville, Georgia's then state capital, was a respectable 44-year-old. Considering the gap in years, the city's unparalleled growth and arrival as a regional power becomes all the more striking.

The lands of Georgia were once Creek and Cherokee Indian territories. Spanish conquistador Juan Ponce de Leon is sometimes cited as the first European to visit these parts, though his travels in 1513 took him farther south to coastal Florida. Contrary to local folklore,

the explorer never set foot anywhere near the future site of Atlanta—even though his name would later grace one of the city's major thoroughfares.

Georgia, the last of the original Thirteen Colonies, was established in 1733 when British Gen. James Oglethorpe founded the port of Savannah. The coastal area was heavily disputed following the Revolutionary War of 1776, with British and Loyalist forces bearing down on Savannah and Augusta. The English recruited Georgia's Creek Indians to help them during the War of 1812, leading to the Creek War of 1813–1814. In the aftermath of those battles, the young United States rushed to build a series of defensive forts in the wilderness

PEACHTREE: WHAT'S IN A NAME?

The late Celestine Sibley, a much-adored columnist for the *Atlanta Journal-Constitution* for 58 years, once wrote, "Only a lunatic would voluntarily and for any length of time leave Peachtree Street." But to hear some other Atlantans tell it, only a lunatic would give every street in town the same name.

A running joke here bemoans the sheer number of addresses in the city featuring some variation of "Peachtree," making the place darn near impossible to navigate for newcomers. It's true that "Peachtree" shows up on at least 71 street signs, including Peachtree Battle Avenue, Peachtree Place, Peachtree Circle, Peachtree Hills Avenue, and Peachtree Dunwoody Road. However, confusion isn't as prevalent as the naysayers claim.

The only Peachtree Street visitors really need to know is the main one, Atlanta's central artery that begins Downtown at Spring Street and runs north through Midtown and Buckhead. (West Peachtree Street runs parallel to Peachtree Street until the two merge at Pershing Point.) In south Buckhead, Peachtree Street's name changes to Peachtree Road, and it becomes Peachtree Industrial Boulevard in Brookhaven. Simple, right? Most of the other "Peachtrees" around town are residential side streets, not easily mistaken for the grand and iconic boulevard.

So why did this town go nuts over a fruit tree almost never seen inside city limits? The phrase comes from Standing Peachtree, a major Creek village founded here before the Revolutionary War. Oddly enough, the "peach" is thought by some historians to be a bastardization of the word "pitch," referring to the sap that flowed from a large pine tree in the area. Had history taken a slight linguistic detour, folks might be complaining today that every street in Atlanta is called "Pitch Tree" – which just doesn't have the same sweetness.

along the Chattahoochee River. One such fort rose close to a key Native-American settlement known as Standing Peachtree, near the present-day Peachtree Creek in Buckhead. Fort Peachtree, built in 1814, became an important site for the area's incoming English, Scotch, and Irish settlers. The hilly terrain's primary Indian paths later became some of Atlanta's main roads (including present-day Peachtree Street), though the Native Americans themselves were systematically removed from the land along 1838's infamous Trail of Tears.

FROM TERMINUS TO MARTHASVILLE

By the 1830s, Georgia was prospering. As the largest state east of the Mississippi River, Georgia had become a viable center of the cotton industry, where massive plantations were worked by African-American slaves. North Georgia had undergone its own boom in 1829 when America's first Gold Rush erupted in the tiny town of Dahlonega. A charge of newcomers to the region soon followed. State powerbrokers decided Georgia needed a new railroad terminus to connect fertile farmland with Tennessee, South Carolina, and the coastal ports to the south. The state sent seasoned army surveyor Stephen Long to the upcountry frontier to choose a practical site for the railroad's development. In 1837, after considering several options, he selected an untamed tract of land where several Indian trails merged. Local folklore says that Long drove a stake into the red clay close to what's now Five Points Downtown and declared the area suitable for "a tavern, a blacksmith's shop, a general store, and nothing else."

A small settlement of railroad workers arrived, and the place was given the unimaginative name of "Terminus." It quickly grew much larger than Long had predicted. By 1842, the village was booming and had attracted scores of new residents, including the wives of the railroad men. As the first train depot rose, Georgia Governor Wilson Lumpkin asked that the community be renamed "Marthasville," after his small daughter. The first railroad engine rolled into town not long after, and by 1846 the railroad connected Marthasville with Augusta, Macon, and Savannah.

For Richard Peters, superintendent of the Western & Atlantic Railroad, the name "Marthasville" just didn't sound like an important transportation hub. He asked his colleague J. Edgar Thompson for ideas, and the engineer supposedly began thinking aloud, "Western & Atlantic, Atlantic masculine, Atlanta feminine. Eureka! Atlanta!" The state legislature quickly approved of the change, and in 1847 the incorporated community of Atlanta was born.

THE CIVIL WAR

Atlanta blossomed over the next 15 years and became known as a rough and randy frontier town, with a bank, a daily newspaper, wooden sidewalks, and a problem with stray livestock blocking traffic. It also earned a reputation for lawlessness. Gamblers, drinkers, and cockfighters ruled over Snake Nation (present-day Castleberry Hill) and Slabtown (near current Decatur Street), flouting the rule of law. In 1851, a group of Snake Nation "Rowdies" stole a cannon from neighboring Decatur and fired a load of gravel and mud at the general store owned by incoming Atlanta mayor Jonathon Norcross—a daring act of defiance. Atlanta citizens were outraged and took it upon themselves to arrest the perpetrators and burn Snake Nation to the ground.

Once the American Civil War erupted in 1861, Atlanta was in a prime strategic position. Four vital railroads converged here, and the place became a center for the factories, machine shops, and foundries that would empower the Confederate Army. In three short years the city's population swelled to 23,000, and its status as a munitions and supply hub made it a target for the Union Army. In May 1864, Union Gen. William Tecumseh Sherman began a major offensive at Chattanooga, Tennessee, with a team of 100,000 soldiers. By June his forces had reached Kennesaw Mountain near Marietta. A major battle ensued and Sherman lost an estimated 3,000 men—compared to Confederate losses of only 800. Still, the Union Army regrouped and trudged southward toward Atlanta. The Confederacy replaced Gen. Joseph E. Johnston with Gen. John B. Hood, a fiery Texan who was told to seize the offensive.

Almost 8,000 soldiers died on July 20, 1864, at the Battle of Peachtree Creek, a crushing defeat for the Confederacy (and present site of an upscale Buckhead neighborhood and Bobby Jones Golf Course). Atlanta was under siege. Residents dug out shelters from the constant shelling. Wounded soldiers were everywhere. The Union forces had targeted railroad tracks outside the city, cutting off General Hood's supply line and leading to a grisly food shortage in town. Finally, on September 1, Confederate soldiers evacuated Atlanta, taking time to blow up seven locomotives and loads of ammunition before they left. General Sherman swept in and ordered his forces to systematically torch any building that might be of future use to the Confederates. Around 5,000 homes burned, along with churches, stores, and factories. Father Thomas O'Reilly, priest at the Church of Immaculate Conception, pleaded with the Catholic soldiers among the Union Army and convinced them to spare five downtown churches and a handful of buildings. On November 16, General Sherman and his men rode out of town via Decatur Street, reportedly singing "The Battle Hymn of the Republic" as they went. Atlanta had achieved the dubious distinction of being the only large American city ever destroyed by war.

RISE OF THE NEW SOUTH

Reconstruction reportedly began almost immediately after the dust had settled from Sherman's horses. Though their city was a smoldering wreck, with wild dogs stalking the streets and dead horses filling the ditches, battle-scarred Atlantans returned and started putting the place together again. The Union occupation actually helped hurry the process along, as Atlanta became a regional headquarters for Northern forces—a boon to its economic recovery. In 1868 the title of Georgia's state capital was transferred from Milledgeville to Atlanta, a mere four years after the inferno.

The area flooded with so-called "carpetbaggers," Yankee entrepreneurs who saw great potential for profit in returning the crippled South to its full production potential. The city also experienced an influx of former slaves, who were seeking gainful employment for the first time in their lives. The Reconstruction Act awarded black men the right to vote. By 1870, Atlanta's City Council included two African-American men, a true sea change. Slaves had been prohibited from learning to read or write before the Civil War. The Reconstruction period saw missionaries and transplanted Northerners making a concerted effort to educate the newly free black population.

An outspoken editor of the *Atlanta Constitution* became the voice of the new era. Henry Woodfin Grady had established a name for himself at the daily newspaper in the 1870s. It was Grady who coined the phrase "the New South," envisioning a region that would prosper not just based upon its cotton and tobacco crops, but through a new epoch of industrialization. He argued for reconciliation between the North and the South, and ventured to New York in 1886 on a mission to attract investors to Georgia. There, Grady delivered what came to be known as the "New South" speech, saying, "There was a South of slavery and secession—that South is dead. There is a South of union and freedom—that South, thank God, is living, breathing, growing each hour." Tragically, the editor died in 1889 at age 38 from pneumonia.

Thanks in part to Grady's efforts, Atlanta mounted three major expositions designed to highlight the region's potential as a manufacturing center. The International Cotton Exposition of 1881, held near today's King Plow Arts Center, featured a model factory for refining cotton into cloth. The Piedmont Exposition, which took place in 1887 on the future site of Piedmont Park, was an expansive world's fair featuring artwork, lectures, and displays of textiles. It drew more than 200,000 visitors, including president Grover Cleveland. But the most lavish of the three events was 1895's Cotton States and International Exposition, a larger-than-life affair that wowed its 800,000 visitors with innovations in agriculture and technology. William "Buffalo Bill" Cody brought in his Wild West Show, and John Philip Sousa performed his new "King Cotton March" for the expo. Booker T.

Washington, a former slave, delivered the legendary "Atlanta Compromise" speech, which inherently supported the "separate but equal" doctrine that became the South's legal custom of the next 60 years. The event also led to the creation of Piedmont Park.

INDUSTRY AND THE JIM CROW ERA

By the turn of the 20th century, Atlanta had become a hotbed for business—and not just cotton and textiles. A local druggist, John Pemberton, had invented a popular headache elixir in 1886, and soon sold the recipe to Asa Candler for $2,000. Candler decided the syrupy liquid might sell better if it wasn't marketed as medicine, and Coca-Cola was born. By 1919, Candler had become Atlanta's mayor, and his family sold the beverage business for $25 million to Ernest Woodruff. The Woodruff family would grow the company into an international powerhouse.

But Coke was not the city's only success story. Downtown's M. Rich Dry Goods had grown from a small shop into one of Atlanta's largest department stores, rivaled only by nearby Davison's. The Rich's chain later expanded across the country. Both Davison's and Rich's were eventually bought by Macy's Inc. Business magnate Amos Rhodes built up a furniture empire here in the late 1800s, which paid for one of the grandest mansions on Peachtree Street, Rhodes Hall. The 1920s saw the opening of the city's first airfield, later site of Hartsfield-Jackson Atlanta International Airport, and the launch of what would later become Delta Airlines, another signature Atlanta brand.

With a population of 90,000 in 1900, Atlanta treated its residents to many modern amenities. Luxurious homes along Peachtree Street had indoor plumbing and electric lights; some even had telephones. Trolley cars carried workers from the "suburbs" (now intown neighborhoods like Grant Park) to new highrises Downtown. Life was good—at least for the white residents. African Americans found themselves living in less ideal circumstances, with all of society segregated by race. After the Civil War, so-called Jim Crow Laws had stripped black Southerners of many of their rights, and African-American involvement in political life vanished.

Though Atlanta had a reputation for tolerance, an ugly race riot broke out in 1906. A play called *The Clansman,* which endorsed the Ku Klux Klan, had fanned the flames of racial tension the year before. Hostile headlines denigrating African Americans began appearing in the local papers, followed by a race-baiting campaign for governor. The ensuing September riot, started by Caucasians, lasted four days and left an estimated 40 black Atlantans dead.

At the same time, Atlanta was becoming a destination for blacks seeking higher learning. The city's most prominent historically black colleges—including Morehouse, Spelman, and Morris Brown—had all been established in the 1800s and helped create a new generation of educated African Americans. Atlanta University professor W. E. B. Du Bois established the National Association for the Advancement of Colored People here in 1909.

THE CITY TOO BUSY TO HATE

In 1936, Atlanta found itself once again in the national spotlight, only this time for a work of literature. Margaret Mitchell—Peggy to her friends—was a former *Atlanta Journal* reporter who was reluctant to share her rambling novel manuscript with an editor friend, but *Gone With the Wind* went on to sell more than 30 million copies. It won the Pulitzer Prize in 1937 and was made into an Academy Award–winning film. Atlanta hosted the movie premiere in 1939, though black actors from the film couldn't attend because the extravagant Loew's Grand Theatre was segregated. Though critics in later years have decried the novel as racist or an apology for slavery, Mitchell used part of the fortune she amassed from the book to create substantial scholarships for medical students at Morehouse College. Mitchell was killed in 1949 after being struck by a taxi while crossing Peachtree Street.

As the civil rights movement gained steam across the South in the 1950s, Atlanta business leaders worked to maintain the city's reputation for tolerance. Unsightly racial incidents in Alabama and Mississippi in 1955 created fears that Atlanta would be next. But black and white community leaders worked behind the scenes to cool the rhetoric and quietly move the city forward. The city's public transit, police force, and public golf courses were all desegregated without major incident. Mayor William Hartsfield famously proclaimed that Atlanta was "the city too busy to hate."

Even still, black families who challenged residential segregation by moving into white neighborhoods were met with physical confrontations and cross burnings. In 1958, a bomb exploded at Atlanta's most prominent synagogue, known locally as "the Temple." The act of terrorism was said to be a response to the U.S. Supreme Court decision Brown v. Board of Education and to Jewish support of the civil rights movement.

A year earlier, Martin Luther King Jr. had returned home to Atlanta and founded the Southern Christian Leadership Conference.

For the next decade, King would be a pervasive national force for civil rights. Atlanta's public school system was successfully desegregated in the early 1960s. Though King died by an assassin's bullet in 1968, his message of social change transformed the nation.

The next two decades saw fundamental demographic shifts. The trend of "white flight" from inner cities led to the dramatic development of Atlanta's northern suburbs. The city elected its first black mayor, Maynard Jackson, in 1974, and the office has been held by an African American ever since.

ATLANTA TODAY

Atlanta continued to grow and prosper during the Carter and Reagan years, when several of the city's signature skyscrapers rose Downtown and in Midtown, including One Atlantic Center, Georgia Pacific Tower, and the Marriott Marquis Hotel. The city's modern preservation movement began in earnest in the early 1970s with an effort to save the Fox Theatre from the wrecking ball, though it was too late to prevent the demolition of many classic buildings. The city was on a mission to boost its credentials on the world stage.

In the late 1980s, a local lawyer named Billy Payne got the idea that Atlanta should bid on the 1996 Olympic Games—a notion that was dismissed as a long shot at first, even with the backing of mayor Andrew Young. But in 1990, Payne's detractors were roundly silenced when the IOC selected Atlanta to host the games, beating out the more likely candidate, Athens, Greece.

A massive building frenzy gripped the metro region in the next six years. The most striking changes happened Downtown with the construction of Centennial Olympic Stadium (now Turner Field) and Centennial Olympic

Park. By the time the summer games arrived, several parts of town had been transformed completely, and events were held in venues as far away as Athens, Georgia. A bomb exploded in the Olympic Village on July 27, 1996, but the city refused to let the incident overshadow the celebratory nature of the games.

The years since the 1996 Olympics have been dizzying. In the late 1990s Atlanta was starting to seem like a victim of its own success: Intown neighborhoods strained with the growing pains of gentrification, while long commutes made many locals wonder where the city had gone wrong. The new millennium has seen the metropolitan area balloon to more than five million people.

In 2002 Atlanta elected its first African-American female mayor, Shirley Franklin, who made repairing the city's infrastructure a top priority—just in time for the tidal wave of new residents moving back inside the Perimeter. Atlanta's notoriously long commutes and clogged highways have caused a greater demand for housing near the city center, with an amazing new building boom of condo towers and loft conversions. Many formerly depressed neighborhoods have become real-estate hot spots, and once-shuttered business districts now buzz with new life. The city boasts $5 billion in new development since 2005 alone, including Atlantic Station, the Georgia Aquarium, and the expanded Woodruff Arts Center. Though serious challenges will face the capital of the New South in the coming years, Atlanta, long known as the Phoenix City, is rising from its ashes yet again.

Government and Economy

GOVERNMENT

Atlanta, as Georgia's capital, is the nerve center of state government. The Georgia State Capitol building, known for its shimmering gold dome, serves as the offices of the governor, lieutenant governor, secretary of state, and the general assembly. Nearby City Hall hosts Atlanta's city government, which is divided into legislative and executive branches. A 15-person City Council serves as the legislative branch, with one representative from each of the city's 12 districts and three at-large positions. City departments, under the direction of the mayor, constitute the executive branch.

The 2002 election of Shirley Franklin has been greeted by many as the dawn of a new era in local politics. For years, City Hall had been accused of being a den of corruption and backroom deals—allegations that gained traction once former mayor Bill Campbell was indicted by a federal grand jury on bribery, racketeering, and wire fraud charges in 2004. Two years later, Campbell was convicted of tax evasion and sent to prison.

Franklin, who had previously held jobs under mayors Maynard Jackson and Andrew Young, inherited a city government with a gaping $82 million budget deficit, forcing her to increase taxes and cut city staff immediately. After a campaign promise to repair potholes in city roads, Franklin has made fixing Atlanta's infrastructure one of her top priorities, including a $3.2 billion overhaul of the aging sewer system. She easily won reelection in 2005, and was named one of America's five best big-city mayors by *Time* magazine.

© TRAY BUTLER

Lady Justice atop the Georgia State Capitol

In presidential elections, the state of Georgia has gone reliably Republican since the late 1960s, except when a Southern Democrat was on the ticket. Georgians rallied behind hometown candidate Jimmy Carter in 1976 and 1980, and gave the state's electoral votes to Bill Clinton in 1992—but not in 1996. No Democratic presidential candidate has prevailed since. Regardless, Atlanta is the deep blue heart in a ruby-red state, with a line of Democratic mayors stretching back more than 60 years. In the 2008 presidential election, Fulton County voted two-to-one for Democrat Barack Obama, and the split in DeKalb County was closer to four-to-one.

ECONOMY

Since its founding as a railroad town, Atlanta has had a love affair with industry and transportation. Georgia was once known mainly as an agrarian state, producing cotton, corn, tobacco, soybeans, eggs, and peaches, and Atlanta traditionally served as the distribution and economic center for the state's crops.

The last 50 years have seen the city rise as a home for international corporations. Atlanta ranked fifth in the 2008 list of cities with Fortune 500 companies. Three Fortune 100 companies are headquartered here: Home Depot, United Parcel Service, and Coca-Cola. Other major employers in the city include Delta Airlines, The Southern Company, Georgia-Pacific, and SunTrust Banks. All told, more than 75 percent of the Fortune 1000 companies maintain offices in metro Atlanta.

Thanks to the efforts of Ted Turner, Atlanta has grown into a leading communications hub and cable television powerhouse. Turner Broadcasting Systems started here in the early 1970s with the launch of the "Superstation," TBS. In 1980, the company premiered the Cable News Network, aka CNN, which has become one of the world's most-watched news sources, reaching an estimated 1.5 billion people. Other members of the TBS family include Cartoon Network, Turner Classic Movies, Boomerang, and Peachtree TV. Outside the Turner empire, the Weather Channel—now owned by NBC—is located here, as well as Cox Communications, the third-largest cable provider in the nation and publisher of a dozen daily newspapers.

The city ranked in the nation's top five for net new job growth over the past decade, adding almost 460,000 new jobs. The metro Atlanta area is forecasted to be America's third-largest job generator over the next decade. According to estimates by the Atlanta Regional Commission, the metro area will add 2 million jobs—and 2.2 million people—in the next quarter century.

EDUCATION

Atlanta's rich concentration of colleges and universities is one of the city's greatest assets. At least 30 institutes of higher learning are located here. The most prestigious of the area's private schools is Emory University, with a total enrollment of 12,000 students. Established in 1836, Emory was named as part of the "new ivy league" in the 2007 *Newsweek How to Get Into College Guide.* Its 630-acre campus sits northeast of Downtown next to the U.S. Centers for Disease Control and Prevention.

Among public schools, the Georgia Institute of Technology is acknowledged as one of the best in the region. In 2008 *U.S. News & World Report* ranked Georgia Tech seventh nationally among public universities for undergraduates. For the past decade, the school has been among the top ten public universities, and its engineering school is the largest in the nation. The 400-acre campus marks the divide between Downtown and Midtown west of the Downtown Connector.

Farther south, the historically black colleges of the Atlanta University Center have traditions dating back to the post–Civil War era, when the state saw its first flowering of African-American education. Located in the historic West End neighborhood near Downtown, the group includes Clark Atlanta University, Spelman College, Morehouse College, and the Morehouse School of Medicine. Combined, the schools enroll more than 13,000 students each year. Nearby, Georgia State University has the unique distinction of being a college campus integrated into the very fiber of Downtown's business district. Known as a commuter school, Georgia State enrolls 24,000 students and is recognized as the state's only urban research university.

Other respected institutions in the area include Agnes Scott College, a women's school near Decatur; Oglethorpe University, a liberal arts school north of Buckhead; and Clayton State University, a public school located 15 minutes south of Downtown. All told, Atlanta-area colleges and universities serve an estimated 196,000 students annually.

People and Culture

DEMOGRAPHICS

With a total population of over 5.2 million people, greater Atlanta was named the nation's ninth-largest metropolitan area by the U.S. Census Bureau in 2007. Of that number, almost 430,000 live inside Atlanta city limits. The population increased by almost 25 percent between 2000 and 2007, making it one of the fastest-growing regions of the country. Atlanta's metropolitan total is projected to top 5.5 million in 2009.

The city's exceptional growth spurt has also led to a more diverse populace. Atlanta's racial diversity is greater than America's as a whole. The city is 61.4 percent African American, 33.2 percent white, 4.5 percent Hispanic and 1.9 percent Asian. Though blacks make up almost two-thirds of Atlanta's demographic, the number flips when compared to the state of Georgia, where African Americans are only 28.7 percent and whites are 65.1 percent.

The ratio of women to men here is virtually equal. The average age in Atlanta is 33.8—younger than the nation's average of 36.

ATLANTA SPEAK

Southern accents just ain't what they used to be. As with other parts of the country, the regional dialect of the South has largely given way to a more universal American cadence, the result of a pervasive media engine that causes folks to sound the same no matter what state they grew up in. This is especially true in Atlanta, which has long felt like a separate entity from the rest of Georgia, overrun with residents from all over the world. Still, visitors here can benefit by learning the local vernacular. A few examples of uniquely Atlanta words and phrases follow:

- **The ATL** – pronounced "A-T-L," a popular nickname for the city. Atlantans will also sometimes refer to "A Town," but locals here will rarely use the term "Hotlanta," which is seen as déclassé and dated.

- **Buckhead Betty** – sarcastic nickname for the well-to-do housewives who live in the wealthy neighborhood of Buckhead, or for anything that's gaudy and over-the-top.

- **Coke** – not just the brand name of the local soft-drink giant, it's also used as a catch-all term. Any carbonated beverage may be referred to as Coke, and occasionally as soda, but never, ever, as pop.

- **The Connector** – the joint section of I-75 and I-85 that runs through Downtown.

- **Dawg** – shorthand for a Georgia Bulldog, aka, a student from the University of Georgia.

- **goobers** – peanuts.

- **grits** – a traditional breakfast food of coarsely ground corn. You're most likely to spot grits on a gourmet New South dinner menu than at brunch.

- **intown** – a catch-all term used to describe locations that are inside the Perimeter and typically south of Buckhead.

- **ITP** – "inside the Perimeter," or within the confines of I-285. It's used as shorthand for anything intown or urban.

- **OTP** – "outside the Perimeter," or beyond I-285. It's often used as a derisive term, meaning "suburban" or, even worse, "alarmingly rural."

- **Ponce de Leon Avenue** – pronounced "PAHNTS duh LEE-on," with no trace of a Spanish accent. It's a handy north-south dividing line, and also known for its seedy street life.

- **Ramblin' Wreck** – the traditional mascot for Georgia Tech (which actually predates the more commonly used Buzz the Yellowjacket), or else a Tech student.

- **Shoot the 'Hooch** – to raft down the Chattahoochee River.

- **Spaghetti Junction** – the busy intersection of I-85 and I-285.

- **Y'all** – the second person plural pronoun, typically used to denote a warm greeting, as in, "Y'all come back now." Never pronounced as "you all."

Residents over the age of 65 comprise 9.7 percent. People born in foreign countries represent 6.6 percent of the population, but the number of families here who speak a language other than English at home is 10.8 percent. Georgia has experienced colossal growth in Hispanic residents in recent years; in 2008, the number of Hispanic people in Fulton County alone was over 967,000. Georgia is listed fourth among the nation's fastest-growing Hispanic markets.

Of the influx of folks who moved to metro Atlanta between 2000 and 2004, a whopping 35 percent came from other states—mostly New

York and New Jersey. No doubt they were lured by the low cost of living and hopes of better-paying jobs; the metro area's median household income was $51,186 in 2004, higher than the national average. Curiously enough, Atlanta has an enviable concentration of millionaires: more than 60,000 in the metro area. Forecasters expect Atlanta to lead the nation in the creation of new millionaires during the next few years, with a growth rate of about 69 percent.

RELIGION

Atlanta is sometimes described as "the buckle of the Bible Belt," a curious distinction given the city's preponderance of strip joints. Which isn't to say Atlantans aren't religious: The metro region has more than 1,000 places of worship, and has long been a stronghold for the Southern Baptist Convention, which makes up the vast majority of the church-going populace. Methodists and Catholics are the two next largest groups, respectively. Recent years have seen the rise of "mega-churches" in the nearby suburbs; for example, Bishop Eddie Long's New Birth Missionary Baptist Church in Lithonia is hailed as the largest African-American church in the Southeast, with 30,000 members. The nation's biggest Presbyterian congregation, Peachtree Presbyterian, has a Buckhead campus that could eclipse some small towns.

The city's traditional home for black churches has long been Sweet Auburn, with the larger-than-life Ebenezer Baptist Church, Wheat Street Baptist Church, and Big Bethel A.M.E. Due to the flood of Hispanic residents, Atlanta has seen a major swelling of its Catholic population in the past decade, and many Protestant congregations here have also started Spanish-language worship services to attract the newcomers. Though many congregations in Atlanta have grown more diverse over the years, Christian churches have remained rather homogeneous groups. As Cynthia Tucker, former editorial page editor of the *Atlanta Journal-Constitution,* once noted, "Devout Christians of different races rarely attend church together; 11 o'clock on Sunday mornings remains among the most segregated hours in America."

Beyond the Christian diaspora, Atlanta also hosts a wide range of other faiths and traditions. The city ranks 11th in the nation for its Jewish population, an increase of 60 percent in just a decade. The area also has seen an increase in Muslim residents, and now supports 35 active mosques. New Thought, Unitarian Universalist, and Existentialist groups also thrive in the city.

THE ARTS
Visual Arts

As home to the High Museum of Art, Atlanta is considered a leading regional nexus for visual art. With a history dating back to 1905, the High serves as an important center of gravity for the Southeast's cultural life. The museum experienced a major boost in 1979 when Coca-Cola tycoon Robert Woodruff promised a $7.5 million challenge grant for the construction of a new facility. The museum responded by raising $20 million, and the High unveiled its new Richard Meier building in 1983, which has since been called one of the greatest works of American architecture of the 1980s. Two decades later, the gleaming white edifice was figuratively bursting at the seams, as the High's permanent collection, attendance, and prestige had all skyrocketed. The museum responded by tapping Italian architect Renzo Piano to design three new buildings, which opened in 2005 and doubled the High's size.

With cheap rents still available and an active gallery scene, Atlanta is known to be hospitable to up-and-coming artists, with many studios operating out of lofts in still-gentrifying in-town neighborhoods like Castleberry Hill. The underground arts scene has long been encouraged by the Atlanta Contemporary Art Center, a multidisciplinary venue that includes studios for artists, as well as Eyedrum, a gallery and performance space famous for its experimental fare. Countless tiny fly-by-night arts collectives, galleries, and exhibitions are constantly popping up around town. The city's artistic life has benefited from the arrival of the Savannah College of Art and Design, which opened an Atlanta campus in 2005.

Commercial galleries here run the gamut from traditional painting to pop-art ephemera. Atlanta is a great place to experience photography and folk art. One of the best-known folk artists to emerge from the state in the past 20 years is the late Howard Finster, a north Georgia preacher who painted grand religious murals, mixing angels with the likes of Hank Williams and Elvis Presley. Though Finster passed away in 2001, many of his works are on display in the High Museum, and fans can also visit his Paradise Gardens Park and Museum in Summerville. The work of local folk artist Nellie Mae Rowe has also received increasing attention in recent years. Rowe, who lived in Vinings and died in 1983, peppered her creations with African and Afro-Caribbean influences. The High Museum now owns many of her best-known works.

In print since 1980, Atlanta-based *Art Papers* magazine has emerged as a nationally read journal of art criticism. With offices in Little Five Points, the nonprofit organization also curates an array of cultural events throughout the city.

Popular Music

Although Athens gets all the credit as a launch-pad for hot bands, Atlanta has played an important role in nurturing the careers of many phenomenal artists of the past 40 years. In the 1960s, the city was a must-hit spot for up-and-coming Motown and R&B stars, with Georgia natives Ray Charles, Otis Redding, and James Brown playing to packed houses. Soul legend Gladys Night was born here and achieved one of the greatest hits of her career, "Midnight Train to Georgia," singing about coming home to the South.

In the 1970s, Atlanta helped kick-start the Southern Rock phenomenon. Lynyrd Skynyrd was discovered playing at a club here in 1972, and Macon natives the Allman Brothers Band made local fans go wild with their song "Hot 'Lanta." The Atlanta Rhythm Section developed a local following in the late '70s. Singer and Atlanta native Jerry Reed capitalized on his homespun eccentricity and whittled a successful film career. Later, Atlanta rock acts like the Georgia Satellites and the Black Crowes took their Southern sound to even wider audiences.

The 1980s and '90s saw the rise of many hometown country hitmakers. Travis Tritt, a Marietta native, started churning out platinum records in 1989. Around the same time, Alan Jackson moved from Newnan to Nashville and became a honky-tonk sensation. More recently, pop-country duo Sugarland has enjoyed breakthrough status. The group formed in Atlanta in 2003 as part of the indie-folk scene at Decatur acoustic venue Eddie's Attic, which had previously helped launch the career of the Indigo Girls. Pop troubadour John Mayer also emerged from the Eddie's incubator and went on to win a heap of Grammy Awards.

The biggest thing to happen to Atlanta's musical standing in recent years is the blockbuster rise of Southern hip-hop. The "Dirty South" rap scene erupted here in the mid-1990s, thanks partly to the efforts of producer Jermaine Dupri's Atlanta-based So-So Def Recordings. East Point duo Outkast achieved fame in 1994 with their album *ATLiens* and went on to record-breaking crossover success. Ludacris, formerly a DJ for Atlanta's 107.9 FM, became an overnight hip-hop sensation who immortalized the scene with his 2001 anthem "Welcome to Atlanta." Other chart-topping hip-hop acts to emerge from the city include India.Arie, Erykah Badu, Monica, T. I., Lil Jon, Usher, and Danger Mouse—to name just a few.

Literature

To hear some people tell it, Atlanta's literary legacy begins and ends with *Gone With the Wind*, a novel with which the city is virtually synonymous. It's true that Margaret Mitchell's Civil War romance ranks as one of the most popular works of fiction of all time, famously hyped as selling more copies than any book other than the Bible. But Atlanta has produced a steady stream of best-selling authors and literary lions over the years.

Eatonton native Alice Walker attended Spelman College here and later won the 1983 Pulitzer Prize for Fiction for her novel *The Color Purple*. Playwright Alfred Uhry, born in Atlanta, won a Pulitzer and two Tony Awards for his Atlanta trilogy, which started with 1987's *Driving Miss Daisy*.

Pat Conroy, author of *The Prince of Tides*, was born in Atlanta and lived in Ansley Park for many years. Hometown author Anne Rivers Siddons (*Peachtree Road*) saw her first wide commercial success in the 1980s, and is still turning out novels today. Local columnists Celestine Sibley and Lewis Grizzard, both staffers of the *Atlanta Journal-Constitution*, also enjoyed prolific careers as authors.

Jim Grimsley, who teaches creative writing at Emory University, has earned a pile of awards for his plays and novels, including 1995's *Dream Boy*. In 1997, West End resident Pearl Cleage became a media darling when her novel *What Looks Like Crazy on an Ordinary Day* was picked for Oprah Winfrey's book club. Cleage's former student Tayari Jones received critical acclaim for her gritty 2002 debut, *Leaving Atlanta*. Prolific horror novelist Karin Slaughter has enjoyed considerable success in the current decade, recently with a series set in Atlanta.

ESSENTIALS
Getting There

BY AIR

Located 10 miles south of Downtown, **Hartsfield-Jackson Atlanta International Airport** (800/897-1910, www.atlanta-airport.com) is often cited as the busiest airport in the world, serving 78 million passengers per year. More than 30 major airlines and smaller carriers fly to Hartsfield-Jackson, and the Atlanta Convention and Visitors Bureau notes that 80 percent of the U.S. population is within a two-hour flight from the city. The airport offers 2,500 daily flights to more than 250 destinations, many of them non-stop.

The airport is the home base and main hub for **Delta Airlines** (800/221-1212, www.delta.com), which, along with its partner airlines, reaches 105 countries. Delta accounts for more than half of the annual travelers passing through Hartsfield-Jackson. In 2008, Delta announced a pending merger with Northwest Airlines, a move that will expand the carrier's offerings even further. The combined company plans to keep its headquarters in Atlanta. Hartsfield-Jackson is also a major hub for **AirTran Airways** (800/247-8726, www.airtran.com), a discount carrier that operates 270 daily flights from Atlanta.

© 2009 KEVIN C. ROSE/ATLANTAPHOTOS.COM

AIRPORT ART

It's easy to get caught up in the rush of passengers hurrying through Hartsfield-Jackson Atlanta International Airport, which features the most heavily used automated people mover in the world. But art lovers with a few extra minutes to spare should make a point of sidestepping the packed underground trains and exploring the airport's unusual assortment of cultural exhibitions. The best example is the permanent exhibition of **contemporary Zimbabwean sculpture** on display in the pedestrian corridor that connects concourses T and A. This collection of striking human-sized stone figures by 12 African artists runs the gamut from playful to solemn – and shouldn't be missed. Meanwhile, the airport's main atrium offers a revolving display of artwork, with exhibits that change every six weeks. The 16 wall spaces feature photography, paintings, and mixed-media works. Elsewhere, artwork by Georgia elementary and high-school students is on rotating display in concourses T, D, and E.

The airport completed a significant expansion in 2006 with the addition of a fifth runway, greatly boosting its capacity. It has 151 domestic and 28 international gates spread out over five concourses; international flights arrive at Concourse E, the airport's most plush wing, but also the farthest from the main terminal building. Commuting between concourses is usually fast and painless thanks to an underground train system and moving sidewalks.

Navigating the TSA security gates at Hartsfield-Jackson can be a frustrating ordeal. Although airlines ask passengers to arrive an hour in advance of domestic flights (and two hours ahead of international flights), it's usually a good idea to build in an extra half hour here. There are about 227 shops and restaurants in the airport—including bars, high-end gift stores, and a post office—so there's plenty to do while you wait. Also, check with an airport agent to see if you can use the North or South security checkpoints, which tend to be faster than the main TSA station. Security wait times are posted on the airport website. Travelers arriving from international destinations also have to go through the tedious process of retrieving checked luggage, passing through customs, re-checking bags, and going through an additional security checkpoint before continuing to other concourses.

The airport connects to ground transportation and MARTA, Atlanta's subway system, at the main terminal. The train ride to Downtown is around 20 minutes and costs $1.50. The same taxi trip takes around a half hour, depending on traffic, and charges a flat rate of $30 for Downtown, $40 for Buckhead. Several rental car agencies are located inside the airport.

Hartsfield-Jackson is the primary airport for the state. The next nearest major commercial airport is Birmingham International in Alabama, about 150 miles west of Atlanta.

BY CAR

Atlanta is easily accessed by car. A web of interstate freeways links the Atlanta metropolitan area with the nation. The two main arteries into the city are I-75 (which runs from Michigan to Florida) and I-85 (which runs from Virginia to Alabama), which converge in the heart of Atlanta (called the Downtown Connector locally). Near the main business district the Downtown Connector intersects with I-20, which reaches from South Carolina to Texas. Another important highway for the city is Rte. 400, a toll road that branches off I-85 in Buckhead and penetrates 50 miles into the northern suburbs. The metropolitan area is encircled by I-285, a 69-mile beltway that intersects with all the major interstates.

BY BUS

Greyhound (232 Forsyth St., 404/584-1728, www.greyhound.com) offers bus services across America. The company also features an **airport bus stop** (6000 N. Terminal Dr., 404/765-9598). It's an inexpensive but time-consuming option for budget travelers.

BY TRAIN

Atlanta's **Amtrak station** (1688 Peachtree St., 800/872-7245, www.amtrak.com) sits at the intersection of Midtown and Buckhead just north of I-85. It's part of the commuter train's Crescent line, which runs from New York to New Orleans. Although rail travel tends to be more expensive than flying, some vacationers prefer the leisurely pace of the experience.

Getting Around

PUBLIC TRANSPORTATION

The **Metropolitan Atlanta Rapid Transit Authority** (MARTA, 404/848-5000, www.itsmarta.com) provides rail and bus service to the city. Visitors from cities with extensive public transportation networks are often baffled by the relatively limited reach of MARTA's subway. The system forms a giant X over the city, with two lines running east to west and two more running north to south. The lines all intersect at the Five Points Station Downtown. While it's true that the subway doesn't access all parts of the city, the bus system covers a much greater area. A single one-way fare is $1.75 for either the train or the bus, and visitors who plan to use the system often should consider buying either the seven-day pass ($13) or the multiday pass ($8–12).

MARTA is a great option for anyone arriving at Hartsfield-Jackson and heading straight to a hotel in Downtown, Midtown, or Buckhead. Sadly, it's not an ideal way to explore the city once you're here, unless all your planned destinations lie in one part of town. The trains are mostly clean and safe, but the routes are imperfect. Bus rides tend to be long and unpredictable.

In Buckhead, the **Buc** (404/812-7433, www.bucride.com) is a free shuttle that connects with MARTA rail stations and some of the area's main destinations, including Lenox Square Mall. The buses run every 8–12 minutes during the morning and evening commute hours. Check the website for routes and a detailed schedule.

DRIVING

Because of the abbreviated scope of MARTA, most everyone drives in Atlanta. Though some parts of town are becoming more pedestrian friendly, this is still a car city. The local love affair with automobiles has had unfortunate side effects on the region: Atlanta's commuters sit in traffic for 60 hours a year, and almost 13 percent of those drivers require more than an hour to get to work.

The good news for visitors is that driving around town can be relatively easy, as long as you avoid the interstates and keep out of rush hour. Navigating the city will require a good street map or GPS system, but Atlanta drivers tend to be more polite than those in New York or Los Angeles. Locals are almost

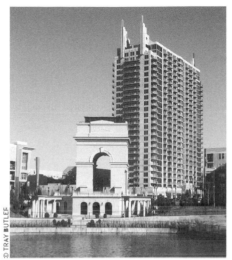
© TRAY BUTLER

Atlantic Station

always friendly and helpful when asked for directions.

On the other hand, parking is a perennial issue here, especially in dense intown neighborhoods. Spots on the street are highly coveted and usually involve paying a meter. Rates and time restrictions vary in different parts of the city, but one factor is constant: The potential for getting a parking ticket is high almost everywhere (the city writes about 13,000 parking tickets a month). In the worst-case scenario, cars that are parked improperly can be towed or booted. When in doubt about a parking space in Atlanta, always err on the side of caution. Fines are steep and the hassle is even worse.

TAXIS

Taxis in Atlanta charge a flat rate of $8 for trips within Downtown, Buckhead, or Midtown, with a $2 fee per extra passenger. Outside of those business districts, metered rates kick in, which are $2.50 for the first eighth of a mile and $0.25 for each additional eighth mile. Fares from the airport range $30–40, more for points outside of I-285.

Finding a taxi is the tricky part. Travelers accustomed to the sea of cabs seen in cities like New York or Chicago will be dismayed at the apparent lack of taxis on the streets. Your best bet is to keep a couple of cab company phone numbers handy and call about 15 minutes before you need a ride. Two services in town are **Atlanta Checker Cab** (404/351-1111, www.atlantacheckercab.com) and **Atlanta Yellow Cab of Georgia** (404/521-0200). A 10 percent tip is customary; more for passengers with heavy bags.

BIKING

Harried Atlanta commuters have been slow to warm up to bicycling. Folks here still tend to see bikes as great for recreation but not for transportation. Sadly, cyclists who attempt to traverse some of the city's busiest streets can expect to be honked or yelled at by passing cars.

The good news is that the city has launched a real effort to create more bike lanes, especially in rapidly growing neighborhoods in Midtown and Downtown. The popularity of bicycling saw a real upsurge once gas prices started climbing, and people who live close to work are starting to see bikes as a better answer. **The Atlanta Bicycle Campaign** (404/881-1112, www.atlantabike2.org) is a grassroots group advocating safer and easier cycling options in the city.

Tips for Travelers

CONDUCT AND CUSTOMS

Although it sounds like a cliché, Southerners deserve their reputation for being more friendly than folks from other parts of the country. Don't be surprised if an agent at the rental car counter strikes up a leisurely conversation with you, asking detailed questions about where you're going and why you're here. This can be off-putting to hurried Northerners or guarded Midwesterners, but it's nothing to take umbrage over. Southerners also pay careful attention to rules of courtesy and look down upon impatient customers who cut in line or yell at waitresses. True, Atlanta is an international city with residents from all over the world, diluting some of its regional propensity for politeness, but city dwellers will almost always stop and offer help to travelers asking questions or needing directions.

SMOKING

Although the rate of tobacco usage is decreasing in Georgia, with smokers making up only 19 percent of adults, the state has been slow to adopt some of the clean-air laws passed in other major cities. Only in 2005 did the state legislature enact a ban on smoking in most enclosed public places that allow minors. Hotels are exempt from the ban, and the law still allows smoking in bars and restaurants that don't serve customers under 18. The City of Decatur went even further by banning smoking in all indoor public places.

Because of the minors clause in the state's ban, almost all Atlanta bars remain tolerant of smoking. Restaurants have phased out their smoking sections, and venues like Hartsfield-Jackson International Airport, Philips Arena, and Turner Field only allow smoking in designated areas.

TRAVELING WITH CHILDREN

Atlanta has long been a popular destination for parents traveling with children. The city has no lack of attractions aimed at the younger crew, from Fernbank Museum of Natural History to the Georgia Aquarium. There's also a vibrant theater scene with performances tailor-made for kids, thanks to organizations like **Young Audiences** (404/733-5293 www.yawac.org) and the Center for Puppetry Arts.

Many hotels are kid friendly, with the exception of a few of the swankier properties, and the same is true of restaurants. When in doubt, call ahead to see if children are allowed. In the past, neighborhoods north of the city were known for being home to more families with small kids, making the businesses there more tolerant of tykes. The past few years have seen a baby boom in more in-town neighborhoods, with strollers suddenly seen on the sidewalks of Midtown and even Little Five Points.

TRAVELERS WITH DISABILITIES

Atlanta has made great efforts in recent years to create a city hospitable to disabled residents and visitors, with new buildings and public spaces that are wheelchair friendly and barrier free. Hartsfield-Jackson is known as one of the most accessible airports in the country. A 2006 survey by the Open Doors Organization ranked Atlanta as one of the 10 most popular cities for travelers with disabilities.

GAY ATLANTA

Atlanta has long been recognized as the gay capital of the Southeast, a tolerant oasis that draws queer residents and tourists from all over the region. The city's enormous annual **Pride celebration** (www.atlantapride.org) began in 1971 and today brings in hundreds of thousands of revelers to the city, with a deluge of events happening around Piedmont Park or the Atlanta Civic Center. The city also hosts one of the world's largest **Black Gay Pride festivals** (www.inthelifeatl.com) each year over Labor Day weekend. **Out on Film** (www.outonfilm.org), Atlanta's gay film festival, takes place each spring.

For decades, the city's most visible gay neighborhood was Midtown – especially around the intersection of Piedmont Avenue and 10th Street – with its concentration of bars and gay-friendly shops and restaurants. The area is home to **Outwrite Bookstore and Coffeehouse** (www.outwritebooks.com), an always-packed gathering spot, and **Blake's on the Park** (www.blakesonthepark.com), a long-standing watering hole. Recent years have found Midtown becoming more mixed and gay Atlantans less confined to any one part of town, with queer bars and businesses popping up from East Atlanta to Marietta. Still, this is the South, so same-sex PDA might draw unwanted attention in any area of the city.

Lesbians in Atlanta have an enviable resource in **Charis Books** (www.charisbooksandmore.com), a Little Five Points landmark that's served the feminist community for three decades. Charis Circle, its programming arm, hosts a vibrant assortment of events and workshops. The city has had less luck keeping a girls-only nightlife scene afloat over the years, though **My Sister's Room** (www.mysistersroom.com) deserves major props for outlasting the odds. The venerable nightspot recently relocated to East Atlanta. **Bellissima Lounge** (www.myspace.com/bellissima_lounge), which opened in 2008, has proven to be a popular newcomer to lesbian nightlife.

For gay men, the bar and club scene in Atlanta may not be as lively as it was a few years back, but there's still lots to do on any given night of the week. **Mary's** (www.marysatlanta.com) in East Atlanta has been cited as one of the best gay bars in the country, drawing an eclectic, alternative audience. **Burkhart's Pub** (www.burkharts.com) is often full of the blue-jeans-and-ball-cap crowd, and it shares a parking lot with two smaller gay bars, **Felix's on the Square** and **The Oscar's. Bulldogs Bar** (893 Peachtree St.) is a long-time favorite for African-American men. The leather scene congregates at the **Atlanta Eagle** (www.atlantaeagle.com) or the **Heretic** (www.hereticatlanta.com), though the latter has become a more mixed dance club recently with more circuit boys and younger guys flooding in.

Gay travelers headed here should check out the **Atlanta Gay and Lesbian Travel Guide** (www.gay-atlanta.com), a portal operated by the Atlanta Convention and Visitors Bureau that features a wealth of listings for lodging, events, and community organizations. The city's two main gay publications, **Southern Voice** (www.sovo.com) and **David Atlanta** (www.davidatlanta.com), are also handy resources.

All of MARTA's 120 bus routes are now equipped with wheelchair lifts or kneeling capabilities. Senior citizens and passengers with disabilities enjoy priority seating at the front of every bus and at one end of each rail car. All rail stations are fitted with wide fare gates for wheelchairs, and elevators on the train platforms.

Health and Safety

HOSPITALS AND PHARMACIES

As home to the national Centers for Disease Control and Prevention (CDC), Atlanta serves as a leading hub for medical research. Near the CDC, Emory University Hospital was named one of the best hospitals in the country by *U.S. News & World Report* in 2008. Emory Healthcare also operates several clinics and medical facilities around the city.

Children's Healthcare of Atlanta is regarded as one of the leading pediatric hospitals in the country; it's the product of a 1998 merger between Egleston Children's Health Care and Scottish Rite Medical Center and operates three hospitals and 15 clinics in the metro area.

For medical emergencies and short-term care, the city has many viable options. A few of the best in Atlanta include Piedmont Hospital, St Joseph's Hospital of Atlanta, Emory Crawford Long Hospital, Northside Hospital, and Atlanta Medical Center. Although hospitals are located all over Atlanta, there's a particular concentration of medical options near the Emory campus and in Sandy Springs north of the city.

Chain pharmacies show up in strip malls and shopping centers throughout the metro area, with the most prevalent being CVS and Rite Aid. The Midtown **Walgreens** (595 Piedmont Ave., 404/685-9665) is one of the few pharmacies intown that's open 24 hours.

CRIME

Atlanta has an unfortunate reputation as an unsafe city, a description that seems to line up with statistics. In 2007, violent crime in Atlanta increased overall, with the city experiencing its highest number of murders in four years, according to FBI data. Anecdotal evidence also suggests a recent rise in robberies and muggings in the city, with a rash of such incidents happening in Midtown and areas around East Atlanta. Overall, cases of aggravated assault have declined in the city. The number of rapes reported in the city has also dipped dramatically.

The good news for visitors is that the vast majority of the city's violent crime is drug related and isolated to metro Atlanta's most desolate neighborhoods—areas that tourists never come anywhere near. As with any major American city, you should take the usual precautions: Stay aware of your surroundings, leave the flashy jewelry at home, avoid dark areas at night, and travel with groups after dark whenever possible.

For years, one of the most annoying aspects of life in the city has been vehicular crime, with cars broken into even in well-lit, heavily trafficked areas. Always lock your doors and never leave any valuables visible in a car, even items that may not seem like they would have much value.

Information and Services

COMMUNICATIONS AND MEDIA
Phones and Area Codes

The metropolitan Atlanta area has three main area codes: 404, 770, and 678. Making a local call always requires 10-digit dialing. Finding a public pay telephone in the city is a real challenge due to the rise of cell phones. Dial "1" before calling toll-free numbers (which start with 800 or 888) or long distance area codes. Many gas stations and convenience stores sell prepaid phone cards. For directory assistance, dial 411.

Internet Services

Finding a Wi-Fi hotspot here is usually no great challenge, if you're prepared to do a little digging. Although Atlanta never launched a municipal Wi-Fi service like some other major cities, most local coffee shops and many restaurants offer Internet connectivity—and in some cases it's even free. **Octane** (1009-B Marietta St., 404/815-9886, www.octanecoffee.com) is a popular gathering spot for laptop-wielding college students and creative professionals. The Wi-Fi is complimentary for customers, so getting a good seat can be a challenge. The same is true for locally owned **Aurora Coffee** (www.auroracoffee.com), which has locations in Virginia-Highland and Little Five Points. Area chains like Starbucks and Caribou offer Wi-Fi, though the free service sometimes comes with a time limit.

Wi-Fi is available throughout Hartsfield-Jackson; it's provided by a handful of carriers with various fees involved. It can also be found

© TRAY BUTLER

Downtown's CNN Center is the national headquarters for the family of news networks.

at almost any major hotel in town, but again, isn't usually a free amenity. For a list of Atlanta businesses that offer free Wi-Fi, visit **WiFi Free Spot** (www.wififreespot.com/ga.html).

Local Publications

Atlanta's largest and most-read daily newspaper, the *Atlanta Journal-Constitution* (www.ajc.com), came about through the merger of two rival publications. The *Atlanta Constitution,* first published in 1868, was traditionally a morning paper with liberal leanings. The afternoon paper, the *Atlanta Journal,* premiered in 1883 and was known for its more conservative bent. The two papers came under the same ownership in 1950 but maintained separate newsrooms until the 1980s. They merged into one publication in 2001, phasing out the afternoon edition. Today the *AJC* has a daily circulation of over 300,000 and reaches 27 counties around metro Atlanta. Like all newspapers in America, the company has struggled to convert declining readership of its print edition into a viable revenue model online. One major push in recent years has involved promoting its popular arts and entertainment site, **AccessAtlanta** (www.accessatlanta.com).

Creative Loafing (www.atlanta.creativeloafing.com) has been Atlanta's default alternative weekly since 1972. Known for its irreverent tone, thorough arts and music listings, and hard-hitting news stories, the "Loaf" has also endured hardship in the new millennium. Months after purchasing the *Chicago Reader* and the *Washington City Paper* in 2007, the paper's parent company filed for bankruptcy protection. Still, the much-loved local publication maintains a loyal readership and a circulation of 130,000. It's also faced the rise of a new competitor in the market, the *Sunday Paper* (www.sundaypaper.com). An alternative to the alternative, the weekly publication tends to take a more mainstream approach in its coverage.

The city has several other daily, weekly, and monthly newspapers of note. The well-respected *Atlanta Business Chronicle* (www.bizjournals.com/atlanta) is a principal resource for Atlanta's corporate community. The *Atlanta Daily World* (www.atlantadailyworld.com) has served African-American readers for more than 90 years. Younger upstart *Rolling Out* (www.rollingout.com) is an opinionated guide to the world of hip-hop, fashion, and urban culture. The free monthly *Atlanta Intown* (www.atlantaintownpaper.com) puts a positive spin on community news, profiling local personalities, businesses, and charities. And *Southern Voice* (www.sovo.com) has been Atlanta's weekly source for gay and lesbian news since 1988.

Radio

Atlanta is the seventh-largest radio market in the country and supports a colorful—and competitive—slate of stations. The FM dial has undergone dramatic changes in the past couple of years, with old favorites abruptly changing formats and morning DJs switching stations. Hip-hop powerhouse **WHTA** (107.9 FM) remains a tastemaker in the market; it's also the station where chart-topping rapper Ludacris got his start as a DJ. The station's main competitor, **WVEE** (103.3 FM), plays a similar mix of hip-hop and R&B. In 2008, Top 40 station **WWWQ** (99.7 FM) replaced the once unstoppable alternative rock giant 99X on the radio dial, boosting its frequency in the process. Around the same time, rival adult contemporary station **WSTR** (94.1 FM) ditched its much-loved morning show and set out to attract a younger market.

Here are some of Atlanta's other noteworthy radio stations:

- talk: WGST-AM (640 AM)
- sports: WCNN-AM (680 AM)
- news: WSB-AM (750 AM)
- college radio: WRAS (88.5 FM)
- indie: WRFG (89.3 FM)
- National Public Radio: WABE (90.1 FM)
- jazz: WCLK (91.9 FM)
- rock: WZGC (92.9 FM)
- alternative rock: WKLS (96.1 FM)
- adult contemporary: WSB-FM (98.5 FM)
- country: WKHX (101.5 FM)
- Spanish: WWVA (105.3 FM)
- oldies: WYAY (106.7 FM)

Television

Affiliates of all the major television networks can be found in Atlanta, which is also home to the Turner Broadcasting family of cable channels.

Atlanta's primary television stations include:

- WSB (channel 2, ABC, www.wsbtv.com)
- WAGA (channel 5, Fox, www.myfoxatlanta .com)
- WGTV (channel 8, Georgia Public Broadcasting, www.gpb.org)
- WXIA (channel 11, NBC, www.11alive .com)
- WPCH (channel 17, Peachtree TV, www .peachtreetv.com)
- WATL (channel 36, My Network TV, www .myatltv.com)
- WGCL (channel 46, CBS, www.cbs46 .com)
- WUPA (channel 69, The CW, www.cw atlantatv.com)

MAPS AND TOURIST INFORMATION

The best place to find brochures, maps, and tips on what to see and do in Atlanta is the **Atlanta Convention and Visitors Bureau Visitor Center** at Underground Atlanta (65 Upper Alabama St., 404/521-6600, www.atlanta.net). The bureau also operates smaller visitors centers at Hartsfield-Jackson (Department of Aviation, Atrium Suite 435) and inside the Georgia World Congress Center (285 Andrew Young International Blvd.) during major events.

RESOURCES
Suggested Reading

HISTORY AND INFORMATION

Allen, Frederick. *Atlanta Rising: The Invention of an International City 1946–1996.* Atlanta, GA: Longstreet Press, 1996. For those lacking the patience to dig through Franklin Garrett's encyclopedic *Atlanta and Environs,* this book makes for a suitable primer on local politics, industry, and culture. Allen, whose previous book detailed the history of Coca-Cola, here delivers a chronicle of Atlanta's breakneck growth in the past half century.

Garrett, Franklin. *Atlanta and Environs: A Chronicle of Its People and Events.* Athens, GA: University of Georgia Press, 1987. The definitive story of Atlanta as recorded by its official historian is probably not ideal for a casual dip into local history. The three-volume set is roughly the size of a cinderblock and goes into meticulous detail about the city from 1820 through the 1970s. The exhaustive scope of the project boggles the mind, but makes it a standard resource for genealogy research and discovering minutiae about the city's past.

Greene, Melissa Fay. *The Temple Bombing.* Cambridge, MA: Da Capo Press, 2006. The 1958 bombing of the Reform Jewish Temple on Peachtree Street is a sometimes overlooked footnote of the civil rights era, a seemingly isolated incident in a city that missed much of the violence of desegregation. Greene's gripping exploration of the event and its aftermath offers a thorough look at the spirit of the times and the major personalities touched by the still-unsolved crime.

Pomerantz, Gary M. *Where Peachtree Meets Sweet Auburn: A Saga of Race and Family.* New York, NY: Penguin, 1997. The author, a former reporter for the *Atlanta Journal-Constitution,* delivers a compelling narrative about the changing roles of race in local politics. He traces the family histories of two of the city's most influential politicians, Ivan Allen Jr., a white mayor of the 1960s, and Maynard Jackson, Atlanta's first African-American mayor. With a reporter's talent for crafting a compelling story, Pomerantz has delivered a book that is a must-read for any student of race relations in the city.

Rose, Michael. *Atlanta: Then and Now.* Berkeley, CA: Thunder Bay Press, 2001. If every picture tells a story, then this handsome coffee-table book of classic photography might be called a nostalgic tragedy. Jaw-dropping black-and-white archival photos of the city are juxtaposed with images of the same scene today—revealing that, in most cases, the graceful, European-inspired buildings of yesteryear were demolished and replaced by considerably less timeless architecture.

LITERATURE AND FICTION

McCall, Nathan. *Them.* New York, NY: Atria, 2007. The slippery questions surrounding gentrification take center stage in this fascinating debut novel by Nathan McCall, a former reporter for the *Washington Post.* Set in today's rapidly changing Old Fourth Ward neighborhood (an area of the city that's seen an influx of upwardly mobile white residents in recent years), the book reveals characters grappling with deeply rooted feelings of prejudice and isolation as the Atlanta they used to know morphs into a different place entirely.

Mitchell, Margaret. *Gone With the Wind.* New York, NY: Scribner, 2007. Modern Atlantans usually cringe when the city's most famous novel gets mentioned, and they're quick to point out how little the book's antebellum setting or clichéd genre-fiction conventions reflect the metropolis of today. Still, there's a reason why Margaret Mitchell's historical romance has developed such a loyal following, and it's not just due to the film (which actually departs from the novel in several key places). Mitchell's insights into the character of the post–Civil War South make for an important time capsule about Atlanta's pedigree.

Siddons, Anne Rivers. *Peachtree Road.* New York, NY: HarperTorch, 1998. Fans of Pat Conroy and Dorothea Benton Frank will lap up Siddons's classic page-turner about Atlanta privilege. Set in Buckhead in the middle years of the 20th century, the richly drawn novel traces the life of a reluctant debutante pulling away from her wealthy family. It also features what may be the best first line of any Southern novel from the past 50 years: "The South killed Lucy Bondurant Chastain Venable on the day she was born."

Windham, Donald. *Emblems of Conduct.* Athens, GA: University of Georgia Press, 1996. Windham, a confidante of Tennessee Williams and Truman Capote, recalls his youth in Depression-era Atlanta. The emotional coming-of-age memoir details his years growing up in a stately Victorian home on Peachtree Street—followed by the family's fall to a public housing project. The writer, best known for his novel *The Dog Star,* captures a bygone era with authority and eloquence.

Wolfe, Tom. *A Man in Full.* New York, NY: Farrar Straus Giroux, 1998. The celebrated author and father of New Journalism shines an acerbic spotlight on Atlanta society. The novel relates the downfall of a good-ol'-boy real-estate tycoon on the brink of financial ruin, and offers an amusing, sometimes brutally accurate view of the city's foibles—from white revulsion over Freaknik to the complicated rules of etiquette among Buckhead bluebloods. Wolfe's agenda is no less than epic; even if the book sometimes falters, it's still an entertaining portrait of Atlanta's propensity for hubris.

Internet Resources

INFORMATION AND EVENTS

Atlanta Convention and Visitors Bureau
www.atlanta.net
The official site of the city's tourism board is a useful portal for finding events, restaurants, hotels, and insider tips to Atlanta. The site's breadth of content is impressive, with loads of information aimed at the convention market, as well as plenty of tidbits for tourists and new residents. Also offers advice for planning reunions in the city.

Atlanta Performs
www.atlantaperforms.com
The go-to guide for a comprehensive list of theater, dance, and kids' events in the city. It's the official site of the Atlanta Coalition of Performing Arts, which has more than 170 member organizations. The user-friendly show calendar lets you search by title, neighborhood, venue, or company. It's also the only place online to purchase half-price same-day theater tickets, via AtlanTix.

Central Atlanta Progress
www.atlantadowntown.com
Central Atlanta Progress, founded in 1941, is a private not-for-profit corporation dedicated to advancing Downtown's business district. The site is an exhaustive resource for local history, entertainment listings, and current city-improvement projects. The neighborhoods section delivers a helpful guide to anyone still learning their way around town.

City of Atlanta
www.atlanta.gov
The official site of the City of Atlanta offers lots of handy information to newcomers, including a downloadable new residents kit. From recycling questions to procedures for obtaining city permits, the site offers a user-friendly response to common concerns. Also includes links to city government offices and county agencies.

Explore Georgia
www.exploregeorgia.org
Anyone considering a day trip outside of Atlanta should first consult Explore Georgia, the state's official tourism site. With a search engine of statewide events, attractions, and accommodations, the eye-catching site makes travel planning easier. Check out the "Special Offers" section to get deals on hotels and tourist spots.

NEWS

Atlanta Daily World
www.atlantadailyworld.com
This daily newspaper is aimed at the city's African-American community, with a history dating back to 1928.

Atlanta Journal-Constitution
www.ajc.com
The city's venerable daily newspaper. Its entertainment and culture coverage falls under the **AccessAtlanta** (www.accessatlanta.com) sister site.

***Atlanta* Magazine**
www.atlantamagazine.com
One of the oldest city magazines in the country, *Atlanta* is a timely journal of local culture

and personalities. The site features a couple of noteworthy blogs.

Creative Loafing Atlanta
www.atlanta.creativeloafing.com

Creative Loafing, the city's main alternative weekly newspaper for more than three decades, delivers an independent take on local news and extensive entertainment listings.

Rolling Out
www.rollingout.com

An urban culture, fashion, and entertainment guide, this is a primo resource for young African-American professionals.

Southern Voice
www.sovo.com

Atlanta's long-standing gay and lesbian newspaper features daily updates on local and national queer happenings. Sibling magazine *David Atlanta* (www.davidatlanta.com) covers gay nightlife.

Sunday Paper
www.sundaypaper.com

An alternative weekly newspaper started by former *Creative Loafing* staffers, the *Sunday Paper* tends to take a conservative slant on the news.

PARKS AND RECREATION

Atlanta Track Club
www.atlantatrackclub.org

Founded in 1964, this running group produces the annual Peachtree Road Race and a handful of other 5Ks and marathons around town.

Centennial Olympic Park
www.centennialpark.com

As one of Atlanta's busiest public spaces, Centennial Olympic Park offers programming year-round. Its official site includes complete event listings, directions, and special deals on area attractions.

PATH Foundation
www.pathfoundation.org

Outdoor lovers will want to spend some time on the official site of the PATH Foundation, an organization devoted to developing local trails for walkers, joggers, cyclists, and skaters. The site includes maps and thorough trail information.

Piedmont Park Conservancy
www.piedmontpark.org

Official site of the nonprofit agency that works to preserve and promote Piedmont Park. Includes detailed listings of events in the park and beyond.

BEST ATLANTA BLOGS AND PODCASTS

The Blissful Glutton
www.blissfulglutton.blogspot.com

For up-to-the-minute news and reviews of Atlanta's restaurant scene, you could definitely do worse than the Blissful Glutton, a spicy journal by food critic Jennifer Zyman. The dish is particularly flavorful for foodies.

Drive a Faster Car
www.driveafastercar.com

Editor Tessa Horehled delivers a delicious blend of happenings and Atlanta gossip, with an emphasis on indie music. Definitely a great read for anyone seeking out underground arts.

Have You Heard
www.haveyouheard.net

This locally produced podcast is one of the best

in town. Weekly shows feature riffs on music news and reviews, live recordings, and tracks from Atlanta artists.

Live Apartment Fire
www.liveapartmentfire.com

Veteran broadcast journalist Doug Richards watches Atlanta's nightly news programs so you don't have to. His entertaining blog supplies biting commentary on local media, written with charm and precision.

Pecanne Log
www.pecannelog.com

Written by a trio of Southern belles who are anything but sweet and submissive, this fiery gossip and humor site takes an irreverent look at life in the city. It's always a witty read.

Index

A

Actor's Express: 95
air travel: 178
Alliance Theatre: 96
amusement parks: 110
APEX Museum: 90
area codes: 185
arts: 90-101
arts and leisure: 88-112
Athens: 159-162
Athletic Club Northeast: 108
Atlanta Ballet: 97
Atlanta Botanical Garden: 36
Atlanta Braves: 111
Atlanta Celebrates Photography: 104
Atlanta Contemporary Art Center, The: 93
Atlanta Cyclorama and Civil War Museum: 27
Atlanta Dogwood Festival: 101
Atlanta Falcons: 112
Atlanta Film Festival: 101
Atlanta Ghosts and Legends Tour: 109
Atlanta Hawks: 112
Atlanta History Center: 41
Atlanta Lawn Tennis Association: 109
Atlanta Opera: 97
Atlanta Preservation Center Walking Tours of Historic Atlanta: 110
Atlanta Pride Festival: 103
Atlanta Symphony Orchestra: 98
Atlanta Thrashers: 112

B

background: 163-177
baseball: 111
basketball: 112
bicycling: trails 106; commuter 181
bike rentals: 107
Bill Lowe Gallery, The: 94
Bitsy Grant Tennis Center: 109
Bobby Jones Golf Course: 107
bowling: 107
Buckhead: 20; map 8-9

C

Candler Park Golf Course: 108
canoeing: 109
Centennial Olympic Park: 27
Center for Puppetry Arts: 90
Chastain Park: 106

Chastain Park Amphitheater: 98
Chastain Park Trail: 106
Château Élan Winery and Resort: 157
Chattahoochee River National Recreation Area: 109
children, traveling with: 182
cinemas: 100
Civil War: 167
climate: 164
CNN Center: 31
Cobb Energy Performing Arts Centre: 98
concert venues: 98
crime: 184

DEFG

Dad's Garage Theatre: 96
dance: 97
Decatur: 21; map 14-15
Decatur Arts Festival: 102
demographics: 173
disabilities, traveling with: 182
Discovering Stone Mountain Museum at Memorial Hall: 155
Downtown: 20; map 4-5
Dragon*Con Parade: 103
East Atlanta: see Little Five Points and East Atlanta
East Atlanta Strut: 104
economy: 172
education: 173
essentials: 178-187
etiquette: 182
events: 101-105
excursions: 145-162
Eyedrum Art and Music Gallery: 94
Fernbank Museum of Natural History: 91
Fernbank Museum's IMAX Theatre: 100
festivals: 101-105
football: 112
Fox Theatre: 36
Freedom Park: 106
galleries: 93
gay and lesbian: 183
geography: 163
Georgia Aquarium: 28
Georgia Capitol Museum: 29
Georgia Governor's Mansion: 42
Georgia Shakespeare Festival: 96
golf: 107
government: 171-172

Grant Park Mothball and Tour of Homes: 104
gyms: 108

H
health: 184
health clubs: 108
High Country Outfitters: 109
High Museum of Art: 37
hiking: 106
Historic Oakland Cemetery: 30
history: 165–171
hockey: 112
Horizon Theatre Company: 97
hospitals: 184
hotels: 131–144; see also Hotels Index

IJKLM
Imagine It! The Children's Museum of Atlanta: 91
Industrialization: 169
Inman Park Festival: 102
Inside CNN Tour: 30
Internet resources: 190
Internet services: 185
itineraries: 22–23
Jai Shanti Yoga: 108
Jim Crow Era: 169
Jimmy Carter Presidential Library and
    Museum: 42
jogging: 106
kayaking: 109
Kennesaw Mountain National Battlefield Park:
    150
Lake Lanier: 157–159
Lake Lanier Islands Resort: 157
Lakewood Amphitheatre: 99
Lighting of Macy's Great Tree: 105
literature: 177
Little Five Points and East Atlanta: 21; map 12–13
Little Five Points Halloween Festival: 105
Lullwater Park: 106
maps, tourist: 187
Marcia Wood Gallery: 94
Margaret Mitchell House and Museum: 39
Marietta: 148–153
Marietta-Cobb Museum of Art: 149
Marietta Gone With the Wind Museum: Scarlett
    on the Square: 150
Marietta Square: 149
MARTA: 180
Marthasville: 166
Martin Luther King Jr. National Historic Site: 31
Martin Luther King Jr. Week: 102
media: 185

Michael C. Carlos Museum of Emory University:
    92
Midtown: 20; map 6–7
Midtown Art Cinema: 100
movie theaters: 100
Museum of Contemporary Art of Georgia: 92
museums: 90
music: 176; see also arts

NOPQR
National Black Arts Festival: 104
neighborhoods: 20–21
New Year's Eve Peach Drop at Underground:
    105
nightlife: 73–87; see also Nightlife Index
parks: 106
Peachtree Road Race: 104
pharmacies: 184
phones: 185
Piedmont Park: 39
planning tips: 20
Plaza Theatre: 100
publications, local: 186
public transportation: 180
radio: 186
rafting: 109
reading, suggested: 188
Reconstruction: 168
recreation: 106–112
religion: 175
resources: 188–192
restaurants: 43–72; see also Restaurants
    Index
Rhodes Hall: 92

S
safety: 184
shops: 113–130; see also Shops Index
sights: 25–42
Silver Comet Trail: 107
Six Flags Over Georgia: 110
Six Flags White Water: 111
Skate Escape: 107
smoking: 182
Southern Museum of Civil War and Locomotive
    History: 151
Spivey Hall: 99
sports: 106–112
Starlight Six Drive-In: 100
State Botanical Garden of Georgia: 160
Stone Mountain: 154–157
Summit Skyride: 155
Sweet Auburn Springfest: 102

T

Tabernacle: 99
taxis: 181
television: 187
tennis: 109
Ten Pin Alley: 107
Terminus: 166
theaters: 95
Theatrical Outfit: 97
tourist information: 185–187
tours: 109
transportation: 178–181
TULA Art Center: 94

UVWXYZ

Underground Atlanta: 32
Urban Body Fitness: 108
Variety Playhouse: 100
Virginia-Highland: 21; map 10–11
visual arts: 175; see also arts
William Breman Jewish Heritage Museum: 92
World of Coca-Cola: 34
Wren's Nest House Museum: 93
yoga: 108
Young Blood Gallery and Boutique: 95
Zoo Atlanta: 35

Restaurants Index

Agave: 68
Agnes and Muriel's: 50
Après Diem: 49
Aria: 56
Atkins Park: 63
Bacchanalia: 50
Bluepointe: 56
Bone's: 60
Cafe Sunflower: 60
Canoe: 70
Carroll Street Café: 65
Chops Lobster Bar: 58
City Grill: 45
Colonnade, The: 59
Daddy D'z: 45
Doc Chey's Noodle House: 61
Dressed: 51
Eats: 62
Ecco: 53
Einstein's: 51
Fat Matt's Rib Shack: 49
Floataway Café : 62
Flying Biscuit Cafe, The: 63
Fogo de Chão Churrascaria: 55
French American Brasserie: 47
Fritti: 67
Front Page News: 64
Geisha House: 48
Georgia Grille: 59
Grant Central Pizza: 47
Harry and Sons: 61
Highland Bakery: 63
Horseradish Grill: 71
JavaVino: 65

JCT Kitchen & Bar: 54
Joël: 57
La Fonda Latina: 62
Las Palmeras: 51
La Tavola Trattoria: 62
Little Azio: 53
Mary Mac's Tea Room: 54
Matador Cantina: 69
McKendrick's Steak House: 72
Mexico City Gourmet: 69
Murphy's: 61
Nan Thai Fine Dining: 49
Nava: 59
No Mas! Cantina: 47
Nuevo Laredo Cantina: 71
Octane Coffee Bar & Lounge: 49
OK Cafe: 56
Paolo's Gelato: 61
Paschal's: 48
Pasta Da Pulcinella: 53
Radial: 64
Rathbun's : 65
Restaurant Eugene: 56
Ria's Bluebird: 45
Roasters: 59
Rolling Bones Barbecue: 45
R. Thomas Deluxe Grill: 60
Ru San's Tower Place: 55
Shaun's: 65
Silver Midtown Grill: 51
Six Feet Under: 48
Slice: 47
Son's Place: 67
Soul Vegetarian: 68

Souper Jenny: 57
South City Kitchen: 54
Sun Dial Restaurant, Bar & View: 46
Sun in My Belly: 66
Swallow at the Hollow, The: 70
Table 1280: 54
Taco Stand, The: 58
Taqueria del Sol: 58
Ted's Montana Grill: 46

Thrive: 46
Thumbs Up Diner: 67
Two Urban Licks: 66
Universal Joint: 68
Varsity, The: 53
Vinings Inn Restaurant: 72
Vortex Bar and Grill, The: 66
Watershed: 68

Nightlife Index

Amsterdam Café: 86
Apache Café: 75
Bar at Trois, The: 85
Bazzaar Urban Bar: 85
Bellissima Lounge: 86
Blake's on the Park: 87
Blind Willie's: 75
Brick Store Pub: 79
Churchill Grounds: 84
Clermont Lounge: 79
Dante's Down the Hatch: 84
Dark Horse Tavern: 79
Earl, The: 75
Eastside Lounge: 85
Eddie's Attic: 76
El Bar: 79
5 Seasons Brewing: 83
Gilbert's Mediterranean Café: 85
Halo: 85
Highland Tap: 80
Leopard Lounge: 86

Limerick Junction Irish Pub: 81
Lobby at Twelve: 86
Local, The: 81
Loca Luna: 81
Manuel's Tavern: 81
Mark Ultralounge, The: 78
Mary's: 87
Masquerade, The: 76
Max Lager's American Grill and Brewery: 83
MJQ Concourse: 78
My Sister's Room: 87
Northside Tavern: 77
Opera: 78
Park Tavern: 83
Red Light Café: 77
Righteous Room: 82
Sambuca: 84
Star Community Bar: 77
Tavern at Phipps, The: 82
Trader Vic's: 82
Twisted Taco: 82

Shops Index

Abbadabba's: 120
A Cappella Books: 116
Alon's: 123
Belvedere: 125
Bill Hallman Men: 118
Blue MedSpa: 129
Boy Next Door: 119
Charis Books and More: 116
Clothing Warehouse, The: 121
Criminal Records: 117
DressCodes: 119
fab'rik: 119
Fickle Manor, The: 120

Green Market for Piedmont Park: 127
Helmet: 129
Highland Pet Supply: 124
Intaglia Home Collection: 126
Jeffrey Atlanta: 120
Junkman's Daughter: 123
Key Lime Pie Salon and Wellness Spa: 129
Knitch: 123
Lenox Square Mall: 128
Luxe Atlanta: 120
Mitzi & Romano: 120
Morningside Farmers Market: 127
Outwrite Bookstore and Coffeehouse: 117

Oxford Comics & Games: 117
Phipps Plaza: 128
Piedmont Bark: 125
Poster Hut: 124
Providence: 122
Psycho Sisters Consignment: 121
Richard's Variety Store: 124
Salon Red & Spa: 130
Sid Mashburn: 119
Sprout: 118

Star Provisions: 123
Stefan's Vintage Clothing: 121
Sugarcoat: 130
Sweet Auburn Curb Market: 128
Traders Neighborhood Store: 126
Twelve Boutique and Flowers: 122
Wax 'N Facts: 117
Wiggle: 118
Yes Home: 126
Your Dekalb Farmers Market: 128

Hotels Index

Atlanta International Hostel: 136
Atlanta Marriott Marquis: 133
Beverly Hills Inn: 139
Country Inn and Suites Buckhead: 139
1890 King-Keith House Bed and Breakfast: 142
Ellis Hotel: 134
Embassy Suites Atlanta at Centennial Olympic
    Park: 134
Emory Conference Center Hotel: 141
Four Seasons Hotel: 136
Gaslight Inn Bed & Breakfast: 141
Georgian Terrace Hotel: 136
Glenn Hotel: 134
Grand Hyatt Atlanta: 140
Highland Inn: 142
Hotel Indigo: 136

Inman Park Bed & Breakfast: 143
InterContinental Buckhead. 140
Laurel Hill Bed & Breakfast: 144
Mileybright Farmhouse Bed & Breakfast : 144
Omni Hotel at CNN Center: 134
Ritz-Carlton Buckhead: 140
Shellmont Inn: 137
Sugar Magnolia Bed & Breakfast: 143
Twelve Hotel Atlantic Station: 138
Twelve Hotel Centennial Park: 134
University Inn at Emory: 142
Virginia Highland Bed and Breakfast: 142
W Atlanta Midtown: 138
Westin Buckhead Atlanta: 140
Westin Peachtree Plaza: 135

Acknowledgments

Many thanks to the staff of Avalon Travel, especially my wonderful editors Naomi Adler Dancis and Jehán Seirafi, who have been a pleasure to work with and consummate professionals from day one. Thanks also to my friends and mentors Suzanne Van Atten, Lucas Miré, and Jerry Portwood, whose encouragement kept me sane and focused during the proposal process. Finally, the biggest thanks of all goes to my partner Brian, whose patience and ambition inspire me daily.

www.moon.com

MOON.COM is all new, and ready to help plan your next trip! Filled with fresh trip ideas and strategies, author interviews, informative blogs, a detailed map library, and descriptions of all the Moon guidebooks, Moon.com is all you need to get out and explore the world—or even places in your own backyard. As always, when you travel with Moon, expect an experience that is uncommon and truly unique.

MAP SYMBOLS

▦ Expressway	◖ Highlight	✗ Airfield	⌕ Golf Course
⋯ Primary Road	○ City/Town	✗ Airport	▣ Parking Area
⋯ Secondary Road	◉ State Capital	▲ Mountain	⬒ Archaeological Site
═ Unpaved Road	⊛ National Capital	✦ Unique Natural Feature	⛪ Church
-- Trail	★ Point of Interest		
⋯ Ferry	• Accommodation	⚑ Waterfall	⛽ Gas Station
⊶ Railroad	▾ Restaurant/Bar	⬆ Park	◌ Glacier
▦ Pedestrian Walkway	▪ Other Location	⬡ Trailhead	▥ Mangrove
⫿ Stairs	⋀ Campground	⅀ Skiing Area	▨ Reef
			▦ Swamp

CONVERSION TABLES

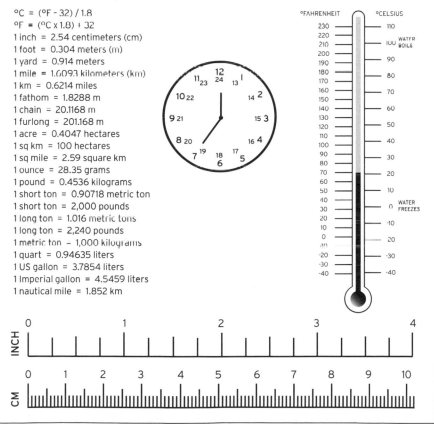

°C = (°F - 32) / 1.8
°F = (°C x 1.8) + 32
1 inch = 2.54 centimeters (cm)
1 foot = 0.304 meters (m)
1 yard = 0.914 meters
1 mile = 1.6093 kilometers (km)
1 km = 0.6214 miles
1 fathom = 1.8288 m
1 chain = 20.1168 m
1 furlong = 201.168 m
1 acre = 0.4047 hectares
1 sq km = 100 hectares
1 sq mile = 2.59 square km
1 ounce = 28.35 grams
1 pound = 0.4536 kilograms
1 short ton = 0.90718 metric ton
1 short ton = 2,000 pounds
1 long ton = 1.016 metric tons
1 long ton = 2,240 pounds
1 metric ton – 1,000 kilograms
1 quart = 0.94635 liters
1 US gallon = 3.7854 liters
1 Imperial gallon = 4.5459 liters
1 nautical mile = 1.852 km

MOON ATLANTA

Avalon Travel
a member of the Perseus Books Group
1700 Fourth Street
Berkeley, CA 94710, USA
www.moon.com

Editor: Naomi Adler Dancis
Series Manager: Erin Raber
Copy Editor: Amy Scott
Graphics Coordinator: Kathryn Osgood
Production Coordinator: Tabitha Lahr
Cover Designer: Kathryn Osgood
Map Editors: Mike Morgenfeld, Kevin Anglin
Cartographers: Lohnes & Wright, Kat Bennett

ISBN-13: 978-1-59880-219-1
ISSN: 1948-5034

Printing History
1st Edition – September 2009
5 4 3 2 1

Text © 2009 by Tray Butler.
Maps © 2009 by Avalon Travel.
All rights reserved.

KEEPING CURRENT

If you have a favorite gem you'd like to see included in the next edition, or see anything that needs updating, clarification, or correction, please drop us a line. Send your comments via email to feedback@moon.com, or use the address above.